Making Policy, Shaping Lives

Power, Dissent, Equality: Understanding Contemporary Politics

The complete list of books in this series is as follows:

What is Politics?
Jef Huysmans

Exploring Political Worlds
Edited by Paul Lewis

Politics and Power in the UK
Edited by Richard Heffernan and Grahame Thompson

Living Political Ideas
Edited by Geoff Andrews and Michael Saward

Making Policy, Shaping Lives
Edited by Raia Prokhovnik

The books form part of an Open University course DD203 *Power, Dissent, Equality: Understanding Contemporary Politics*. Details of this and other Open University courses can be obtained from the Course Information and Advice Centre, PO Box 724, The Open University, Milton Keynes MK7 6ZS, United Kingdom: tel. +44 (0)1908 653231, e-mail general-enquiries@open.ac.uk

Alternatively, you may visit the Open University website at http://www.open.ac.uk where you can learn more about the wide range of courses and packs offered at all levels by The Open University.

For availability of other course components visit the webshop at www.ouw.co.uk, or contact Open University Worldwide, Michael Young Building, Walton Hall, Milton Keynes MK7 6AA, United Kingdom for a brochure. tel. +44 (0)1908858785; fax +44 (0)19088 58787; e-mail ouwenq@open.ac.uk

Making Policy, Shaping Lives

Edited by

Raia Prokhovnik

The Open University

This publication forms part of the Open University course DD203 *Power, dissent, equality: understanding contemporary politics*. Details of this and other Open University courses can be obtained from the Student Registration and Enquiry Service, The Open University, PO Box 197, Milton Keynes MK7 6BJ, United Kingdom (tel. +44 (0)845 300 60 90; email general-enquiries@open.ac.uk).

Alternatively, you may visit the Open University website at www.open.ac.uk where you can learn more about the wide range of courses and packs offered at all levels by The Open University.

To purchase a selection of Open University course materials visit www.ouw.co.uk, or contact Open University Worldwide, Walton Hall, Milton Keynes MK7 6AA, United Kingdom for a brochure (tel. +44 (0)1908 858793; fax +44 (0)1908 858787; email ouw-customer-services@open.ac.uk).

The Open University
Walton Hall, Milton Keynes
MK7 6AA

First published 2005 by Edinburgh University Press, Ltd; written and produced by The Open University.

This edition published by The Open University.

Edited, designed and typeset by The Open University.

Printed in the United Kingdom by Bell & Bain Ltd, Glasgow.

The paper used in this publication is procured from forests independently certified to the level of Forest Stewardship Council (FSC) principles and criteria. Chain of custody certification allows the tracing of this paper back to specific forest-management units (see www.fsc.org).

ISBN 978 1 8487 3465 4

2.1

Mixed Sources
Product group from well-managed forests and other controlled sources
www.fsc.org Cert no. TT-COC-002769
© 1996 Forest Stewardship Council

FSC

Contents

Preface   vii

INTRODUCTION   1

Powers & structures

CHAPTER 1
How is policy made?   7
Deborah Mabbett

Centre & periphery

CHAPTER 2
Challenging centre–periphery relations in health policy   43
Julie Charlesworth and Wendy Humphreys

Participation & dissent

CHAPTER 3
Welfare, participation and dissent in public policy   79
Richard Freeman

Equality & difference

CHAPTER 4
Fair policy or special treatment? Disability politics   113
Nick Watson

Evidence & argument

CHAPTER 5
Talking about policy   145
Raia Prokhovnik

Acknowledgements   183

Index   185

The Open University course team

Geoff Andrews, *Staff Tutor in Government and Politics*

Brian Ashcroft, *Associate Lecturer Panel*

Pam Berry, *Compositor*

Karen Bridge, *Media Project Manager*

Vivienne Brown, *Professor of Intellectual History*

Julie Charlesworth, *Lecturer, Open University Business School*

Martin Chiverton, *Media Production Specialist*

Stephen Clift, *Editor*

Lene Connolly, *Print Buyer*

John Craig, *Associate Lecturer Panel*

Michael Dawson, *Course Manager*

Marilyn Denman, *Secretary*

Andrew Dobson, *Professor of Politics*

Lucy Flook, *Course Manager*

Fran Ford, *Course Secretary*

Liz Freeman, *Copublishing Advisor*

Robert Garson, *Reader in American Studies*

Pam Garthwaite, *Course Manager*

Carl Gibbard, *Graphic Designer*

Bram Gieben, *Staff Tutor in Government and Politics*

Janis Gilbert, *Graphic Artist*

Richard Golden, *Production and Presentation Administrator*

Montserrat Guibernau, *Reader in Politics*

Lisa Hale, *Compositor*

Celia Hart, *Picture Researcher*

Richard Heffernan, *Lecturer in Government and Politics*

Wendy Humphreys, *Staff Tutor in Government and Politics*

Jef Huysmans, *Lecturer in Government and Politics*

Bob Kelly, *Staff Tutor in Government and Politics*

Paul Lewis, *Reader in Central and European Politics*

Joanna Mack, *Media Production Specialist*

David Middleton, *Staff Tutor in Government and Politics*

Jeremy Mitchell, *Lecturer in Government and Politics*

Raia Prokhovnik, *Senior Lecturer in Government and Politics and Deputy Course Team Chair*

Michael Saward, *Professor in Politics and Course Team Chair*

David Shulman, *BBC Producer*

Lynne Slocombe, *Editor*

Mark J. Smith, *Senior Lecturer in Government and Politics*

Grahame Thompson, *Professor of Political Economy*

Consultant authors

Richard Freeman, *Senior Lecturer in Politics, University of Edinburgh*

Deborah Mabbett, *Lecturer in Politics, Brunel University*

Mads Qvortrup, *Professor of Sociology and Public Policy, The Robert Gordon University, Aberdeen*

Judith Squires, *Senior Lecturer in Politics, University of Bristol*

Nicholas Watson, *Professor of Disability Studies, University of Glasgow*

External assessor

Michael Moran, *Professor of Government, University of Manchester*

Preface

Tumultuous events such as '9-11' and the war and its aftermath in Iraq have reminded people how critical – and sometimes how deadly – the world of politics can be. Even the local, everyday politics of council services, schools and hospitals can affect people's lives powerfully. The Open University, with its unique tradition of interdisciplinary work and its mission to reach and enthuse a hugely diverse student audience, has set out to show why and how politics matters. It aims to shed light on the inner workings of power, decision making and protest, covering politics from parliament to the street, from ideas to institutions. *Making Policy, Shaping Lives* teases out and interrogates the many faces of public policy and policy making, drawing on case materials ranging from the single European currency to disability politics. Through engagement with case materials the book explores different theories of policy making, examines the links across the public and private sectors in policy making, and tracks recent attempts at restructuring modern welfare states. It is a highly readable and accessible introduction to a range of debates around public policy.

Series preface

This book is one of the five texts which make up the new *Power, Dissent, Equality: Understanding Contemporary Politics* series from The Open University. Each book in the series is designed for students and others who have not studied politics before, and can stand alone as a short introduction to key areas of debate within political science. However, if you wish to use the series as a whole, there are a number of references to chapters in other books in the series and these are easily identifiable because they are printed in bold type.

Each book offers a distinctive angle on the character and analysis of politics today. *What is Politics?* offers a critical overview, showing the often surprising faces and locations of political life. *Exploring Political Worlds* examines comparative politics, asking what we can learn by looking at one country or context in the light of another. *Politics and Power in the UK* questions how we might make sense of major developments and debates in UK politics, such as devolution and constitutional change. *Living Political Ideas* is an accessible introduction to key topics in political theory and ideology, such as legitimacy, national self-determination, dissent and social justice. *Making Policy, Shaping Lives* teases out and interrogates the many faces of public policy and policy making, drawing on case materials ranging from the single European currency to disability politics.

For all of the books, apart from *What is Politics?*, the chapters follow a common thematic structure. There are five organizing themes. *Powers and structures* explores the meaning and location of power in contemporary societies – what it is, and who has it. *Centre and periphery* looks at issues from the role of the state in our lives to the revival of nationalism in the post-Cold War world. *Participation and dissent* leads us to look, on the one hand, at voting and elections, and on the other hand at new and unconventional forms of political protest and dissent. *Equality and difference* examines how we are seen as 'equal to' and 'different from' each other and how this matters politically. The *evidence and argument* theme focuses attention on the ways in which the study of politics involves both explanation and recommendation.

Courses produced by The Open University are very much a team effort, and *Power, Dissent, Equality: Understanding Contemporary Politics* is no exception. Each member of the course team has made his or her mark on these books, and the work was done with goodwill and good humour. Some special thanks are owed. Raia Prokhovnik's tireless and dedicated contribution as Deputy and Acting Course Chair has been of huge benefit to the course. Mike Dawson has been a superbly calm, tactful and efficient Course Manager. Lucy Flook, Course Manager in the early days, played a significant role in getting the team up and running efficiently and ahead of schedule. Pam Garthwaite kept the momentum going in the period between Lucy's departure and Mike's arrival. The editorial skills of Stephen Clift and Lynne Slocombe and designs by Carl Gibbard have been key to the quality of the texts. Fran Ford has been a great support as course secretary, ably supported at different times by June Ayres and Marilyn Denman. John Craig and Brian Ashcroft have constituted a 'tutor panel' which has commented most helpfully on draft chapters. Robert Garson (Bobby) of Keele University was an influential and insightful member of the course team for two years. Professor Mick Moran of the University of Manchester has been the ideal external examiner – sharp and committed, he has been a tremendously positive influence on the content of these books.

Michael Saward, Course Team Chair

Introduction

Raia Prokhovnik

This book is about public policy and how policy decisions shape the lives of citizens. 'Policy' refers to one aspect of politics – not elections, nor party politics inside or outside parliament, nor dissent, but the making and delivery of laws, rules and guidelines. It is a distinctive feature of modern politics that governments are expected to make policies and implement them effectively, and that plans for policy provide the electorate with a means of distinguishing different parties at elections. Public policy is that part of politics concerned with government decisions, and their administration and implementation. Note an ambiguity straight away – 'policy' can refer to what parties or governments *plan* to do, as well as to what governments actually do when in office.

All politically significant matters will have a policy addressed to them, so the idea of policy strongly affects ways we understand how we are governed. Parties, governments and interest groups 'having a policy' about things such as social problems, levels of immigration or interest rates indicates that these issues are political. The issue is debatable or contestable, or a problem, and it mobilizes values. Alternatives are considered and the issue is addressed by doing this rather than that. The outcome also says something about the power relationships among policy actors. Establishing whether something results from a policy or from individual action (for instance the extreme mistreatment of Iraqi prisoners at Abu Ghraib jail by US soldiers in 2004) can be vitally important to determining what it means.

There are other important features of the policy process. Policies are forward-looking rather than retrospective, and there is a specialization of tasks among policy makers (for example, one policy maker responsible for industry and another for the environment). A government might have a preference for raising the level of taxation, but a *policy* puts that preference into practice. Also, 'having a policy' means that, rather than having to think up something in an ad hoc way, there is an authoritative answer or strategy for all cases of a certain kind. A policy provides general guidelines and rules for how to react to particular cases, and a 'policy' signals a response made in the name of the government, and not just owned by an individual politician or official. Another thing a policy does is to establish an authoritative language for talking about that issue, and a government-sanctioned knowledge about it that legitimizes further policy choices. Policies can arise in response to events (such as '9-11'), by translating a dominant discourse into action (for instance the 'citizen consumer'), as a result in shifts in ideas (the 'third way', 'new public management') or power (after an election), or by updating a previous policy.

'Policy', then, refers to various things that are linked to each other – a *decision* founded upon a general *orientation*, that leads to a course of *action* or outcome that affects ordinary people. Policies can also establish *goals* within a certain context of economic *circumstances*, political *demands*, social *values* and authoritative *vocabulary*. They are designed to accomplish collective purposes, and seeing an action in terms of a 'policy' labels the action as a specific kind of outcome. 'Having a policy' both explains an action and gives it a sense of credibility. Policies in the form of laws can come about through legislation, or by being enacted through other, sub-legislative forms or by a precedent set by a court.

All of this makes policy sound like a clear product of ordered, rational procedures. But we also need to remember that policy making is not generally a neat, rational process. Policy making is about power, as well as problem solving. Policies can be deliberate choices for *inaction* rather than action, and can *resist* change rather than bring it about. Policy objectives may not be achieved, and political bargaining and accommodation can muddy or distort them. Policies can be symbolic, formulated more to give the *impression* of government action than to address social and other issues. They can be driven by political considerations, such as the dominance of one interest group over others, rather than by the public interest. Moreover, the origin and character of a policy can be fuzzy. It can be difficult to specify exactly what the key decision was or at which precise point the policy emerged. Policy can arise out of a set of decisions by a community of actors involved in policy debate, rather than from one decisive choice. A policy can also persist due to bureaucratic inertia rather than deliberate choices by a government. New policies cannot easily shift existing routines and structures. Sometimes, policy is expressed in a *series* of decisions; policy can also evolve over time, incrementally rather than according to rational plans. And policy decisions are interpreted and adapted when they are implemented in practice. It is not always easy to draw a clear line between policy *making* and policy *implementation*.

Over the past two hundred years, the time and energy devoted by modern states to policy making has dramatically increased, as a way of managing complex, mass industrial societies. There has been a rapid increase in policy initiatives, and the turnover rate of policies has escalated. Policy making involves not just public issues such as taxation and foreign policy, but an extended range of public goods such as roads, rubbish collection, and street lighting. Modern policy making also covers greater regulation of the economic marketplace (for example, to prevent monopolies and limit environmental damage), and more and more areas of 'private' life such as welfare issues and family life. Increased policy making has meant a more intervening state, and there are two prominent voices in the debate about the extent of state intervention and policy making. Some of those on the right call for no more than a 'minimal state' with the barest of welfare safety nets, while some on the left advocate extensive and systematic state action to regulate the market, distribute generous welfare benefits, and redistribute more wealth through taxation. In recent years, these ideological lines have become blurred in many countries with, for example, parties of the left embracing more market-oriented notions of 'choice'.

Having considered what 'policy' means, let's turn to 'public'. The term 'public' in this context generally refers to policy making and delivery by government. Sometimes non-state bodies are involved in policy delivery too – for example, the British Medical Association plays a role in regulating medical standards in the UK. Recent years in Western states have seen an increase in the delegation or contracting-out of some governmental functions to agencies, semi-government bodies, and public/private partnerships. This development blurs the boundary between public (state) and private (profit-making or voluntary) organizations. Policy control is shared between public and private bodies. It can be more difficult for the citizen, patient, pensioner, tenant, benefits holder or customer to find out who is accountable for problems with a policy (managerial accountability), and to hold the government to account for a policy at election time (democratic accountability). On the plus side, increasing links between public and private bodies might foster new opportunities for democratic participation. The move from government (a more formal, top-down model) to governance (a more diffuse and informal model) in this sense thus has important repercussions for how citizens' lives are shaped by policy making. In some senses 'public' policy making may not differ from any other kind (for instance by a private company or a family), but it carries a special responsibility in that it applies to everyone and is compulsory.

Now that we have a sense of what 'public policy' is, we can think about how to study it. Political scientists approach the study of public policy in different ways: there are studies of the policy *process*, of policy *outputs*, of the way *information* is used in policy making, of policy *advocacy* by various groups and interests, and studies *evaluating* the effectiveness of policy.

In this book we are primarily concerned with the first of these, the policy process, though the book also touches on questions raised by other areas of public policy analysis. This policy process is dynamic rather than static and, in theory at least, the process is a sequence of events over time. The policy process is also a system, a practice, an activity and a language. It is propelled by new ideas, debate and ideological prescriptions or aspirations. It flows through information gathering, canvassing experts and listening to interested parties, to the formulation of the issue and setting up of policy objectives. The process goes on to forecast likely impacts and consequences, to an options analysis, to bargaining, and from there to a decision-making phase. The process then reaches implementation and delivery, and on to monitoring, evaluation and feedback, and finally to maintaining, reviewing or ending the policy.

In the following chapters four policy areas are explored. Chapter 1 examines the policy process leading to the single European market, and Chapter 2 studies policy making for the health service. The third chapter discusses welfare state policy debates, while Chapter 4 considers how the issue of disability came onto the policy agenda. However, in the following chapters the four policy areas are viewed as *case studies* in policy making. The focus of this book is on the different policy areas as *examples* of policy making, rather than on the details of the case studies. We hope that readers will draw from the chapters general principles and features of the public policy-making process through case studies which bring them to life and 'make vivid' to the reader questions of public policy making in the real world. Chapter 5 differs from the other chapters in taking up this issue and reflecting upon what has gone on in the previous four chapters.

Chapter 1, 'How is policy made?', shows how different actors and various structural opportunities and constraints affected the policy-making process in the run-up to the single European market decision. The interaction between politics and policy is clear when the issues of power, and the new and old structures within which power is exercised, come into play. Deborah Mabbett focuses on the EU as a new arena of systematic policy making. Her chapter centres on the question: what were the processes that went into the decision about how far the European Union and its member states should seek to regulate the economic market? She emphasizes the different stages that a piece of policy making goes through.

In Chapter 2, 'Challenging centre–periphery relations in health policy', Julie Charlesworth and Wendy Humphreys show how a range of geographical, functional and political positionings can be construed as different centres and peripheries. Policy for the health service, and the distribution of health inequalities, are both influenced by where the centre and periphery are thought to be. The chapter also indicates how international influences, and policy making at the European level, now have an impact on health policy in Britain. The authors describe how the post-war model of a hierarchical bureaucracy – following standard operating procedures and having a top-down perspective on policy making – is being modified. They discuss a new model of more flexible, open and fluid policy design and delivery, with inputs from the market and the community as well as from the state. The chapter asks: does the idea of 'multi-level governance' successfully characterize recent attempts in health policy to move from one model to another? One of the points about public policy that this chapter highlights is that policy making can crucially involve administrators, powerful interest groups, and perhaps citizens, at regional and local levels as well as centrally based actors and venues.

Chapter 3, 'Welfare, participation and dissent in public policy', examines the diversity of welfare states across different countries, and the varying patterns of participation in them, against the background of the radical changes and retrenchments that have reduced the role of the state in welfare. In terms of state policy making, are we witnessing the retreat of the welfare state or new opportunities for participation and dissent? Richard Freeman tackles the scope for participation in welfare state politics, in the light of the claim of the state to distribute welfare goods on non-market principles in the name of social justice. Freeman shows how ideological and institutional frameworks in different countries affect how they react to the factors driving restructuring – such as globalizing pressures, politicians' assumptions about how much citizens are prepared to pay for welfare, the neo-liberal logic, and the dilemma of spiralling welfare costs. This chapter also highlights, in terms of the politics of participation and dissent, that the policy process can involve a whole range of actors, including patients and tenants, and is not restricted simply to national decisions by civil servants and the participation of experts.

Chapter 4 examines the way disability has become a policy issue, and the approaches to policy making in this area. The title of the chapter, 'Fair policy or special treatment? Disability politics' points to a major debate discussed by and about disabled people, and informing public policy questions – whether disability policy should focus on granting disabled people equal rights, or whether they deserve special treatment. Nick Watson considers the strengths and weaknesses of the social model of disability. The chapter compares debates on disability policy making in the UK with developments in other countries. By showing how disability has become visible on the public policy agenda, this chapter deals with a very dramatic way in which politics and policy interact. The case study about disability politics also shows the wider political framework influencing policy in this area, beyond the narrow 'black box' that gives priority to the decision-making phase of the policy process. Watson discusses the process that led to the Disability Discrimination Act of 1995 in the UK.

The final chapter of the book, 'Talking about policy', steps back from the particular case studies in the book and asks: what kinds of arguments and what range of evidence have been used in the previous four chapters? Here again, it is not the details of the case studies that are at issue, but the more general points about the policy-making process that are important. The chapter is also concerned with insights into how policy is *studied*, as well as with understanding the policy *process*. It revisits particular examples of evidence, unpacks some of the issues they contain, and considers some of the methods used and the implicit methodological assumptions they contain. The chapter discusses these topics under four headings: aspects of political science, the importance of values, the use of models, and the gap that can occur in policy making between what is 'thinkable' and what is actually 'doable' in practice.

How is policy made?

Deborah Mabbett

chapter 1

Contents

1	Introduction	8
2	Who governs?	12
3	Actors and venues	16
	3.1 Policy communities	16
	3.2 From policy communities to issue networks	18
	3.3 Venues	21
4	The role of ideas	23
	4.1 The rational choice model	23
	4.2 The role of expertise	25
	4.3 Norms and values	26
5	Problems of interest representation	28
	5.1 Interests, democracy and the media	28
	5.2 Bias in policy communities	30
6	Implementation	33
	6.1 Power and implementation	34
	6.2 Evaluation	36
7	Conclusion	38
	References	39
	Further reading	41

Powers & structures

1 INTRODUCTION

This chapter provides an introduction to the process of public policy making, and the powers and structures through which it develops. Public policy concerns the choice, adoption and implementation of courses of action by state authorities. Thinking of the policy process as involving the passing of a law is not a bad place to start, but policies involve a wider class of instruments than laws. A policy may involve a series of laws, or it may be possible for the government to introduce a policy within existing legal powers – that is, without going before parliament. Policies may also involve changing administrative practices or establishing new institutions.

The idea of policy making denotes something *purposive*: a policy is intended to produce outcomes, although, as we will see, the intended outcomes do not necessarily occur! Policy making is also a process: it involves stages of formulation, decision and implementation. The stages may be hard to identify and we may have to hunt around for them, not least because policies are often under continual development, so that often the reformulation takes place before the initial formulation is fully implemented. However, the idea of stages in the process is still useful, because it draws our attention to the different *venues* (see Section 3.3 below) that are involved at different stages. For example, formulation may take place in government departments and cabinet, decision in parliament, and implementation in agencies.

Studying the policy process in a general way presents us with a difficulty, in that the content of each policy presents its own unique political problems. It is hard to see how the same framework might inform an analysis of policy on, say, asylum seekers and pension reform. Immigration issues have high political visibility, and the policy debate is dominated by visceral fears and insecurities. Pension reform is important to long-term welfare but that does not mean that the general public is prepared to spend time gathering information and debating the issues. The economic complexity of pension problems means that the policy space is largely left clear for economists and others with high levels of technical knowledge to engage in esoteric debate.

However, by comparing these two very different policy areas, it is possible to begin to identify some key aspects of the policy process. First, it is notable that some policy issues get a great deal of public attention and others do not. Governments make thousands of policy decisions during their terms of office but only some will prove important for the outcome of the next election, by becoming the focus of contestation among the political parties or the subject of media attention. Second, some areas are readily colonized by experts and technocrats while others are much more open to public debate. Third, groups may be mobilized around particular political issues because they have a great deal to gain or lose from a decision (such as the location of a resettlement centre); conversely, mobilization is much weaker around issues with thinly spread, uncertain and long-term consequences, such as pension reform.

On closer scrutiny, the two issues prove to have some elements in common, too. National policies on the acceptance of refugees and asylum seekers are governed by international conventions. These conventions recognize that the decisions of one state will have an impact on others. If national governments act independently, the result may be 'beggar-thy-neighbour' policies that, in the end, have an adverse outcome for everyone. Some policy problems cannot be addressed effectively at national level at all: in economic policy, in particular, some national policy instruments have been rendered ineffective by international economic integration ('globalization'). Pension reform has become an international political issue because particular reform or non-reform strategies affect international macroeconomic stability. Several national governments in Europe had to push through pension reforms in order to comply with the Maastricht convergence criteria that provided the ground rules for European monetary union.

This discussion identifies, then, some of the themes that an analysis of the policy process can address in order to give insights into who has power and the structures through which power is exercised. The analysis can identify the *stages* in the policy process and establish how power is exercised at each stage (Section 2). It can examine who the *actors* (individuals or organizations) are, and how they come to participate in the policy process (Section 3). It can look at the role of *ideas*, whether these are technical or political, and ask how the various parties in the policy process come to develop views about which policies are in their best interests (Section 4). It can ask how policy processes relate to *democratic* political processes (Section 5). By examining how policy is implemented, the analysis can identify some reasons why the best-laid plans do not necessarily have the intended outcomes, and how *implementation* is itself a stage at which power is exercised in important ways (Section 6).

This chapter uses a variety of specific examples to illustrate important features of the policy process. It also looks in detail at a case study of the policy process leading up to the development of the single market in Europe, the Single European Market or SEM (see Box 1.1). This process is sometimes referred to as the '1992' initiative; 1992 was the end date for the removal of barriers to the free movement of goods, services, labour and capital. The initiative brought to a close a long period in which the process of European integration had stagnated, and it set the stage for the adoption of economic and monetary union and the eastward expansion of the European Union (EU). The SEM makes a good reference point for thinking about the policy process. Its technical and economic nature made it a prime candidate for 'capture' by a specialized policy community. In public political debate it got nowhere near the attention of the subsequent Maastricht Treaty, even though it is arguable that Maastricht was just the logical outcome of the 1992 process. The acceptance of the SEM by the member states reflected the tidal wave of ideas about the benefits of market liberalization that swept across many states

BOX 1.1 The development of the Single European Market (SEM)

The creation of the SEM revitalized the process of European integration, which had become sluggish in the 1970s. By removing all obstacles to economic transactions across European borders, the SEM was intended to make the European economy more dynamic, competitive and efficient. It required member states to change some cherished national institutions and practices, and it was therefore susceptible to 'backsliding' during implementation. Setting 1992 as the target date for the removal of barriers had symbolic importance, but in reality implementation is continuing in the twenty-first century.

As with many policy processes, it requires some care to identify all the relevant elements in the single market policy. The 'four freedoms' (free movement of goods, services, labour and capital) were set out in the Treaty of Rome (1957), but this legal agreement did not remove the many technical and regulatory barriers to a single market. The European Commission had long been engaged in a slow and tortuous process of 'harmonization' of rules and regulations affecting trade. This process involved the preparation of directives that had to be unanimously accepted by the Council of Ministers. The 1992 initiative accelerated this process through three main devices:

1   First, the changes needed in over 300 areas of trade were outlined in a White Paper prepared by the Commission. Member states accepted the proposals in the White Paper *as a package*. While all member states had reservations about parts of the package, they all perceived that, taken as a whole, the proposals in the White Paper were in their best interests.

2   Even after agreeing the package as a whole, individual directives still had to be formulated and agreed on, and the process could be stalled at this stage as it had been before. The second critical element in the initiative was, therefore, the introduction of majority voting in place of unanimity for measures needed to complete the single market. This element was contained in the Single European Act (SEA, 1986).

3   The third element was the creation of a new legal doctrine that opened up national markets in the absence of harmonization. The doctrine of 'mutual recognition' stated that the satisfaction of the regulatory requirements of one state makes the product or service legitimate for the purposes of trade with other states. Mutual recognition gave states a new incentive to agree. It meant that, if the member states did not agree on harmonized regulations, the principle of mutual recognition might operate by default. States had a new incentive to agree on harmonized standards, as otherwise the least-regulated state would gain a competitive advantage and regulatory standards would gravitate to the 'lowest common denominator'.

These elements were not all put in place at the same time. The White Paper was agreed by the European Council at a summit in Milan in 1985. At the Milan summit the states also agreed to convene an intergovernmental conference (IGC) on the voting reforms that were later embodied in the SEA. The IGC took place in autumn 1985; the SEA was ratified in 1986 and came into effect from July 1987.

in the 1980s. The implementation of the SEM was full of difficulties, as good intentions had to be translated into measures by member states. Box 1.2 sets out the structure of the key institutions in the EU (see Heffernan, 2004).

But before turning to the intricacies of policy making, it is worth recalling the big question that motivates the study of the policy process, which is summed up in the title of a famous book by the American political scientist Robert Dahl: *Who Governs?* (1961). Dahl picked up the gauntlet thrown down by Marxists and others who analysed the fundamental economic inequalities of the Western capitalist democracies and argued that democracy was a veneer, a facade behind which real political power was exercised by the corporations and capitalists which had economic power. One important way of assessing who really exercises power, is to look at the policies that governments implement and ask how those policies are formulated, who influences them and who benefits from them. The next section briefly reviews Dahl's approach to answering these questions and introduces some of the problems involved in identifying where power really lies.

BOX 1.2   **Structure of the key institutions in the EU**

The European Council

The European Council is the senior, most authoritative body in the EU with legislative and executive powers. It brings together the Heads of Government of the member states and the President of the European Commission. The foreign ministers of the member states plus one other member of the Commission attend to provide assistance.

The Council of Ministers

The Council of Ministers (also referred to as 'the Council') exercises the day to day legislative responsibilities of the EU. It is composed of one representative at ministerial level from each member state, empowered to take decisions on behalf of their government. It is the main meeting place of member-state governments, and as such it is the EU's principal decision-making authority.

The European Commission

The European Commission is the permanent bureaucracy of the EU and the guardian of the treaties. Although the Commission can make proposals, the ministers of the member states take legislative decisions in the European Council and the Council of Ministers, sometimes in co-decision (or, in some cases, consultation) with the European Parliament. Working in close partnership with other European institutions and the governments of the member states, the executive powers of the Commission are restricted to the power of initiative, not decision, but it is charged with enforcing treaties already agreed to, and legislation previously implemented.

The European Parliament

The European Parliament lacks the formal powers of most national legislatures and it has no power to legislate alone, having to work with the Council of Ministers by scrutinizing proposals from the Commission and the Council of Ministers, being consulted on future legislation, and making recommendations. Nonetheless, its powers have increased in recent years and it has formal responsibilities for scrutiny of the executive and exercises budgetary and co-legislative powers.

The European Court of Justice

The Court of Justice enforces EU legislation agreed to by treaty or by the regulations, directives and decisions enacted by the Council of Ministers. It is the final arbiter of inter-union disputes between European institutions, between institutions and member states, and between member states. The Court is comprised of 25 members, one judge per member state, and 8 advocates-general.

(Heffernan, 2004, pp.3, 4, 6, 9, 11)

SUMMARY

- We can think of policies as going through the stages of formulation, decision and implementation, although in many complex areas of policy the stages overlap.

- In studying the policy process, it is possible to identify some general themes about how power is exercised in public policy making, which can be applied to many different types of policies.

---

2   WHO GOVERNS?

In *Exploring Political Worlds*, Paul Lewis looked at the problem of defining and identifying power. At first sight, the meaning of power in the policy process is aptly summed up by Bertrand Russell as 'the production of intended effects' **(Lewis, 2005, Section 4.2)**. Studying the policy process reveals some of the issues behind this definition. Policy goes through stages – but which stages matter most in producing effects or outcomes? The intentions of those involved in the policy process are not always clear and, indeed, different parties may have different intentions while agreeing on a common policy.

The way in which Dahl posed the question 'who governs?' avoided many of these complexities by focusing on the *decision-making* stage of the policy process. Dahl noted the tension that appears in democratic states between the broadly equal allocation of voting rights (the universal franchise) and the unequal allocation of power resources – such as 'knowledge, wealth, social position, access to officials, and other resources' (Dahl, 1961, p.1). On the basis of case studies of three areas of policy making in New Haven, Connecticut, Dahl rejected the idea that a small elite determined policy. Despite voter apathy and the concentration of power resources, city politics responded to demands put forward by diverse groups of activists, provided that they were sufficiently organized and persistent. 'Pluralism' is the term coined to describe this permeability of the policy process to diverse interests.

A key feature of Dahl's approach, which has since given rise to a great deal of debate and controversy among political scientists, was that it concentrated on what political actors *did*. Specifically, Dahl's 'behaviourist' method focused on the decision-making stage of the policy process. This is the stage where an issue has been identified and a proposal developed which is being put to a vote or subjected to some sort of approval process. Dahl looked at who (or which interests) prevailed at this stage. 'Success', and therefore power, was indicated by having a policy proposal accepted.

Critics of Dahl's analysis argued that power might be exercised very effectively at previous stages in the policy process. In particular, they pointed to the importance of controlling the policy agenda, and thereby influencing the way that issues are identified and proposals are formulated. For example, a large polluting corporation could exercise power more effectively if it could exercise its influence over politicians by keeping environmental controls off the public or political agenda rather than by opposing such controls at the decision-making stage. A key point made by Bachrach and Baratz (1962) was that some interests are never mobilized in the political process: some potential policies are never on the agenda. Power may be exercised by confining the scope of decision making to relatively 'safe' issues. Bachrach and Baratz argued that 'non-decisions' (that is, decisions to keep issues off the public agenda) are as important as decisions, so to really understand power, one has to look at what is *not* being discussed.

Steven Lukes, in a famous critique of the theories of power of Dahl and Bachrach and Baratz, highlighted a 'third dimension' of power (Dahl's decision-making focus is described as 'one-dimensional', and the introduction of agenda setting by Bachrach and Baratz provides a 'two-dimensional' view). Lukes (1974) focused on how the preferences of the actors involved in the policy process are developed and shaped. An 'interest group' is a collection of actors who have a common set of preferences or policy aims. Interest groups do not come into the world ready-formed. The recognition of a common interest may involve a good deal of leadership and persuasion. Issues are framed in particular ways, and causal theories are developed to trace through the impact of a policy on the well-being of the group. Even before decisions are made and agendas are set, there is 'latent' power over how people think, what they regard as common sense, and what is seen as politically workable and feasible and what is not. Power which operates at this level is difficult to see or quantify – and Lukes's work has been criticized on this score – but it can have profound effects. From Lukes's perspective, dominant values in society condition our thinking about what is right and wrong, possible and impossible. These values do not just magically appear; ideas about the common interest may involve a great deal of leadership and persuasion.

The example of the single market illustrates very clearly the strengths and limitations of Dahl's approach, and the significance of some of the criticisms made of it. The decision-making phase of the single market took place between June and December 1985. In June the leaders of the member states agreed to convene an extraordinary IGC, which took place in Luxembourg in the autumn. At that conference, government ministers formulated drafts of amendments to be made to the treaties that govern the EU (then still called the European Economic Community) which were incorporated into the SEA. These measures were subsequently approved by the heads of government and then, in the early months of 1986, ratified by the member states.

Two things are noticeable about this process. First, it is very difficult to identify how power was exercised in these decision-making forums. This is partly because they are not open to public scrutiny, but even if they were the main finding would probably be that a great deal of wheeling and dealing went on, with multiple 'side bargains' being struck by the participants (Figure 1.1). Because the member states all had to agree to adopt the SEA (unanimity was required), there was no voting, so it is not possible to identify clear winners and losers. All states saw themselves as winners overall, but some made more concessions than others.

FIGURE 1.1   Wheeling and dealing in the EC: power is exercised as much in 'side bargains' as in formal decision-making forums

Second, the events between June and December 1985 described above do not seem to be the most important events in understanding how the single market came about. Prior to June, proposals were put which set the decision-making wheels in motion. When the heads of state met in June they had before them a White Paper setting out measures to remove barriers to the free movement of goods, services, capital and labour, along with a report suggesting changes to the decision-making process in the Community. The process that led up to the creation of these documents, which set the agenda for the events that followed was, arguably, more significant than the schedule of meetings at which the decisions were taken.

'Winding back' from June 1985 widens and deepens the perspectives that can be developed on the policy process. More actors and interests are introduced into the analysis, and it is possible to look not only at the positions they took and the decisions they made, but also at the ideas that were developed and disseminated. By winding back it is also possible to take a more open view of the venues in which power is exercised, for example by looking at the way

TABLE 1.1   Stages of the SEM policy process

Date	Event	Key actors
1979	*Cassis de Dijon* judgement	European Court of Justice acting on complaint from German importer
1980–85	Lobbying by business interests, resolutions passed by European Parliament	Leading industrialists (Roundtable of European Industrialists formed 1983), representatives from member states
June 1985	Publication of White Paper	European Commission
June 1985	Milan summit	European Council: heads of state plus President of European Commission (Delors)
December 1985	IGC to finalize and agree SEA	Delegations from member states
1986	Ratification of SEA	National legislatures (referendums in some states)
1987–92 and after	Implementation	Technical committees, European Commission (drafting directives), Council of Ministers (passing directives), national governments (transposing directives into national law)
ongoing	Enforcement	European Commission (compliance actions), national courts, European Court of Justice

the Commission works. A decision-making orientation narrows the focus: in the European context, the European Council (comprising heads of government of the member states) occupies the central place. We will see (in Section 6), that it is also interesting to 'wind forward' to the implementation of the policy, another domain in which power is exercised. Table 1.1 shows the timeline of the SEM policy process, taking into account the 'winding back' and 'winding forward' perspectives.

The discussion in Section 4 below reviews the ideas that underlay the single market and shows how their formulation can also be seen as a domain for the exercise of power.

SUMMARY

- Power is exercised in different ways at different stages of the policy process.
- Having one's proposals accepted (e.g. by winning votes) is one dimension of power.
- Influencing the agenda for decision making – including keeping some issues off the agenda – is a second dimension of power.
- Power can also be exercised through broader societal values, prior to decision making and agenda setting; for example, through the ways that participants in the policy process frame problems and interpret the evidence about possible solutions. These are aspects of the third dimension of power.

3   ACTORS AND VENUES

Having noted the different stages at which power can be exercised, in this section we look at the different actors involved in policy making, and the different venues where policy making takes place. We consider policy communities and issue networks and the role of the 'dominant actor' and 'policy entrepreneur'.

3.1 Policy communities

Before we can think about the kind of actors involved in the development of the SEM, it's useful to highlight a distinction between 'low' and 'high' politics. Studies of the policy process tend to focus on 'low politics' issues, such as managing the economy and providing benefits and services to the population, rather than on the 'high politics' of international diplomacy, defence and security. This is not to imply that there are no policy processes in 'high politics'. The decision by the US and UK governments to go to war with Iraq in 2003 involved a policy process. However, high politics processes tend to suit a different type of analysis from those of low politics. The former processes combine a blaze of publicity and journalistic commentary with intense secrecy. We often do not know what has really happened until papers are released thirty years after the event. Low politics processes are not so heavily reported in the media, but large parts are accessible to researchers. Low politics attracts researchers who are interested in the 'daily life' of government. Frequently the processes are lengthy and attenuated, suiting the more measured pace of academic research. High politics fits better with the frenetic style and quick-response capacity of journalism. The process of European economic integration has been dominated by low politics with occasional high interludes. The creation of the SEM required the resolution of innumerable small technical problems relating to the conduct of trade. It also raised high politics issues of national sovereignty that occasionally attracted media commentary.

So how can we work out who are the important actors in the policy process? In 1969 Jeremy Richardson published an important account of the process by which the Restrictive Trade Practices Act 1956 had been passed (Richardson, 1969). The Act was used as a case study to illustrate how the policy process in the UK worked. At the time, Richardson's study was unusual in giving a relatively high profile to the influence of interest groups on the policy process. This compared with a narrower traditional view that looked to the institutions of government (government departments, the cabinet, parliament) as the central players in the policy process, with only walk-on roles for political parties, public opinion and the media. As Richard Freeman explains in Chapter 3, a wide range of organizations participate in policy processes, lobbying on issues which are of particular concern to their members. These organizations can be seen as making up a 'policy community' or 'issue network'.

The UK tradition is for policy communities to be informal, although there are some examples of the formal incorporation of interests into the structure of policy-making bodies. For example, the Monetary Policy Committee at the Bank of England, which makes decisions on interest rates, comprises people from business, trade unions and the City of London alongside academics and other experts. In some European countries this structure would be more strongly embedded by giving certain corporate bodies (the Confederation of British Industries and the Trades Union Congress, for example) the right to nominate a fixed number of members of the committee. The dominance of policy communities, whether formal or informal, is connected with a consensual style of policy making, whereby informed participants can agree on desired developments or, if necessary, make 'non-decisions' to avoid embarking on conflictual paths. It is this consensual quality that allows policy communities to keep the overt politics out of policy.

Often, it is those involved in implementing the policy who are prepared to devote most resources to participating in a policy community. One example that has been studied in depth is Britain's roads policy, where the road building companies enjoyed a close relationship with the Department for Transport (under its previous titles) for many years. This small, stable policy community agreed on the desirability of building more roads and developed and implemented roads policy accordingly. **Thompson (2005, Section 4)** suggests that we still find tight policy communities in, for example, education and agriculture, but the once-comfortable transport policy community has been challenged by new organizations, particularly motivated by environmental issues.

3.2 From policy communities to issue networks

Political scientists in the UK and the USA have argued that policy communities are becoming less cohesive. This partly reflects changes in structures for the implementation of policy (discussed in Section 6 below); implementing agencies are now sometimes deliberately excluded from the formulation stage of the policy process, allowing more radical ideas to come onto the agenda. Communities may be opened up in other ways too. Conservative governments from 1979 onwards reduced their dependence on the civil service by bringing in proposals that were initiated and developed by people and organizations that had no connection with established communities, such as executives from big businesses and intellectuals from think-tanks. New Labour has continued this practice.

In the USA in the 1960s, the image of an 'iron triangle' was used to describe the close relationship and shared language among government agencies, special interest lobbies and members of congressional committees. However, by the 1970s this pattern was changing. Heclo (1978) argued that the tight policy communities that used to characterize US policy making had been opened up by new interest groups. The style of politics in Washington, DC, was becoming less clubby, the public policy agenda 'congested', and the interactions 'a merry-go-round', calling to mind a Jacques Tati film in which drivers on a roundabout 'spend their time socializing with each other as they drive in endless circles' (Heclo, 1978, p.97). The concept of 'issue networks' is used to describe these more open and fragmented structures.

We can find both 'policy communities' and 'issue networks' in EU policy making. A great deal of the work of the single market programme went on in committees, which had to formulate detailed proposals for regulatory harmonization and to facilitate mutual recognition of national regulations. Membership of these regulatory committees is generally drawn from the equivalent regulatory bodies of the various states. There are plenty of examples of conflict and paralysis in these committees, with each national representative defending their own national regulatory approach. However, the procedural and decision-making changes introduced as part of the SEM helped to steer the committees away from bargaining from national positions and towards negotiation and problem solving – the style of interaction characteristic of policy communities.

We can also see looser issue networks operating in European policy making. The processes leading first to the SEM and then to Maastricht were widely criticized as secretive and undemocratic, and the Commission has responded to this criticism by consulting more widely on its proposals. While this often involves consulting with established elites such as business leaders and academic experts, the Commission has also established links with 'new social movements' such as the disability rights movement (discussed by Watson in Chapter 4). However, finding a policy agenda that responds to the aims of new social movements but is also acceptable to national governments is a challenge. There is pressure to bring forward new initiatives and a tendency to neglect the more mundane task of implementing existing policies.

One way in which an issue network can be galvanized is by the activities of a 'dominant actor' who is able to coordinate the different interests involved and formulate the sequence of measures that will produce effective policy. The obvious candidate for the position of dominant actor in the SEM process is the President of the Commission, Jacques Delors (Figure 1.2). Delors had the 'vision' to carry others along and find the necessary compromises and settlements to turn the vision into an agreed policy. This is not the same as saying that Delors 'created' the SEM or even that the SEM would not have happened without Delors. Rather, it is to acknowledge that particular individuals may shape the policy agenda and influence the interactions among different interest groups.

FIGURE 1.2   Jacques Delors was a 'dominant actor' in the policy process

A related idea is of a 'policy entrepreneur', who finds the proposals that can mediate between different interest positions. **Thompson (2005, Section 5.1)** explains how Delors was the key policy entrepreneur in promoting monetary union. Often in national government the civil service is an important policy entrepreneur, aided by its institutional role in formulating the details of policy (drafting laws, etc). Analysts of the EU have debated the Commission's role as a policy entrepreneur. The Commission's key power lies in its role in initiating policies and thereby setting the agenda for the member states in Council. While the Commission occupies the same place as a national civil service in formulating policy (for instance in drafting directives), it is different from a national civil service in (at least) two important ways. First, the lines of political authority are much less clear than in national governments, giving the Commission more autonomy to pursue its own agendas. This implies that the Commission has more freedom in policy entrepreneurship than the civil service. The Commission is 'a bureaucracy with a mission: ... the mission of promoting the integration process' (Cram, 1997, p.31).

However, this image of a powerful and autonomous Commission is countered by the second difference: the relatively small size of the Commission. The Commission does not have the resources to research and develop policy internally. Rhodes and Marsh (1992) argue that policy networks are partly created from such 'resource dependencies'. Commission officials need the contributions of academics, business experts and indeed national officials in related policy fields. Viewed from this perspective, the Commission does not have a high level of autonomy, and so cannot act effectively as a policy entrepreneur.

The concepts of policy communities and issue networks draw attention to the range of participants who may have influence over how a policy is developed, from intellectuals and academics to businessmen and civil servants. However, the wider the view we take of participation in the policy process, the harder it is to identify how power is really exercised. It is necessary to distinguish between advocacy and influence: advocates of a particular policy do not always have influence over the policy. It might also be necessary to distinguish consultation processes from the real business of policy making. UK governments have developed a habit of consulting widely, but there is often little sign of policies being changed as a result of consultation.

Commentators who have analysed the single market initiative disagree with each other about which actors were most influential. For example, one might expect that multinational businesses would be influential, as they have much to gain from the removal of barriers to trade. Sandholtz and Zysman (1989) say that business leaders were important, wielding influence through their personal contacts with national and Community political leaders. Moravcsik (1991) says that they were not: he sees the negotiation of the SEA as being primarily an intergovernmental process, motivated by a convergence of views in the member states (particularly Germany, France and the UK) on the desirability of privatization, deregulation and economic liberalization. The difference of view partly arises from focusing on different stages of the policy process: Moravcsik looks most closely at the decision-making stage (June–December 1985), while Sandholtz and Zysman take a wider view of how the single market agenda was developed.

3.3   Venues

Just as some actors have more power than others in the policy process, so venues matter too. The policy process involves venues ranging from parliamentary debates, cabinet meetings and select committee hearings through to public enquiries, seminars and conferences and court cases. Groups that are excluded from the policy process may open up new venues such as street demonstrations or direct action. The conditions of access to different venues and the rules governing their operation comprise the institutional structure of the policy process, and they can have a strong influence on how power is exercised and by whom.

We can understand the EU institutions as a completely new set of policy venues. These new venues are not necessarily colonized by the same actors who are influential at national level. Participants in the European Council (where heads of government meet) and the Councils of Ministers (made up of ministers from member states who hold the relevant portfolios) could be seen as bringing national positions to the European bargaining table, but the reality is more complicated. Politicians and senior civil servants who find their ideas blocked by their national policy communities can seek a more fruitful environment in Brussels. For example, the German representation at the Commission is generally more oriented in favour of market liberalization than its counterparts in national German politics. German liberalizers saw the single market initiative as a way of out-manoeuvring the domestic policy community, which maintained a restrictive regulatory environment in areas such as banking, finance and insurance in Germany.

What can we learn about venues in policy making from the SEM example? Well, crucially, the SEM initiative was helped on its way by the development of a new venue, the European Council. The heads of government (prime ministers or presidents) of the member states of the EU had been meeting sporadically for some years, but the meetings became more regular in the 1980s. With the formal creation of the European Council, Jacques Delors became the first President of the Commission to enjoy regular access to national leaders, through the group meetings. While much of the SEM process was based on the work of bureaucrats and regulators, the European Council gave the initiative high-level leadership, which facilitated and speeded up the lower-level processes.

Another important venue for the development of the single market was the European Court of Justice (ECJ). Generally the courts do not figure much in UK accounts of the policy process, but in some other countries they are leading actors. The ECJ has played an important role in the development of the single market. Many ECJ cases originate in attempts by businesses to overturn government policies that restrict their access to markets. One such case was brought by the German importer of a French liqueur, *Cassis de Dijon*. The importer was prevented from selling the liqueur in Germany because it did not meet German standards regarding alcohol content. In 1979, the ECJ ruled that, if the cassis met French standards for a liqueur, it could be sold as such in Germany. The Cassis decision was quickly picked up on by the European Commission, and its potential in promoting market integration developed in the course of launching the SEM initiative (see Box 1.1 above).

The ECJ has also proved to be an important venue at the implementation stage of the SEM policy process. Generally (as Section 6 explains), the implementation venues for EU policies are national institutions: EU institutions formulate and decide on policies but member states implement them. This 'venue shift' creates a rich set of opportunities for modifying and evading the policy. However, both private individuals and the Commission can bring legal actions against member states for non-compliance with directives, and the ECJ has succeeded in improving the effectiveness of EU law in a number of cases.

Why are courts significant in this discussion? Courts are interesting venues because the conditions for gaining access to them are quite different from the conditions for successful lobbying inside the political process. Resources are needed – court cases are expensive – but participants do not have to recruit a mass membership or demonstrate that their position has wide public support. This makes courts particularly suitable venues for big businesses to defend their interests. Court action is also attractive to minority groups whose interests may be neglected in majoritarian democratic processes. As Watson shows in Chapter 4, disabled people have sought anti-discrimination legislation that can be enforced through the courts.

SUMMARY

- Interest groups may participate in the policy process in a variety of ways: as advocates, position takers, bargainers or negotiators who work towards finding consensual solutions.

- A 'policy community' is a group, which may encompass diverse interests but shares a common vocabulary that has the capacity to develop detailed policy formulations which are workable and acceptable to the participants.

- Whether or not civil servants dominate policy communities depends on the size and resources of the state bureaucracy and its relationship to the government.

- Venue shifts may change the composition of policy communities and allow different interests to be represented more effectively.

4 THE ROLE OF IDEAS

In Section 3 we saw that many actors invest resources in the policy process. While they are sometimes engaged in a conservative process of defending their established interests, they may also seek to promote innovative policies that provide new solutions to old dilemmas. This section examines the role of ideas in policy making in the following three senses. How useful is the rational choice model? How do 'experts' shape the language and choices that are made? And what is the influence of the norms and values held by the actors? Winning the 'ideas game' has become an important route to power and influence in the policy process, particularly in policy areas where transnational networks of experts play a major role, as in the creation of the SEM.

4.1 The rational choice model

Herbert Simon's influential book *Administrative Behaviour* (1957) offers an account of how policy decisions might be understood through a process of rational choice. 'The task of decision,' Simon suggested, 'involves three steps: (1) the listing of all alternative strategies; (2) the determination of all the consequences that follow upon each of these strategies; (3) the comparative evaluation of these sets of consequences' (Simon, 1957, p.67). Simon abstracts from the hurly-burly of the policy process and constructs a model of pure rational choice. This is an idealized view of how policy might be determined, rather than a description of how decisions are actually made. The rational choice model is often introduced to civil servants engaged in policy work as an ideal framework for giving policy advice to ministers.

But how well does this model 'fit' with what really goes on? Well, for a start, even the most loyal and diligent civil servant will fail to give the minister a complete 'information set' for making policy choices. It is not really possible (or even useful) to list all alternative strategies: only the strategies that are deemed plausible and realistic will be given. Nor can all the consequences be anticipated – the analysis is likely to focus on the consequences in which the minister is primarily interested, for example those which are politically sensitive. There is likely to be a host of unnoticed and sometimes unintended consequences that are outside the policy frame of interest. These limitations in the information that might be used in making a rational choice are captured in the concept of 'bounded rationality'.

Once we establish that rationality is necessarily bounded, the next step is to understand how the boundaries are drawn. How is the set of alternative strategies determined? One answer is that the policy process proceeds incrementally. Decisions always start from the existing situation and involve comparisons of possible small steps in various directions from the status quo. This does not mean that major policy changes do not or cannot happen. Rather, it suggests that they will happen through an accumulation of small steps. One advantage of small steps is that the range of consequences that has to be considered is kept within manageable bounds; however, a succession of small steps can lead to outcomes that were not envisaged or desired at the time of the first step.

Looking across different examples of the policy process, we often find incrementalism in situations where the decision and implementation phases of policy are quite closely linked, so that small changes are quickly implemented and feedback about the effects of the policy is soon available to the decision maker. This may be one reason why EU policy processes do not usually seem particularly incremental. On the contrary, they often involve big decisions that are radical breaks with the past. While Europe had been moving slowly towards the creation of a single market before the SEA, the SEM involved several new moves to speed up the process. A big gesture was made in setting the date of 1992 for completion, and mutual recognition was moved to centre stage as a means of accelerating implementation.

Another reason for adopting policies that involve big shifts rather than incremental moves is the difficulty of obtaining agreement among all of those who are entitled to participate in the decision-making process (the member states). It might be thought that agreement is easier if the changes envisaged are small, but this is not necessarily so. The EU decision-making process makes extensive use of 'package deals' in which a number of policy decisions are linked together. This facilitates agreement because member states who oppose one part of the package are persuaded to give up their opposition in return for getting other parts of the package which they support. The SEM was a package deal par excellence. Each state might have preferred to choose accelerated market liberalization in some sectors and limited reform in others, but they were forced to choose between acceleration and stasis across the board.

Once we recognize the importance of issue linkage and package deals, we can see that the policy process has moved a long way from the rational model. Decision makers are not presented with a wide range of alternatives; on the contrary, the number of alternatives is deliberately suppressed in order to promote a decision. Furthermore, the wide scope of the package deal makes it very difficult to give a full account of its consequences. Rather than proceeding by rational evaluation, policy makers agreed to the SEM out of a sense that it was a big idea whose time had come.

To understand how this climate of opinion came about, we need to consider Lukes's third dimension of power, whereby interpretations of the issues are framed and preferences formed. This process is the prelude to setting the agenda (the second dimension) and making decisions (the first dimension).

4.2 The role of expertise

How did the idea of greater economic integration come to be lodged in the imaginations of European actors? The single market initiative was based on a set of ideas about the benefits of market liberalization, extension of competition policy and the reduction of state subsidies. These ideas constituted an *ideology* in the sense that they were believed to be true independent of evidence and verification. By the mid 1980s, this ideology was so pervasive that it is hard to associate its advocacy with any particular group of actors. It had become part of the received wisdom of elites in international organizations. The European economies were all in difficulties, facing accelerating inflation and deeper recessions. While more right-wing governments came to power in several European states in the early 1980s, it was perhaps even more important that parties of the left began to reject the interventionist policies, notably in France. Most of the governments participating in the negotiation of the single market had a broadly similar market-oriented perspective on economic policy.

Several commentators argue that the poor economic performance of many states in the 1980s gave an impetus to market liberalization policies. It is a structural imperative of public policy to promote the health of the economy. Since the European economies are capitalist economies, this means responding to capitalist interests and creating the conditions under which capitalism can thrive. As global capitalism has grown in strength, European governments sought to ensure that their countries were competitive in the global economy. The adverse comparison of European with US economic performance particularly preoccupied them.

One of the key ways in which capitalist interests are internalized by governments is through their reliance on the advice of economists. Economists promise policies that comply with the structural imperative of promoting the health of the economy but, unlike that of the business lobby, their position is not compromised by (apparent) self-interest. Economists were influential in promoting the idea that failure to develop the single market would be costly, particularly in a study known as the Cecchini report, entitled *The European Challenge 1992: The Benefits of a Single Market* (Cecchini *et al.*, 1988). This study was requested by the single market commissioner, Lord Cockfield, and sought to quantify the extent of the economic benefits which might flow from integration.

What made this report so influential? There are several features of the report that illustrate how ideas can be influenced by selection and 'framing'. The primary idea in the Cecchini approach was that national government regulation was costly, and that a minimal European-level framework of regulations would therefore be beneficial. It was widely held that many obstacles to freer trade were unintentional: customs procedures, product standards and tax regimes had evolved differently in each state, but many differences were just historical institutional legacies and were not important for achieving national policy aims. Reflecting this view, the Cecchini report neglected many of the good reasons why governments might want to regulate (for example, to prevent environmental degradation). Only in the later, implementation stages of the SEM policy was it realized that many more aspects of national regulatory frameworks had to be preserved than the Cecchini report had assumed.

The Cecchini report was based on heroic assumptions about how output and prices would respond to competition and deregulation. Analyses of the effects of a policy are hypothetical by their very nature. Lindblom suggests that 'policy is analysed not in an unrealistic attempt to reach conclusive determinations of correct policy, but simply to persuade' (Lindblom, 1968, p.117). The report could be understood as presenting favourable scenarios, or stories, about how the single market might work.

Some commentators take a positive view of the role of experts and technocrats in EU policy making. Economists are skilled in finding efficient solutions to certain types of problems, creating 'positive sum' situations in which everybody benefits from a policy. Critics argue that popular preferences are suppressed under the cloak of efficiency by substituting 'the voice of the expert for the voice of the people' (Bernstein, 1955).

4.3 Norms and values

As well as considering the roles of the rational choice model and of experts in generating the ideas that frame policy making, we need to bear in mind that participants in the policy process interpret the evidence in the light of their own norms and values. In Europe, there is a value difference between those who favour deeper European integration and those who seek to preserve national autonomy. The formation of the single market crucially required that this value difference was put to one side, and other values – related to economic dynamism and growth – were brought to the fore.

The first commitments to economic union were made as early as 1969, and throughout the 1970s the European Council expressed concern about the slow progress of market integration. Armstrong and Bulmer (1998) emphasize how the ideas of the single market became embedded through repetition. '*Repeated* rehearsal of policy commitments can lead to the embedding of ideas in institutions; to the creation of new norms and values' (Armstrong and Bulmer, 1998, p.17). What we need to realize here is that national governments did not work their way carefully through the Cecchini report and add up the costs and benefits of opening markets. They signed up because they had, in a more general way, accepted the ideal of market integration.

The Cecchini report adopted a 'European frame' in assessing the benefits of the single market. Estimates of output and income growth were presented for Europe as a whole, rather than state by state. In other words, the Cecchini report invited policy makers to think of problems in a European rather than a national context. It might be thought that members of the Council of Ministers cannot be expected to 'think European' while they remain accountable to their national electorates. But, as we have seen, only a small subset of policies is salient in national elections, allowing plenty of scope for policy makers to adopt norms and values that deviate from those of the electorate.

Compared with the rational calculation of interests, the influence of norms and values can be rather ambiguous. There was certainly an essential ambiguity about the framework of norms and values informing the SEM. Some (such as Jacques Delors) adhered to the theory that there must be 'spillover' from economic integration to social and political union, while others (including Margaret Thatcher) regarded economic integration as a process that was entirely separable from political and social union. Thatcherite norms and values emphasized liberalization and competition; for those adhering to the wider European ideal, the values centred on the strengthening of Europe as an economic and political force. These values were sufficiently similar to facilitate agreement on the SEM, although their differences soon led to major ruptures over the Maastricht Treaty.

SUMMARY

- Ideas are crucial – both for political scientists to understand what is going on in the policy process, and for policy actors in framing policy making.

- 'Bounded rationality' refers to the way that policy makers necessarily consider only a limited set of policy choices and have limited information about the consequences of those choices.

- In order to facilitate agreement, agenda setters may deliberately constrain choices by linking together separate issues and constructing package deals.

- Expert advice is important, not only in providing information for the rational calculation of interests, but also in providing the frames through which policy makers view their interests.

- In considering large and complex policy initiatives, the parties may not be able to calculate their interests precisely, and may adopt general norms and values to guide their actions and decisions.

5 PROBLEMS OF INTEREST REPRESENTATION

In Section 3 we saw that the policy process is dominated by policy communities and issue networks, while Section 4 suggested that experts exert a profound impact on policy by shaping ideas and framing policy choices. These observations raise important issues about how power is exercised in the policy process. We turn now to look at the problem of how policies can be aligned with the preferences of the electorate when democratic institutions apparently play little role in the policy process, and to the question of bias in policy communities.

5.1   Interests, democracy and the media

How much can you and I, or even our democratic institutions, participate in policy making? A sanguine view might be that constraints on interest representation in policy making are a natural consequence of the effort involved in acquiring information, developing ideas, engaging in coherent debate and organizing an efficient policy process. Governing the country would grind to a halt if *all* interests had to get a hearing and *every* stage of policy making had to be debated in parliament. Most policy communities are clubs that the general public does not want to join. A refinement of this idea is that, while policy communities may be selective and indeed elite, there is contestation and debate among elites. So long as (say) both capital and labour are represented at elite level in the policy process, the outcome should represent a reasonably fair consensus that takes account of different interests in society.

Another answer might be that the institutions of representative democracy *do* provide a safeguard against policy processes being completely hijacked by vested interests. Provided an issue is important enough, governments will, in the end, be accountable to the electorate for their policy decisions. However, there are some problems with this claim. Without adequate information, voters cannot choose policies that are in their best interests. As soon as we acknowledge the problem of 'educating' the voters, we also have to acknowledge that the participants in the policy process are unequal, either because they have unequal information, or because some have the skills and vocabulary to process and interpret that information and others do not.

Where does that leave you and me? The general public relies on the media for information about policies, but there's a problem here too because the media report particular things in particular ways. The media may be 'primed' or manipulated by policy makers to raise issues – the media are rarely agenda setters. Also, they are interested in conflicts and disagreements that make good stories: if policy makers are able to proceed consensually, the policies they develop will attract limited media coverage. Moreover media interest in most subjects is sporadic, creating an 'issue attention cycle'. Public opinion may affect the behaviour of policy makers when the media spotlight is on them, but the spotlight will in due course move on. Finally, media coverage will tend to simplify the issues, stirring public interest by highlighting the symbolic content of a policy rather than undertaking detailed analysis of its real effects.

Another problem for democratic representation, as shown in the SEM process, was that there were few ready symbols to galvanize our interest. European makers evoked a 'borderless Europe', but it was hard to get the general public excited about the abolition of customs paperwork. In contrast, the policy of monetary union (the adoption of the European single currency) has huge symbolic content, resulting in a much more intense public debate, even though the effect on the allocation of resources may well be smaller than the effect of the SEM. Very late in the day, long after the SEM was a done deal, the UK media found some symbols of market integration to attack. They created a powerful image of a meddling Brussels bureaucracy, concerned with the straightness of bananas and intent on abolishing UK clothes sizes and imperial measures. Small parts of the single market that conformed to this image were publicized, often with a gleeful disregard for accuracy in the details. The European Commission's Press Office in London devotes an entire section of its website to the rebuttal of 'Euromyths', but its efforts lack the elements of human drama and absurdity which the tabloid press can bring to its Brussels bureaucrat stories.

A further limitation on democratic participation resulted from the relatively quiet consensus of the European states in adopting the SEM. This meant that the SEA (containing the treaty amendments necessary for the SEM) attracted much less attention than the subsequent Maastricht Treaty negotiations, where there was a high-profile disagreement between the UK and Denmark and the other states. During the time of the single market negotiations, the UK public was absorbed in the conflict over the UK's financial contribution to the European budget. While this may have been an important issue in itself, it was also politically very 'saleable' and was valuable for reassuring Euro-sceptics, both in the Conservative Party and in the electorate.

Even if stronger public preferences on the SEM had been formed and shaped, it is not clear that these preferences would have influenced government decisions. The single market case study reveals (at least) three problems in identifying any influence of electoral preferences over governments' decisions to sign up to the 1992 initiative. The first problem is that policies may become politically salient too late in the day to change direction. Policies are 'path dependent', which means that the policy options available now depend on those chosen previously. The single market was a very important initiative with significant consequences for the future of European integration, but by the time these consequences were fully understood, it was too late to reverse the policy (although adjustments were made at the margins).

The second problem is that public opinion affects electoral outcomes through the mechanisms of party politics. Sometimes, political parties divide clearly on a major policy issue, enabling a signal to come from the voters about their policy preferences. Often, however, parties scramble for what is perceived to be the 'middle ground' in order to maximize their vote, or alternatively adopt ambiguous stances on policies where the risk of splitting the party and/or losing voters is too great. European integration has fallen into the latter category in UK politics. Political preferences over European integration cut across existing party alignments: both Labour and the Conservatives are internally divided on the issue.

A similar pattern can be found elsewhere in Europe. One variant is that, in a number of states, the main parties are united in favouring European integration, enabling governments to participate in European policy making without being much concerned about the domestic political consequences. However, this pattern has given rise to some major political scares. In Denmark, the pro-European positions of the main parties are not matched on the ground and the Danes have, through referendums, thrown out two proposals for deeper integration. In France, the shock success of Jean-Marie Le Pen coming second in the first round of the 2002 presidential elections was attributed in part to the failure of any other party to offer an anti-European platform to the French electorate.

A third problem is that a government's interest in getting re-elected (and therefore taking notice of public opinion) may not be its only interest. It is possible to think of parts of the state as having their own interests. For example, bureaucrats may be interested in expanding their powers and budgets. Ministers in the government may be interested in gaining respect and recognition from their peers (including ministers in other governments) or in having a place in history. Then again, some theories of European integration conceive of each member state as having preferences that are relatively autonomous of direct political concerns, and are instead located in culture, history and economic structure.

5.2 Bias in policy communities

The discussion so far suggests that the policy process is only rather weakly connected to the institutions of democratic government. Furthermore, we have seen that policy communities are made up of agents who have substantial vested interests in certain policy outcomes. This section examines whether the choice of policies will be systematically biased or constrained as a result of these two factors.

One of the most famous theories of bias in policy communities was put forward by Mancur Olson in *The Logic of Collective Action* (1963). Olson argued that small interest groups were more likely to be active and effective than large ones. Large groups, according to Olson, would have difficulties maintaining participation, and so in that sense have a bias or predisposition to mobilize less effectively (see Figure 1.3). Large groups would suffer from 'free rider' problems: the free rider leaves it to others to expend resources on actions (campaigns, lobbying, etc) which are also in the free rider's interest. Olson's theory had a particularly sharp application to economic policy. Generally, policies to liberalize trade will impose large costs on the domestic industries that suffer from exposure to competition. Both employers and unions in these industries will mobilize to campaign against liberalization. In contrast, the main benefits from trade liberalization are spread thinly, almost invisibly, across consumers who have a wider range of products supplied under more competitive conditions, leading to lower prices. Mobilizing consumers is very difficult. The conclusion was that economies with small sectoral union and employer organizations were fated by the logic of collective action implied that costly protectionist policies would prevail if unions and employers were organized to defend narrow sectoral interests.

FIGURE 1.3   Large groups are not necessarily effective in influencing policy outcomes

Critics of Olson have pointed out that large groups will have more political legitimacy and more resources than small groups. In practice this last claim is arguable: large numbers cannot be equated with large resources. The wealth of group members matters more. Groups of businesses and employer interest associations are likely to be smaller and therefore easier to coordinate (overcoming free-rider problems) and better resourced than consumer groups. Furthermore, they are likely to be recognized as legitimate because of the importance of business and employment to economic well-being in a capitalist society.

So how does Olson's theory fit with our case study of the SEM? The single market is exactly the type of policy that, in Olson's analysis, will suffer substantial resistance from organized interest groups. Olson's analysis could be used to explain the long period of stagnation in European policy making that preceded the 1992 initiative. There are several strands to explaining how this opposition was overcome.

First, Olson's analysis characterizes the main business interests as protectionist. His model was built with the US case in mind, where exports are a small part of the economy and exporters' interest groups are not very influential. Exporters have an interest in trade liberalization. In Europe, companies which saw trade liberalization as providing opportunities to enter new markets constituted an important political force. Furthermore, multinational companies perceived that the SEM would involve shifting power over market regulation (product standards, trademarks, etc) to the European level, where well-organized business interests could have a big influence over how market regulation was conducted.

Second, trade unions were not uniformly opposed to the 1992 initiative, despite the fears of specific groups of workers who were vulnerable to competition. Olson has noted that if trade unions are sufficiently large to encompass both sheltered and competitive industries, then they may advocate policies that are in the interests of workers generally. Since workers are also consumers, this is one way in which consumer interests may begin to count in the policy process. In practice, trade unions are multi-level organizations, with 'peak' confederations (such as the Trades Union Congress) inclined to take an 'encompassing' view, while trade unionists in particular sectors may see things rather differently.

However, the main limitation to the application of Olson's analysis is a deeper one. His analysis assumes that the actors can identify their interests clearly. This requires that they can predict the outcomes of the policy with confidence. The outcomes of some policies are obvious and direct, but the SEM was not such a policy. Its very scope introduced uncertainty, which interest groups responded to by taking very general pro-European or anti-European positions. These positions were themselves built on predictions about the nature of the entity that Europe might become. Some pro-European trade unionists believed that greater economic integration would 'spill over' into the strengthening of European social policy, which might in turn improve the ability of workers' organizations to bargain effectively with multinational companies. Others opposed the single market because they saw it as the first step towards full economic and monetary union (EMU) that would involve ceding power over monetary policy to a European central bank, which would be locked into monetarist policies. These examples show the importance of Lukes's 'third dimension' of power, whereby ideas and theories play a fundamental role in shaping the interest group structure.

Nevertheless, Olson's theory of the political weakness of large groups with diffuse interests can illuminate the role of the media in public policy. We considered in Section 5.1 that the media will tend to address the symbolic content of a policy rather than examining its real effects. This reflects the difficulty of getting the public interested in policies that will have small impacts on most people, even when the total effects are important. This tendency to apathy might be overcome by finding appropriate symbols which people feel strongly about. However, symbols can be used to deflect as well as to mobilize public concern. As Section 6 explains, policy makers can mollify public opinion by making appropriate symbolic declarations about the aims and values of a policy, which are then not necessarily reflected in the details of implementation.

SUMMARY

- Representative institutions such as parliaments often have a limited role in the policy process, particularly in the early stages of agenda setting and policy formulation.

- Electoral preferences may still affect the choice of policies, but the impact of electoral preferences depends on whether policies are sufficiently politically salient, how the political parties align on the policy issue, and whether the politicians making the decisions are primarily interested in getting re-elected.

- There are likely to be biases or systematic tendencies in interest group formation, such that a small group that is strongly affected by a proposal is likely to mobilize more effectively than a large group that is weakly or diffusely affected.

6 IMPLEMENTATION

Once policies are formulated and decided upon, they have to be implemented. Laws governing the action of businesses or individuals have to be enforced. Measures involving government expenditure have to be budgeted for and spending authorizations given to bureaucracies or agencies. Different agencies and government departments have to recognize the impact of the policy on their work and coordinate changes to their activities. In the last twenty years, the UK government has changed its implementation structures a number of times to try to achieve better delivery of its policies. For instance, the health service has been repeatedly reformed, the structure of education governance and funding has changed, and the Department of Social Security has disappeared. Clearly implementation, and evaluation of the policy once it has been implemented, are important domains for the exercise of power in the policy process.

6.1 Power and implementation

Wilson (2005; first published 1887) argued that it was important to draw a clear distinction between policy and administration. Policy involves politicians making choices from alternative courses of action on the basis of their aims and values, while administration is done by officials whose role is to implement the delivery of the chosen policies. Like the rational choice model discussed above, the idea of a clear distinction between policy and administration is influential on civil servants' understanding of their role; but as an account of what actually happens, this idea is rejected by analysts of the policy process. In practice, implementation generally involves value-laden decisions, for a number of reasons. It may be that conflicts between aims or values have not been resolved at the policy-making stage, so that politicians have in effect delegated some of the hard choices to administrators. Sometimes, it is felt that administrators are better informed than politicians or have special expertise, and that it is therefore a good idea to leave them some flexibility. The policy may involve a succession of detailed choices in particular situations that cannot be anticipated by high-level policy makers. It may be inefficient to be highly prescriptive, if the resulting policies are over-centralized and lacking in flexibility.

In the UK, the government has moved away from a hierarchical model of implementation towards a 'rational goal model' – of setting targets for its agencies rather than prescribing to them exactly how they should achieve the government's aims. The limitations of this model have in turn contributed to the development of new models of self-government and open systems (see Chapter 2), in which there is no clear distinction between policy making and implementation.

Moreover, in European policy making, the idea of a distinction between policy and administration has no credence because the implementing authorities are themselves elected governments that have legitimacy to determine aims and values. A key idea in European implementation is 'subsidiarity', a concept that reflects the difficulty of developing precise policies at the European level which are appropriate for application in all the member states. European directives have to be 'transposed' by the adoption of national laws to put them into effect. A degree of subsidiarity is inherent in the procedures for transposition of directives, which are 'binding, as to the result to be achieved' but leave to member states 'the choice of form and methods'. However, this is not as permissive as it may sound. The SEM directives were relatively detailed and tightly drafted, and the ECJ has found in a number of cases that they were inadequately transposed. More recently, the EU has moved towards the adoption of more 'framework directives' which leave member states greater flexibility in how to achieve the specified aims.

Is implementation a part of all policies? There is one subcategory of policy that is formulated without any intention that it should be implemented. Symbolic policies may be adopted when politicians want to be seen to be in favour of certain measures or goals without wanting them to be carried through into resource allocation or coercive enforcement. Symbolic policies are attractive if politicians are judged by the electorate on the basis of their declarations rather than on outcomes 'on the ground'. They may also be adopted deviously. The symbolic measure may satisfy its earnest but poorly informed advocates; cynical and well-informed opponents may in their turn be content with assurances that the policy will not be implemented.

Not all symbolic policy making is devious and manipulative. Some goals are not really susceptible to organized state action, but involve gradual changes in the hearts and minds of the public at large. The aim of making us all into 'good Europeans' may fall into this category. Some concrete measures can be taken, such as facilitating exchange programmes among universities, but there is also a more general effort to persuade the public that Europe stands for good things, such as fundamental human rights. These measures are primarily declaratory: such enforcement as there is relies on the uncoordinated actions of individuals taking cases before courts.

Sometimes, there is uncertainty or ambiguity among the participants about whether the policy is meant to be symbolic or not, or about the nature of the desired implementation. We saw in Section 4 that there was uncertainty about the eventual scope of the SEM initiative. For those participants who sought political as well as economic integration, the important elements in the SEM initiative were those that created momentum towards EMU, notably the changes in voting rules to speed up agreement on some key measures. From this perspective, the important part of implementation was the development of the EU's institutional capacity to create the legal framework for the SEM. Implementation 'success' could be measured by the number of directives pushed through and their coverage of different sectors.

For the UK government, in contrast, implementation meant improvement in the access of UK firms to European markets and the exposure of sheltered parts of the economy to competitive pressures. This implied that the directives creating the single market should be properly transposed and enforced across all the member states. The result was the apparent paradox that the UK, the reluctant European, took a hardline stance on the enforcement of European law. In 1992, when the rule-making part of the SEM process was largely complete, a high-level report on the operation of the single market (the Sutherland report) highlighted numerous failures to translate the rules into 'facts on the ground'. The report outlined a strategy for keeping the momentum of the SEM going, through monitoring and enforcement actions by the Commission. The UK government itself set up a Single Market Compliance Unit to monitor compliance with SEM legislation by other member states.

6.2 Evaluation

As we saw earlier, part of the rational choice model of the policy process was that policies should be evaluated, enabling systematic 'policy learning' to take place. Some theories postulate a 'feedback loop' whereby the results of evaluating a policy are incorporated into the formulation of revisions to the policy.

The SEM example illustrates some of the practical problems that arise in evaluation and policy learning. A number of evaluations of the SEM have been done. However, even by the turn of the century, evaluators hedged their findings with caveats about the long timescale that would be necessary for the full effects of the SEM to emerge. The period for evaluation is generally much longer than the period for policy making, so policies are often revised before evaluations are available. Alternatively, by the time the evaluation can be done the policy has dropped out of the current policy agenda and there is little political interest in undertaking revisions.

To evaluate the SEM (and indeed to evaluate most policies), economists had to formulate ideas about the *anti-monde*, that is, what the world would have looked like in the absence of, in this case, the SEM. To do this, they developed ideas about the possible effects of the policy and looked to see if these effects could be matched in time with the implementation of the SEM. Not all these ideas corresponded to those put forward in the Cecchini report. The evaluators discovered various positive effects of the SEM which Cecchini (and others) had not forecast. Most notably, there was considerable convergence between the rich and poor members of the EU in the 1990s, which evaluators argued could be attributed to the SEM. Convergence was not forecast by Cecchini. Indeed, in the 1980s there was concern that the single market might increase the gap between the core and the periphery in Europe.

The evaluation studies for the SEM have been used to prevent 'backsliding' on the policy and to maintain pressure for its full implementation. The studies have played a persuasive role, in much the same way as the Cecchini report used analysis as a form of persuasion (see Section 4.2 above). (See also the celebratory postcard in Figure 1.4.)

FIGURE 1.4   The European Commission works to promote the continued development of the SEM

SUMMARY

- Many important aspects of what a policy involves may not be resolved until the implementation stage.

- Implementation involves venue shifts, giving opportunities for actors who may have been excluded from the formulation and decision stages to exercise power.

- Policies may be implemented through a hierarchically organized bureaucracy, but often agencies with an element of autonomy are involved. In the EU, member states have considerable autonomy in implementation.

- Evaluation may be undertaken to examine whether a policy has achieved its aims, but a 'feedback loop' from evaluation into policy making is unlikely to be found in practice.

7 CONCLUSION

In the Introduction, I remarked that it can be hard to study the policy process in a general way, when every policy has its own specific and unique features. Table 1.2 summarizes how different approaches to the study of the policy process have illuminated the SEM case study. Agenda setting plays a key role, as discussed in Section 2 on dimensions of power and Section 4 on the role of ideas.

TABLE 1.2   Approaches to studying the policy process

Aspect of the policy process	Concepts and theories	Case/context
Setting the agenda	Three faces of power; non-decisions as power The role of ideas	How did the SEM get on the agenda? Ideas about the benefits of market liberalization and competition
Actors: who was involved?	Policy communities and issue networks Dominant actors and policy entrepreneurs	How did business interests affect policy? How important was Delors? Is the Commission able to act as a policy entrepreneur?
Venues: where was the policy formulated, decided upon and implemented?	Different actors are influential in different venues	The role of the ECJ: who has access to the Court? Opportunities for slippage from SEM commitments at the implementation stage
Content of the policy: what was decided and how was it decided?	Rational actor model Politics of expertise Role of norms and values Repetition Ambiguity	The Cecchini report: how did it influence policy makers? Were its predictions accurate? Adoption of a European 'frame' Was the SEM just about trade or would there be a social dimension?
Implementation	Separation of policy and administration	No separation in Europe: implementing authorities are elected governments

Ideas have to be promoted by powerful *actors* in influential *venues*. Ideas can swim around in the 'policy soup' to use Kingdon's phrase (Kingdon, 1984, p.21), but until they are taken up in appropriate ways they are not authoritative: they do not compel actions or direct resources. Section 3 discussed how actors may be linked in policy communities and issue networks, and also showed how venues may shape policies.

One of the main aims of studying the policy process is to work out where power really lies and identify the structures through which it is exercised. In the 1960s and 1970s, UK government ministers were wont to complain about the tight grip exercised by Whitehall mandarins over the policy agenda. The character of Sir Humphrey Appleby in the TV series *Yes Minister* provided a compelling example of this view of the policy process. Compared with Whitehall, the European institutions are much more open to external influence. The European Commission has little capacity to formulate policy autonomously. Instead, it facilitates the formation of issue networks, which produce policy proposals. The institutions of the EU, too, cannot implement policy autonomously – they are reliant on member states to transpose directives (although there are sanctions if states fail to do so).

Studying the policy process is a good way to get a sense of how changes in the *structure of government* may have effects on the *exercise of power*. This chapter has shown how a supra-national institution such as the EU makes policy. Subsequent chapters will look at other aspects of policy making in the context of multilevel governance. The opening-out of the policy process beyond the nation-state has contributed to changes in the way that power is exercised and the structures in which it operates. Today, it is more important than ever to 'stretch' our view of the policy process both at its beginning and its end, by 'winding back' and 'winding forward'. And at the beginning of the process, it is important to acknowledge the role of ideas – in particular, the contribution of ideas by lobbyists, think-tanks and international organizations to the government's language or discourse in which policy making takes place. At the end of the process, the realities of implementation can significantly affect our view of who has power and how power is most effectively exercised.

REFERENCES

Armstrong, K. and Bulmer, S. (1998) *The Governance of the Single European Market*, Manchester, Manchester University Press.

Bachrach, P. and Baratz, M. (1962) 'Two faces of power', *American Political Science Review*, vol.56, pp.947–52.

Bernstein, M. (1955) *Regulating Business by Independent Commissions*, Princeton, NJ, Princeton University Press.

Cecchini, P., Catinat, M. and Jacquemin, A. (1988) *The European Challenge 1992: The Benefits of a Single Market*, Aldershot, Wildwood House.

Cram, L. (1997) *Policy-making in the European Union*, London, Routledge.

Dahl, R. (1961) *Who Governs?*, New Haven, Yale University Press.

Heclo, H. (1978) 'Issue networks and the executive establishment' in King, A. (ed.) *The New American Political System*, Washington, DC, American Enterprise Institute.

Heffernan, R. (2004) *The Architecture of the European Union*, DD(ZX)200 *Governing Europe*, Milton Keynes, The Open University.

Kingdon, J. (1984) *Agendas, Alternatives and Public Policies*, Boston, Mass., Little Brown.

Lewis, P. (2005) 'Politics, powers and structures' in Lewis, P. (ed.) *Exploring Political Worlds*, Edinburgh, Edinburgh University Press/The Open University.

Lindblom, C. (1968) *The Policy-making Process*, Englewood Cliffs, NJ, Prentice Hall.

Lukes, S. (1974) *Power: A Radical View*, London, Macmillan.

Moravcsik, A. (1991) 'Negotiating the Single European Act' in Keohane, R. and Hoffman, S. (eds) *The New European Community: Decision-making and Institutional Change*, Boulder, Colorado, Westview Press.

Olson, M. (1963) *The Logic of Collective Action: Public Goods and the Theory of Groups*, Cambridge, Mass., Harvard University Press.

Rhodes, R. and Marsh, D. (1992) 'Policy networks in British politics' in Rhodes, R. and Marsh, D. (eds) *Policy Networks in British Government*, Oxford, Clarendon.

Richardson, J. (1969) *The Policy-making Process*, London, Routledge.

Sandholtz, W. and Zysman, J. (1989) 'Recasting the European Bargain', *World Politics*, vol.42, no.1, pp.95–128.

Simon, H. (1957) *Administrative Behaviour* (2nd edn), New York, Macmillan.

Thompson, G. (2005) 'Policy networks and interest representation' in Heffernan, R. and Thompson, G. (eds) *Politics and Power in the UK*, Edinburgh, Edinburgh University Press/The Open University.

Wilson, W. (2005; first published 1887) 'The Study of Administration', http://teachingamericanhistory.org/library/index.asp?document=465 (accessed January 2005).

FURTHER READING

Cram, L. (1997) *Policy-making in the European Union*, London, Routledge.

Rhodes, R. and Marsh, D. (1992) 'Policy networks in British politics' in Rhodes, R. and Marsh, D. (eds) *Policy Networks in British Government*, Oxford, Clarendon.

Richardson, J. and Jordan, G. (1979) *Governing Under Pressure: The Policy Process in a Post-Parliamentary Democracy*, Oxford, Martin Robertson.

Challenging centre–periphery relations in health policy

Julie Charlesworth and Wendy Humphreys

chapter 2

Centre & periphery

Contents

1	Introduction	44
2	Restructuring health care	47
3	Health policy and citizenship	51
	3.1 Health inequalities	52
	3.2 Equality and equity	55
	3.3 Rights and responsibilities	55
4	International influences	60
5	Health policy inputs: actors, networks and processes	64
	5.1 Health policy actors	64
	5.2 Health policy making and implementation – visualizing the centre–periphery model	66
	5.3 From health policy community to issue network?	68
	5.4 Challenges to the health policy community: a shift to multi-level governance?	70
6	Conclusion	75
	References	76
	Further reading	78

1   INTRODUCTION

In this chapter we use the case study of the National Health Service (NHS) in the UK to explore the politics of policy making, drawing in particular on the concepts of centre–periphery relations and multi-level governance. These concepts provide a means of understanding where different sources of power and influence lie, and especially the extent to which power and influence are centralized and/or dispersed.

To focus on centre–periphery relations is to highlight the contrast between the concentration of power and influence at the centre and their comparative absence at the 'margin'. As **Guibernau (2005)** states, we can think of centre–periphery relations from different perspectives. A geographical perspective would focus on which places (cities/regions) were at the centre or on the margins of policy making. Alternatively, we might examine which organizations (government or professional bodies) are most powerful, and those others that appear to be excluded from policy making. Then again, centre–periphery relations can be conceived in terms of identities, to see what effect factors such as gender, ethnicity and class have on the constitution of actors and non-actors in health policy making. The concept of multi-level governance signifies partnership and networks linkages between different tiers of government and other agencies (in both the private and voluntary sectors). The idea of multi-level governance also signifies an aspiration towards increased participation in policy making by different groups in society.

Although we are presenting centre–periphery relations and multi-level governance in this chapter as two models, elements of both may be apparent in any policy-making contexts, with shifts in emphasis of dominance at different times and in different contexts. A further important distinction between the two models is that politicians sometimes talk explicitly in terms of seeking multi-level governance, so it is both a way of organizing policy making and management of public services and an academic model for understanding change.

We can say that the centre–periphery relations model of power and policy making has provided appropriate explanations of health policy in the UK in the period following the Second World War. It has operated at three dimensions – functional, spatial, and through identities (see Table 2.1). First, on the functional dimension, central government and the medical profession have traditionally dominated policy making. This interdependent relationship developed during the early part of the twentieth century and was consolidated after the war with the setting up of the NHS. It has traditionally proved difficult for other professions and groups to break into this power relationship. Again in the functional dimension, there is a central versus local division. In this respect, local agencies (local hospitals, local government and other welfare providers) as the implementers of policy have been on the periphery of power and influence, together with local communities and patients.

Second, at a spatial (or geographical) level, London was the centre of policy making and the regions were on the periphery. However, measures of devolution to Scotland and Wales have had an impact here, as they now have their own departments responsible for health. In addition, although much of the UK's health care policy making is formulated within the UK, there are also international influences, for example through the European Union (EU), the World Health Organization (WHO) and international legislation and guidance relating to health care. UK actors have an input to these policy-making bodies but their sphere of influence is likely to be less in the international context. The growing importance of international influences on health care policy making illustrates that centre–periphery relations have a number of spatial contexts.

Finally, cutting across these different dimensions are issues of identity connected with individuals' levels of influence and the effects of ethnicity, class and gender for instance, leading to an imbalance in representation within and between policy-making groups.

However, we also need to take into account the fact that changes to traditional centre–periphery power structures have been taking place. As a result the concept of multi-level governance is gaining importance as a means of understanding policy making. In some cases, different organizations, pressure groups or individuals have been successful in breaking into key policy-making forums. Various governments have attempted to reduce the traditional role of the public sector as sole provider of public services by bringing in other partner agencies, and also by ensuring that policy making is more inclusive and responsive to the needs of citizens or consumers. The concept of community has been used to highlight how public services can become more integrated (or 'joined-up') and better able to tackle the needs of local people. In other words, these developments challenge the orthodoxy that only the centre can plan services. There is greater recognition that communities are diverse, and that local policy makers are often better able to understand the local interplay and mix of factors such as health, social deprivation, poverty, crime, housing conditions and employment.

TABLE 2.1   Dimensions of health policy making in the UK

	Functional	Spatial	Identities (such as ethnicity, gender, class)
Centre–periphery relations	dominance of medical profession central–local government relations (reduced autonomy for local agencies)	London/England at centre, regions on periphery within localities, dominance of public sector nation-states resist convergence in health policy	lack of representation from minority and marginalized groups in policy-making centres
Multi-level governance	enhanced role for managers and other health professionals increased autonomy for local organizations joined-up government, partnership and participation	devolution within UK local partnerships international influences on health policy	greater awareness of the need to involve more representatives of a wider variety of groups in society in policy making

Table 2.1 sets out the key characteristics of the centre–periphery relations and multi-level governance models of explaining health care policy making. However, we also need to consider the interaction of these dimensions. The evidence is that, in health policy making, particular mixes or combinations of these factors occur at different times to create concentrations of power, whether in particular places, institutions or groups.

The question of whether policy making is becoming more inclusive and multi-level in practice, or whether inclusivity remains government rhetoric, will be explored later in the chapter. Arguably, for there to be a stronger shift towards multi-level governance, there needs to be increased devolution of power from the centre to regional and local levels. This would facilitate the dispersal of access to power and influence to groups formerly excluded from policy-making structures. However, such a development requires a different context and set of relationships between actors. As **Thompson (2005)** notes, multi-level governance refers to how activities are co-ordinated between the different dimensions of governance involving vertical and horizontal co-ordination, which could include negotiating and bargaining. This idea can bring greater accountability, equity and equality, but also more fragmented and complex arrangements. In spite of the increased rhetoric of working more in partnership, the question remains as to whether powerful groups are prepared to forgo privileged positions and work in a less hierarchical way.

The main questions for discussion in this chapter are:

- What influence do different groups have in the policy-making process?
- Where are the main sources of power now located?

In particular, we examine the dilemma of how to describe and explain possible realignments of relations over time, and whether the concept of multi-level governance is more applicable today than it has been previously. Alternatively, are we seeing evidence for the co-existence of both centre–periphery relations and multi-level governance? In this chapter, we consider a number of interrelated issues in order to help us understand these questions about the nature of change. First, we provide an overview of changes to health care in the UK. We then move on to discuss how citizenship is perceived in health policy, particularly in terms of the notions of health inequalities, equity and equality, and rights and responsibilities. The influence on UK health policy of wider – international – sets of centre–periphery relations is also examined, and lastly we look in detail at the nature of, and challenges to, the health policy community in the UK.

2 RESTRUCTURING HEALTH CARE

The purpose of this extended case study is not to develop in-depth knowledge about the inner workings of the NHS. Rather it is to see health policy in the light of wider political structures and processes, and to understand and explain change in health policy in the context of centre–periphery relations and multi-level governance.

Why is health policy a good example for assessing the value of the models of centre–periphery relations and multi-level governance in an effort to understand contemporary policy making? Health policy has experienced substantial change in recent decades, providing a useful indicator of whether, and how, the policy making process is being transformed, and the impact of this on traditional sources of power. Historically, policy making was conducted by the centre (spatially, functionally and in terms of most prominent identities), dominated by particular elements of the medical profession, thereby giving an image of a strong centre–periphery model (although the reality was more complex than this). Public services in the UK have been subjected to waves of restructuring in the name of making them more cost-effective, efficient and accountable, and the NHS in particular was targeted during the 1980s for its unwieldy bureaucracy, hierarchical structures and high costs. Thus, the restructuring of the health service epitomized the new culture of reform for public services based on:

- an emphasis on competition
- elements of privatization
- contracting out of services to other providers (private, voluntary, 'arm's length' public sector organizations)
- the introduction of internal markets (by dividing organizations into purchasers and providers)
- partnership with other public sector, private and voluntary sector organizations
- regulation and monitoring by central government.

The process was governed through the introduction of the idea of 'new public management', to replace the perceived bureaucratic ineffectiveness of the previous regime of managers. The new system focused on goals, outcomes, choice and empowerment for customers. Other key elements of new public management were the decentralization of authority to lower tiers of management and a shift away from the dominance of clinicians in managing services. In addition, public sector managers were expected to learn from the private sector.

In 1997, the Labour government introduced a strategy of modernization and partnership which, although presented as a break from the past (and as a 'third way'), was to some extent a modification and reconfiguration of the previous government's policies. The idea, in theory at least, was to make public services and policy making more inclusive for all groups in society, and public services more efficient and integrated. Partnership with the private and voluntary sectors was supposed to replace competition, thereby facilitating a more constructive environment in which to collaborate and to move beyond contractual relationships (perhaps to the point of merger). However, an emphasis on public management from central government continues for the purposes of managing modernization and evaluating performance measures.

In health policy, these ideas have translated into a variety of initiatives, particularly associated with continuing the trend of involving a wider range of agencies in public services. Examples of such initiatives include private finance for public services infrastructure, and creating autonomous hospitals (Figure 2.1). These autonomous 'foundation trust' hospitals are, according to government rhetoric, to be governed by local people, staff and patients. But alongside the introduction of private finance and a greater say at the local level, central regulation and inspection of standards of public service provision continue, on the grounds that central monitoring best ensures quality and performance measurement. Health and social care professionals are increasingly required to operate within national service frameworks. The medical profession has traditionally enjoyed a strong power base in health policy making but doctors, too, have been subject to tighter controls: changes to their contracts and working hours are under negotiation.

FIGURE 2.1   Restructuring health care – a new foundation hospital in the UK

The above discussion provides an indication of the extent of recent restructuring – particularly since the 1980s – affecting public services in general and health care in particular, and we will return to these themes later. This trend is not peculiar to the UK, as the cost and difficulty in running many other health care systems are providing one reason for this kind of reform process. What we need to draw out from this discussion and to bear in mind for the rest of this chapter, is the extent to which the claims of different government policies to be realigning the balance of power in policy making towards greater inclusion, measure up against what actually happens in practice. Despite the rhetoric, is it business as usual? Or do the new policies result in a meaningful extension of citizenship and useful new concepts of 'health'?

A further important point in this discussion is that health care is an emotive issue. In contrast with some areas of policy making, most people have first-hand experience of the health service from the vulnerable position of the patient, and very few people get through life without ever visiting a health care professional (whether hospital doctor, general practitioner (GP), nurse, optician, physiotherapist, dentist, health visitor, etc). In consequence, many people feel confident about expressing an opinion on the efficiency of the system and the quality of care delivered, on the basis of personal and anecdotal evidence. Health care is an emotive issue for another reason as well. In the context of the UK, the NHS retains a strong identity as a key part of the welfare state. The NHS was a central element in the physical and psychological rebuilding of the nation after the Second World War. It is still important to the identity of the NHS that it transformed the pre-war system of fragmented and unequal provision into the first system in the world to provide free health care (at point of use) for the whole population through state-provided services. Many people feel passionate about the NHS because of its history and universal and egalitarian principles, and thus changes to the character or shape of the system are frequently decried. On the other hand, patients also want new treatments and better provision than was available when the NHS was first set up – for example, shorter waiting lists, higher quality care and local providers. These factors help to explain why poor performance and scandals such as those that have occurred at the Bristol Royal Infirmary and Alder Hey hospital, and the case of the GP Harold Shipman (see Box 2.1), produce national outrage and condemnation, and provide fuel for the media's criticism. Health inquiries are one source of influence on health policy.

BOX 2.1   Examples of health inquiries

The Bristol Royal Infirmary Inquiry focused on the management of the care of children receiving complex cardiac surgical services at the Bristol Royal Infirmary between 1984 and 1995. The inquiry was set up to examine why there were failures in care and a higher mortality rate than normal. Two hundred recommendations resulted from the inquiry, which focused on the needs of sick children, the competence of hospital consultants, how health care professionals work together, the availability of information to patients, the standards of care and how they are monitored. Three hospital consultants were disciplined by the General Medical Council for professional misconduct.

(adapted from Bristol Royal Infirmary Inquiry, 2001)

An inquiry into the Royal Liverpool Children's Hospital at Alder Hey in Liverpool investigated the retention of human organs by clinicians for research purposes and, in particular, their failure to determine whether parents of deceased children had objections to their actions. The investigation focused on the actions of one hospital consultant for 'the unethical and illegal retention' of organs, falsification of reports and statistics, and lying to parents about the use of their children's organs. The managers were also severely criticized for their appointment, management and appraisal of the consultant concerned, and for the management of his department.

(adapted from Royal Liverpool Children's Inquiry, 2001)

Harold Shipman was a GP who was given 15 life sentences in 2000 for murdering fifteen of his elderly female patients. An inquiry into the case suggested that he had probably killed another 200 patients. Recommendations focused on reviewing the coroner service, including its training provision and organization, and improving monitoring and investigative procedures into deaths.

(adapted from Harold Shipman Inquiry, 2003)

Inquiries into such events can provide the stimulus for policy change – in care provision, in inter-organizational and professional working relationships, and for systems of professional accountability. In particular, the Bristol and Alder Hey inquiries highlighted the disregard shown by doctors to parents, by failing to provide them with adequate information about their children's medical condition. Salter (2003) argues that where such inquiries uncover poor practice there is an opportunity for pressure groups to use the information to force a shift in the power base away from professionals, particularly doctors. We will return to this debate again later in the chapter, as an element of understanding multi-level governance.

SUMMARY

- There have been major changes in health care.
- The models of centre–periphery relations and multi-level governance can be useful in evaluating the restructuring of the health service and reforms in health policy making.
- Health is an emotive issue.
- Health inquiries can provide a stimulus for policy reform.

3 HEALTH POLICY AND CITIZENSHIP

In this section, we explore how governments and pressure groups have sought to change the basis of policy making in health care in order to make the process more inclusive. Key elements of this move towards inclusivity relate to a shift in attitudes about health and illness – away from reactive health care for the ill patient and towards pro-active health promotion. More ambiguous is the government's keenness to instil a heightened sense of the rights and responsibilities of citizens with respect to health care. People are now encouraged at an individual level not only to be better informed about their health and the care available, but also to take responsibility for their health instead of regarding the doctor as a cure-all. However, it has long been recognized (although only recently acted upon by government policy) that persistent structural inequalities in health exist. There is a strong correlation between people's social and economic circumstances and their levels of health, although some health inequalities are due to genetic make-up. These points then raise two questions: how to address social inequality in policies that alleviate its effects on health, and how to address intrinsic differences that may need to be considered in terms of equity of access to services required.

3.1 Health inequalities

There is a heated debate about health inequalities and how this issue should be addressed by government policy making. There is an increasing recognition that a person's chance of health and illness has a number of determinants. In particular, people with low incomes, poor housing and living in run-down environments, for example, are more likely to experience ill health and higher mortality rates (Figure 2.2). (Mortality rates measure the number of deaths in the population, accounting for geographical differences in age structures.) This correlation is confirmed by a Department of Health report, which acknowledged that the mortality gap between the highest and lowest social classes has in fact *widened* since the 1930s, with the unskilled group experiencing 1.2 times the mortality rate of the professional classes in 1930–32, increasing to 2.9 times in 1991–93 (Department of Health, 2003a, p.7).

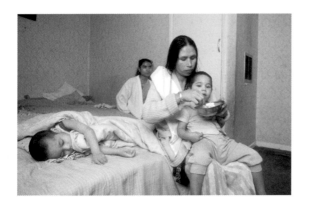 

FIGURE 2.2   Health inequalities: children in disadvantaged economic circumstances in East London and a picnic at Henley regatta

Inequality is not, however, just about class or economic position. For a start, certain groups are more likely than others to find themselves in poverty, with all of its attendant disadvantages. A disproportionate number of those from ethnic minorities have lower than average income levels and are more likely to reside in poorer areas and in substandard housing, which then has a knock-on effect in terms of inequalities in health among ethnic groups. Women also are disproportionately represented within those living in poverty and this is often connected to their tendency to be the main carers within families, whether for children, the elderly or infirm. The purpose of the NHS is to provide care for all members of society but it has become apparent that there is a wide gap between those with health needs and their capacity to access health service provision. It makes sense to examine health inequalities in the context of centre–periphery relations since we find that disadvantaged people are less likely to make an equal contribution to policy making and thus remain on the periphery of key decisions.

Understanding the contribution of inequalities to poor health is nothing new: the Black Report (Department of Health and Social Security, 1980) on inequalities uncovered evidence of differences in health status between social classes, and it suggested reasons why these occur. It made various recommendations for reducing inequalities, such as redistribution and increasing public expenditure and taxation. The Conservative Government at the time played down the finding and gave it only a limited release. In 1992, they introduced The Health of the Nation legislation that set targets for health improvement and built in the expectation that health authorities would work with other agencies. So despite largely ignoring the Black Report at the time, there were glimmers of recognition of the importance of the need for health authorities to look beyond their traditional boundaries in order to tackle the causes of ill health.

In 1998 the Acheson Inquiry revisited and confirmed the significance of health inequalities to poor health and highlighted that inequalities had worsened during the 1980s and 1990s (Ham, 1999). As we saw in the previous section, inquiries and reports can impact on policy making, often leading to policy or legislative change or, at the very least, generating wider public interest through the media. In 1999 Labour revisited the Black Report in *Saving Lives: Our Healthier Nation* (Department of Health, 1999), making the problem of health inequalities a cornerstone of their programme of health reform. In particular, the legislation picked up on the wider social, economic, and environmental factors in poor health. It highlights the 'complex interaction between the genetic make-up and behaviour of individuals and social, economic and environmental factors in the community' (Department of Health, 1999, Section 4.1). It acknowledges the importance of health inequalities based on social class, geography, gender and ethnicity, all of which can be understood in terms of centre–periphery relations.

However, disturbingly, the legislation also identifies individual behaviour as centrally important in 'improving, safeguarding or damaging health' (Department of Health, 1999, Section 4.1). It is a major problem if government is placing more responsibility on individuals with regard to their own health, when those most disadvantaged are likely to be least able to access effectively the information needed to improve their position. Furthermore, by moving the emphasis onto the individual, there is some suspicion that this personalization of responsibility, despite a stated policy of service improvement, will be used as an opportunity to shift blame for continued inadequacies away from the government and onto individuals.

The change in the role of local agencies is also double-edged. In terms of their significance in the health policy process, local agencies are now required to work in partnership to produce local strategies for health improvement based on target setting and measurement of improvements. The local targets (for example, reducing coronary heart disease and smoking-related illness, and for promoting a healthy diet and nutrition) are required to relate to national targets but there is some scope to shift emphasis depending on the needs of the local community. Although welcomed by local agencies, the burden of meeting a range of government indicators can inhibit innovative local action.

Differential access to health care continues to be a key issue, relating to geography, wealth, gender and ethnicity. Reference to cases of the 'postcode lottery' in health, whereby one's level or type of treatment may depend on area of residence rather than on what is clinically needed, are frequently brought to the public's attention by the media. Clearly such examples point to regional differences, but these are not necessarily a reflection of centre–periphery relations in health policy. Gaining better treatment for Alzheimer's disease or cancer in one area does not necessarily indicate greater access to the policy-making process. Such inequalities, however, may be devastating for the individuals concerned, and when it comes to weighing up the balance between rights and responsibilities, individuals may well feel cheated when the system fails to provide for their particular need.

In certain cases these inequalities may be considered a form of indirect discrimination, a term frequently used in the fields of gender and ethnicity relations. A gender-based example would be an area curtailing resources or failing to invest in resources for breast cancer. For example, a survey by a pharmaceutical company producing an effective drug for breast cancer found that only a third of the women eligible for it were actually taking it (*The Guardian*, 2003, p.11). Breast cancer could affect both men and women, but women as a group are likely to be disproportionately affected and so may feel discriminated against. Indirect discrimination within health provision also occurs in the context of ethnic minority health needs. There are certain conditions that particularly affect certain ethnic groups. For example sickle cell anaemia, which is found predominantly within the African-Caribbean population, or thalassaemia, found in the UK mainly within the Asian community. Whilst such conditions may be deemed peripheral in terms of the proportion of the entire population, because they disproportionately affect particular ethnic groups, those campaigning on behalf of ethnic minorities, such as the Commission for Racial Equality, argue that services such as screening must be provided.

These are just a few examples and you may well be able to think of other conditions that affect certain groups more than others. One of the important issues here is the different positions of differently placed individuals and groups in relation to the policy-making process, particularly in circumstances where health citizenship (especially when narrowly defined as the linking of rights and responsibilities in health) has been made a prominent principle. Some groups feel that meaningful citizenship in the wider economic, social and political context is outside their reach, with 'health' being just another area where they do not quite 'belong' and are placed on the periphery of society.

Despite these negative examples, one does occasionally come across evidence of fairer treatment. A London Health Observatory Report (2003) comments on the higher proportion of coronary surgical interventions for most south Asian groups (excluding Bangladeshis) in comparison to white people, saying that 'this might suggest that NHS care is not as inequitable as might have been anticipated' (London Health Observatory, 2003, p.18). People of south Asian origin suffer disproportionately from serious heart problems and there is some evidence that health provision has responded directly to this.

3.2 Equality and equity

So far we have looked at inequalities in health care, but are the notions of equality and inequality the best principles to guide health policy? As Barker (1996) explains, a major dilemma in health care policy has always been that of achieving equity or fairness in provision. In terms of health care it is not necessarily equality that is required – many people are healthy most of their lives and only occasionally require health services – so therefore not everybody needs an *equal* level of service. How then do policy makers decide the criteria of equity or fairness? Often, they base their judgments on geography: for example, it is easier and less costly for the state to provide services (particularly specialist services) for those living in densely populated areas rather than for a dispersed population in rural areas. However, this logic leads to a situation of inequity of access to services, and the cost and burden of travel to services in towns and cities is then usually borne by the patient.

So, given a limited pot of resources, how can you ensure that the people needing the health care actually receive it? In order to answer this, it would be useful to have a clear definition of 'need'. But the discourse on defining 'need' in health policy has been extremely problematic. Specifying need can be highly subjective: people have different perceptions of pain and suffering and of their capacity to cope. Furthermore, some of those people needing health care are not necessarily able to articulate their problems or even come forward to use health services. Medical definitions are also inadequate because they do not take into account the interplay of social and economic factors in people's poor health. Barker makes the case that if the goal of health care is to create equitable redistributive policies, then the onus is on policy makers to ensure that they know who and where are the people in need. People in need should be given a stronger voice in policy making as they tend to be the least powerful members of society (Barker, 1996).

3.3 Rights and responsibilities

There appear to be moves at the EU and UK levels to make health policy more inclusive, accountable and responsive to patients' needs. As we have seen, these moves arise in part from a changing understanding of the concept of 'health' and the role of patients' rights and responsibilities within health care. A shift in attitudes has occurred from the dominance of a medical model of health to a social model. The traditional medical model emphasized the biological and physical aspects of the patient, whereas the social model of health focuses attention on the social and psychological dimensions. As a result the social model stresses health over sickness and takes a holistic approach to people's well-being. This shift stems from the recognition that the causes of poor health are often connected to wider social and economic issues, such as poverty and deprivation, housing, employment, the environment, and crime.

The idea of patients having rights and responsibilities has developed over time, and the balance between the two categories has changed. In the UK, the Conservative Government developed the Patients' Charter in 1990. This provided information on patients' rights and on the standards of care patients should expect, and it included league tables on the relative performance of health trusts, with a particular focus on waiting lists (Ham, 1999). The emphasis of the Patients' Charter was on rights rather than responsibilities. The language of responsibilities together with rights, as components of citizenship, has been part of the Labour Government's agenda since 1997. Their idea of a 'contract' (or 'deal') between the individual and society is meant to be about awarding rights and opportunities but in return demanding obligations and responsibility. According to the contract, 'healthy citizens' can fulfil their obligations, as they are better able to work and make an economic contribution to the nation, and therefore not become a burden on the state (Petersen and Lupton, 1996). However, critics note that it is often difficult for the most vulnerable members of society to take part in this new environment and thus fulfil their 'duties'.

How does this language translate into health care in the UK? An examination of the language used in health care policies would seem to suggest that patients ought to occupy a key position in health policy. There has been a shift of emphasis from a paternalistic model of health towards one that focuses on the patient as an individual. For example the NHS Plan (Department of Health, 2000) describes 'a health service designed around the patient' (see Box 2.2). In broad terms this means that services should be responsive to patients' needs, provide greater choice, and that patients should generally have an enhanced voice in policy making. These provisions help to fulfil the rights and opportunities aspects of the citizenship contract. But in return patients are 'obliged' to take greater responsibility for their health. The document *Saving Lives: Our Healthier Nation* (Department of Health, 1999) laid out an action plan for tackling poor health and placed the responsibility for achieving this on a partnership between individuals, communities and the government. The plan placed a strong emphasis on self-regulation. According to the plan, individuals are required to take responsibility for improving their health, through: physical activity, diet, reducing smoking, dealing with stress, ensuring that children were not subjected to generational patterns of ill health, and understanding risk. Furthermore, detailed guidelines are provided on the actions required by individuals, communities and government to tackle the key areas of cancer, heart disease, mental health and accidents.

BOX 2.2   **A health service designed around the patient**

'Services will be available when people require them, tailored to their individual needs.'

'Step by step over the next ten years the NHS must be redesigned to be patient centred – to offer a personalised service.'

'[The NHS] will provide a growing range of products and services to help people adopt healthier lifestyles.'

'The frontline in healthcare is the home. Most healthcare starts with people looking after themselves and their families at home. The NHS will become a resource which people routinely use every day to help look after themselves.'

(Department of Health, 2000, pp.17–18)

While these reforms are presented as a radical and positive new agenda, encouraging citizens to take responsibility for their own health is not particularly new. What *is* new is the potential for erosion of the NHS commitment to universal health provision, on the grounds of individual responsibility for some aspects of health. The potential for greater surveillance of individuals, to ensure compliance with their responsibilities, is also worrying.

Health education has a long history, originating in the public health movement of the nineteenth century, which emphasized cleanliness in the home and improving sanitation as a means of tackling disease. Now the message of health education focuses on the individual and risk avoidance and 'encouraging' people to change their lifestyles. Professionals impart extensive information about risk to health to the public and expect them to comply, but these information campaigns are not always successful. One reason concerns the cost of a healthy and aspirational lifestyle. Gym membership, organic fruit and vegetables, vitamin supplements and so on are too expensive for many people on basic salaries. Hogg outlines other reasons for unsuccessful campaigns (Hogg, 1999):

- health education messages are complex and often based on conflicting evidence (and the media also bombards people with conflicting and therefore confusing information)

- messages focus on risks that the individual takes and ignores risks imposed on them by society (for example, pollution)

- campaigns do not always take into account why people act as they do (for example, young people are more likely to take risks and find it difficult to think about the future).

Another aspect of health policy changes also has beneficial and troubling effects. A focus on local communities is prevalent in the language of the citizenship rights and responsibilities of patients too, in terms of understanding their health needs and enabling the planning of public services accordingly, but also in facilitating their participation in this process. Such a focus is not exclusive to health. Other areas of public policy have also attempted to become more centred on the service user and the distinctive needs of different communities. In health policy making, the focus on local communities implies that health policy designed solely at the 'centre' would be unable to fulfil these locally based objectives and that the dispersal of power to the 'periphery' is a necessary requirement of the new approach. As a result the implementation of health policies at a local level has been widened, but in a specific sense. Health organizations in a community (for example, hospital trusts and doctors' surgeries) are now required to work with other organizations such as local government (including social services and housing) and the police. The idea behind this move is to ensure that public services are working in partnership, encouraging a holistic and integrated approach, and increasing accountability to citizens.

In addition to this form of widening the implementation of health policies, it is government policy that broader representation of ordinary people should be encouraged. According to government policy, this should be happening at national and local levels with people participating in different consultative and policy groups, thereby facilitating a process of multi-level governance. Indeed, if the citizenship language is to be fully meaningful, representation is needed from the voluntary sector, pressure groups and the general public, as well as politicians, government departments and the medical professions, in order to address these interconnected issues.

However, the rhetoric of empowerment, participation and citizenship employed by the Labour Government does not always translate well into reality. Critics note that it is difficult to include representation from all interested parties in policy making or consultative forums for the obvious reason that the groups would be too big and thus unable to reach decisions. In addition, Hogg (1999) suggests that the broader language of rights and responsibilities does not always transfer effectively into the individual relationship of patient and professional. Patients often do not feel sufficiently empowered to question the care they are offered, as they may feel scared and vulnerable when faced with professionals and illnesses they do not understand. We can regard this situation as another dimension of centre–periphery relations, with professionals at the centre and patients on the periphery. However, there is a class division at play here too, with better-informed and more articulate patients closer to the centre than others. This clear difference *between* patients illustrates the complexity of centre–periphery relations in health policy.

Improving access to information (either through health education networks or via the Internet) can sometimes help this situation. The Internet, however, also has a downside because it can be the means of acquiring too much information or even misinformation. Moreover, and related to the class division noted above, some people feel more comfortable than others in using Internet information to challenge the health system and professionals, for this is again an instance where people's background and resources affect their ability to act. However, there has been an increase in the number of complaints against the health service in recent years, and more complaints are leading to litigation (McSherry and Pearce, 2002). There is a number of reasons for this: greater knowledge of complaints procedures; patients growing in confidence in their role as consumers and therefore more likely to complain about poor services; and increasing awareness that claims could lead to financial compensation (although these would have to be serious negligence cases).

Governments frequently argue that their rationale for introducing a more mixed provision in health care (both in terms of private finance and in terms of local services) is to increase choice, which leads to greater capacity and ultimately to improvements in equity. However, this argument does not always carry weight with ordinary citizens and patients. Government policy that results in changes to the providers of services is often controversial, particularly where it leads to greater private sector involvement or competition for resources. For example, Foundation Trusts in England are perceived by their opponents as privatization 'through the back door', and liable to create conflict and exacerbate existing difficulties in provision.

Despite the rhetoric of extending patient choice, the reality of funding problems in the health service, both nationally and locally, frequently affect choice and availability of services. The outcome is that what patients consider is their right is not necessarily deliverable under the current system. In addition, critics have discerned a gender inequality arising in practice from the language of extending patient choice. The focus on the individual and community often shifts the burden of care on to women as 'unpaid' carers (Doyal, 1998), with the real effect of reducing state expenditure on health care. Moreover, while some initiatives have received new money, in many cases the designated money is simply a reallocation of existing funds.

We have seen in this section how changing ideas and imperatives about health, social contracts and rights and responsibilities relate to policy making. In particular, we have critically assessed the impact of the changes on the input of different actors to policy making, and found that in some cases the reality does not match the language of change constituting a shift away from the power and influence of traditional groups.

SUMMARY

- In order to understand health policy making, we need to explore the different aspects of health and citizenship (especially need, equity, equality, rights and responsibilities).

- Ill health often relates to wider social and economic inequality and people in greatest need may be the least able to participate in policy making.

- A workable definition of 'need' is crucial to effective health policy making but remains unavailable.

- Differential access to health care continues and even where improvements are made at the local and individual level, this does not necessarily affect the imbalance of power in policy making.

- The way in which patients are 'required' to fulfil their duties as 'healthy citizens' and take responsibility for their own health, is problematic.

4 INTERNATIONAL INFLUENCES

So far we have focused largely on health policy within the UK. We turn now to consider how policy-making structures in the UK do not operate in a vacuum. Individual states increasingly need to liaise and co-develop policy at an international level on risks to health – from infectious disease to bioterrorism. Health problems do not stop at national boundaries, and outbreaks such as the SARS virus in 2002 and 2003 clearly illustrate the need for international collaboration on health issues. However, despite the international conferences and media attention to global health problems such as HIV/AIDS, a spatial divide persists in terms of patients receiving equal access to the best – or cheapest – drugs and procedures, with patients in developing countries frequently on the periphery. It is beyond the scope of this chapter to discuss the international arena for health in depth, but here we outline the impact on UK health policy making of international influences and UK policy making in a European perspective, within the context of the models of centre–periphery relations and multi-level governance.

As we saw in the previous chapter, EU legislation exerts influence, or even has jurisdiction over, different areas of UK public policy. The situation with health policy, however, is not so straightforward. The EU has a number of committees, regulations and statements on health including rights of access. The 'Charter of Fundamental Rights of the European Union', for example, states that: 'Everyone has the right of access to preventive health care and the right to benefit from medical treatment under the conditions established by national laws and practices' (quoted in European Commission, 2001, p.5). But while the EU has a broad mandate for health, individual member states have traditionally maintained sole authority for their own health services, and have resisted convergence across EU member states.

There are two main reasons why it is difficult to conceive of a common health system across the EU. First, health care systems exhibit wide variation both in terms of how they are financed and in provision. Box 2.3 gives details and examples of systems of health funding through social insurance, taxation, a mix of these, or private insurance. European countries also differ in the provision of health care, for example, by public ownership or a mixed economy of public and private providers. Consequently, important structural differences in policy making have emerged across these different countries. Second, and this applies beyond the EU, 'health policies are embedded in contexts that are often highly specific to individual countries' (Blank and Burau, 2004, p.209). These contexts include demography, biomedical technology, social values and cultural factors, legal and political systems, social structures, the mass media and public expectations (Blank and Burau, 2004).

BOX 2.3   **Funding for health care (2004)**

Social insurance model (compulsory health insurance funded by employer and individual contributions): Croatia, Czech Republic, Estonia, France, Germany, Hungary, the Netherlands, Slovakia, Slovenia, Japan

Taxation model (funded from general taxation/National Insurance): Albania, Denmark, Finland, Italy, Kazakhstan, Latvia, Norway, Poland, Portugal, Romania, Spain, Sweden, the UK, New Zealand

Dual (mix of social insurance and taxation): Belgium, Greece, Switzerland

Private insurance (purchase of private health insurance financed by employers and/or individuals): USA

European member states have made attempts at reform, in part in response to the pattern of spiralling costs and ever increasing demand that developed in many health care systems during the 1980s. The widespread scope of such attempts at reform across states illustrates that both taxation and social insurance systems share weaknesses. Policy makers traditionally concentrated on cost containment, but are now focusing on revenue policies and ideas for how to fund health care 'on a sustainable basis' (Mossialos and Dixon, 2002, p.1). However, even where states with similar health systems have engaged in reform, they have approached it in different ways. Blank and Burau (2004) provide an interesting comparison of the examples of Sweden and the UK. Sweden has traditionally focused on decentralized governance of health, whereas the UK continues to be perceived as highly centralized and hierarchical despite greater autonomy being awarded to local health trusts and health authorities.

Restructuring of health care in modern industrialized states has, in common with the UK, concentrated on four key areas (in addition to funding issues). These are: organizational and managerial improvements such as internal market reform (for example, in Sweden and Spain); extending patients' rights and choice (for example, in Norway); emphasis on primary care (for example, in Sweden and Germany); and increasing autonomy to more local levels (for example, in Sweden and Finland).

There is a longstanding recognition in the EU of the contradictions between health care being restricted to member states, and the free movement principle for persons, goods, services and capital of the Single European Market (SEM). Part of the problem arises from treating health as a 'market' even though patients are not conventional consumers of services (in that medical professionals largely make decisions about consumption), and there is a strong possibility of an 'inefficient and inappropriate supply' of care services (European Commission, 2001, p.7). The European Court of Justice (ECJ) has ruled in favour of several individual cases concerning reimbursement of health care costs for treatment in other member states. These rulings were upheld under regulations on the free movement of goods and services (European Commission, 2001). However, concerns were raised about the implications of this principle for the autonomy of individual member states in health care. Meanwhile the UK started to send its patients for treatment to hospitals abroad in 2003, in order to reduce waiting lists for common operations and offer greater choice. These examples illustrate that in the future the EU may need to increase its influence over UK health policy (and that of other member states) and set clearer guidance as consumers continue to demand greater choice and access.

Attempts have been made in the direction of clearer guidance as the EU has developed an official health strategy, particularly around public health. The origins of promoting a cross-national public health strategy lie with WHO programmes such as the Healthy Cities legislation (1980). The most recent EU strategy aims to provide better information and knowledge for patients, professionals and health authorities. It is also designed to supply an improved response to major health threats, and to address health determinants (through health promotion and disease prevention). The latter issue is also a key element of UK health policy, in the form of health promotion programmes. These programmes, planned and implemented by multi-agency teams, include a variety of targets for reducing inequalities (Department of Health, 1999). Other countries such as the Netherlands, Italy and Germany have also adopted this approach.

A further source of connection between the EU and individual member states' health policies is through sources of funding for economic, social, environmental and regeneration projects. Although such funding is not directly for health services, these projects engage with the broader remit of understanding the causes of poor health and health inequalities. Furthermore, the structures are in place for pressure groups to exert a wider representation in policy making, with organizations such as the European Public Health Alliance (representing non-governmental and not-for-profit organizations), the International Alliance of Patients' Organizations, and patient representatives on G10 health groups (Figure 2.3). However, there are still concerns at both international and national levels that patients, citizens and voluntary groups are not adequately represented.

FIGURE 2.3   International influences on health policy making – the European Public Health Alliance

So which of the two models – centre–periphery relations and multi-level governance – best accounts for the impact on UK health policy making of these international and EU influences? There are strong grounds for arguing that some aspects of health policy making in the UK and other EU states have become part of a wider set of centre–periphery relations. On one level, UK policy making has to take account of wider legislation and trends. Whether the UK is at the centre of these debates or on the periphery will inevitably vary depending on the issue involved. Furthermore, policy making for the UK involving actors from different countries suggests, for instance, that UK doctors, who have traditionally held a strong power base in a national context, are required to share their privileged position. It may only mean that UK doctors are required to negotiate with other doctors. But even if this is the case, it could well place UK doctors in a different set of centre–periphery relations where they might be on the periphery.

At the international level, before multi-level governance could replace the centre–periphery model in explaining UK health policy, other groups apart from doctors, such as other health professions and patient and citizen groups, would have to be more strongly represented. Otherwise it will be 'business as usual' with health policy dominated by the medical profession. Moreover, despite a trend toward international influence over policy-making structures and processes, we can still regard the national context as the key site for developing UK health policy.

SUMMARY

- External influences on UK health policy making emanate from the need to legislate and collaborate at the international level: ill health, infectious disease and social inequalities traverse national boundaries.

- Individual states have resisted convergence in health care systems and retain much autonomy in developing their own internal policies.

- Many states have experienced problems of rising health care costs and have implemented programmes of reform and restructuring.

- A wider set of relations in health policy making exist at the international level at which there are attempts to be more inclusive but differences in power and influence persist between nations and groups.

5 HEALTH POLICY INPUTS: ACTORS, NETWORKS AND PROCESSES

Having considered UK health policy making in national and international contexts, in this section we look in more detail at the actors, networks and processes in health policy making within the UK and the ways in which they interrelate.

5.1 Health policy actors

We have already mentioned many of the actors involved in health policy making and started to explore the different degrees of influence of actors (some, especially doctors, having high levels of influence). There now appears to be a recognition at least that the balance of power relations in policy making needs to shift in order to incorporate a wider range of interests and thereby increase accountability. We saw earlier that the concepts of centre–periphery relations and multi-level governance are useful in understanding the nature of policy making. How can we utilize these ideas to explain shifts in the power and influence of health policy actors?

Before we can assess what relative influence different groups have, and what their divisions and allegiances are, we need to examine who are considered to be the main 'actors'. Box 2.4 outlines the main 'inputs' to health policy making in the UK. But remember that the details are less important here than the overall point that health care policy involves a range of inputs with different degrees of influence (which we return to in Figures 2.4 and 2.5).

BOX 2.4   **Health policy-making inputs in the UK**

Pressure groups (producer and consumer) – professional organizations (such as doctors' groups), issue (such as anti-smoking) groups, groups representing particular service users/patients

National regulatory and inspection agencies – e.g. NICE (National Institute for Clinical Excellence)

Parliament – e.g. select committee reports, MPs' questions, private members' bills

Mass media – are increasing their role in exposing poor standards in health care

NHS bodies (local health authorities and trusts) – these implement policies following national guidance but also have a limited amount of flexibility to ensure they can meet the particular needs of their localities; local government should also be included here as it has now regained some shared responsibilities for health; and there are also national groups representing their members' interests.

Consultative machinery – advisory groups, ad hoc working groups, inquiries, formal consultation with NHS bodies

Ministers and civil servants – demands from ministers and civil servants within the departments of health (England, Wales, Scotland, Northern Ireland)

Industrial and commercial interests – providers of private health care; providers of goods, equipment and services to the NHS; companies producing goods which may be harmful to health; organizations providing investment through public–private partnerships

Academics and researchers – provide ideas and information which may influence health policy, for example in the Black Report on inequalities

(adapted from Ham, 1999)

The actors involved in health care and policy making are constantly in flux, with organizations often changing their names, structures and responsibilities. Measures of devolution within the UK have also created variations in health care arrangements as well as new actors. Traditionally, the centre of health policy making (as with other areas of public policy) in the UK was considered to be London, but now policy is determined by equivalent departments of health in Wales, Scotland and Northern Ireland. In general, there are strong similarities between the broad policies of the different national health departments (and they frequently work in partnership) but also scope for each national region to respond to their particular health needs, thereby enabling greater local 'ownership'.

5.2 Health policy making and implementation – visualizing the centre–periphery model

The discussion of health policy actors outlined some of the key groups involved in policy making. Later we will look in more detail at how they work together, but it is also useful to consider here how we might understand health policy-making formation and implementation in the context of centre–periphery relations and multi-level governance.

If we think about policy making in broad geographical and functional terms (national–local) and in the light of dominant identities, it still makes a lot of sense to conclude that policy devised at the national level by dominant identity groups sets the broad context and framework for health care. This is the case for decisions on overall funding, stipulating the actual organization of the health service, and national guidelines for standards of care established. In theory, the input of voluntary groups at this level is supposed to be representative but critics would contest the extent to which this happens in a meaningful way. Despite different governments' rhetoric, many groups continue to be excluded or, where they have been invited to a policy-making forum, feel that their presence is tokenistic and holds no real power. Figure 2.4 depicts the dominance of the centre over the periphery in health policy making and implementation at the national level. Figure 2.5, mirroring the situation at the national level, portrays the dominance of the centre over the periphery at the local level. Figures 2.4 and 2.5 provide an indication of how the explanatory model of centre–periphery relations in health policy might be represented visually, highlighting the different degrees of influence of different actors, with the outer circles having less influence. We need to remember, though, that the model is complex and dynamic rather than static. The influence of different actors may shift over time and depending on the issue – for example, the impact of the media and different campaign groups can at times be very important in affecting policy.

Figure 2.4, then, models the central role of ministers and civil servants, together with doctors and the government regulatory agency, NICE, in contrast to the peripheral role played by individual patients. Figure 2.5,

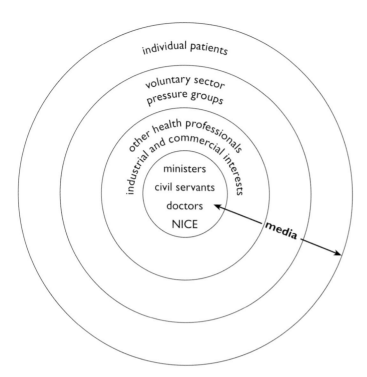

FIGURE 2.4   Actors in centre–periphery relations (national level)

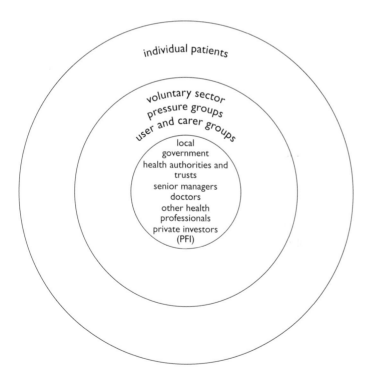

FIGURE 2.5   Actors in centre–periphery relations (local level)

focusing on the local level, describes how the centre is comprised of statutory organizations (local government, health authorities and trusts), with voluntary organizations, patients, carers and local people on the periphery.

Within the national framework, local organizations are charged with formulating local policy, deciding on priorities, allocating funding, and implementing the national policies. In reality, there is limited autonomy at this level and thus the relationship between the national and local levels is one of power centre to power periphery. **Thompson (2005)** refers to this as a 'command economy'. Local organizations have statutory requirements to meet in terms of how their health care is organized (through health authorities, hospital trusts, primary care trusts and so on) and meeting national targets and care standards. Local organizations are increasingly required to work in partnership with other bodies (such as social workers) in terms of policy making, consultation and delivery of services, and much of this is mandatory (for example, in child protection).

However, there is some flexibility to develop a range of policy-making and consultation forums appropriate to the particular needs of the local community, and it is in this context that innovative practices may occur. But in reality, local organizations have often found it difficult to co-ordinate such forums and, with squeezes on resources, have attempted to control their own organization's involvement in the spiralling number of partnerships. In terms of working with voluntary agencies, local authorities and health trusts increasingly prefer to consult 'umbrella' groups representing different voluntary and user and carer groups instead of large numbers of individual groups. The difficulties for marginalized groups in finding a voice in policy making at the national level thus also occur at the local level. The local periphery itself contains centre–periphery power relationships (there are wheels within wheels). Voluntary and community agencies and user and carer groups often complain that they are excluded from key policy-making forums and that consultation is often conducted in a cursory manner – so that statutory organizations can tick the box to say they have consulted the 'voluntary sector'.

5.3 From health policy community to issue network?

We have described how the model of centre–periphery relations represents the way policy making in the health service was structured in the post-war period, and how it continues to accurately account for some of the reforms and restructuring that has taken place. But does that model still accurately represent health policy making overall? Some political scientists now think that the complexity of the situation in health policy, particularly the differential power among the groups and inputs to policy making, is best represented through the theory of policy networks. The term network is often used synonymously with 'partnership', thereby suggesting more equal power relations. However, networks can also be elitist and exclusive. Therefore, if we want to understand how networks function, we need to examine different types of network. **Thompson (2005)** explains the key features of this approach and the distinction between a policy community and an issue network (the same distinction was also made in the previous chapter):

> A *policy community* is characterized by a largely stable set of interdependent participants, co-existing in a bounded network, who build up a set of shared values and norms and hence form a community that is difficult to break into.
>
> An *issue network* involves a more open and fragmented network structure, one which is less discriminatory and exclusive. In this case a wide circle of 'policy activists' drawn from interest groups, government personnel, academics and concerned individuals – who are constantly changing – form loosely articulated network groups around specialized issues.

(Thompson, 2005, Section 5.3)

Historically, health policy making in the UK has been described as taking place through a 'policy community' (Smith, 1993; Salter, 2003). As Mabbett explained in the previous chapter, those who implement the policy were often part of the community. In the case of health, there has been a tight policy community comprising the government and the medical profession (in particular hospital consultants). We need to take an historical perspective to examine the reasons for this. Even before the introduction of the NHS, the state entered into negotiations with the medical profession to help set up and run the health insurance schemes. After the Second World War this dependency was heightened when the doctors were needed to help establish the necessary infrastructural power in order for the state to become more interventionist (Smith, 1993). This led to even more dependency on doctors in devising and implementing policy.

These negotiations led to compromises by the state in the shape of the emerging system, doctors' clinical autonomy and salary arrangements. Smith (1993) suggests that although negotiations were generally conducted with the British Medical Association (BMA), the real source of doctors' power was state policy rather than their professional body. Many of the early negotiations involved civil servants who lacked political authority and the resources to take the upper hand with the doctors and, consequently, they tended to compromise, creating an 'institutionalised relationship' in policy making between the doctors and the state (Smith, 1993). However, other actors were also involved in negotiations, including local government, voluntary hospitals and insurance companies.

With the election of the Labour Government in 1945, the new health secretary, Aneurin Bevan, had a much clearer vision of what the NHS could be and was in a strong position to implement it. However, he still needed to negotiate with the doctors and there ensued difficult discussions and conflict among the BMA, general practitioners and hospital consultants. Despite his political authority, Bevan acknowledged the interdependence of the state and doctors in developing the NHS and, consequently, compromises were made in the doctors' favour. It was at this stage that a policy community was created, based on the Ministry of Health, the BMA and the Royal Colleges (Smith, 1993). Of course, doctors were not the only professionals involved in health care but doctors were at the *centre* of this community, with other health professionals (and patients) on the *periphery*. Doctors have tended to be male, white and middle-class, which reinforces the inequalities in policy making.

Overall, minority ethnic groups form 8.4 per cent of the total workforce (Department of Health, 2003b). Surveys of health staff in the UK suggest that about one third of hospital doctors are from minority ethnic groups (which is high given that they make up only 7.9 per cent of the total population). However, they are largely concentrated in lower staff grades and only comprise 20 per cent of hospital consultants. Racism is cited as a reason why doctors from minority ethnic groups fail to attain coveted consultant posts. A survey of graduates (Cooke *et al.*, 2003) uncovered several key aspects that contribute to racist attitudes:

- recruitment continues to be based on patronage ('who you know') and recruiting familiar types of staff
- lack of time and energy to change attitudes
- junior doctors reluctant to complain in case it hinders their recruitment elsewhere
- a perception that overseas doctors have poor language skills.

Despite the fact that men and women graduate from medical school in equal numbers, women comprise approximately one-third of all practising doctors and are less well represented in senior hospital posts. The 'working all hours' culture that doesn't fit well with bringing up children has been picked out as one reason for this (*The Guardian*, 2001). However, it is clear that both male and female doctors are dissatisfied with the way the medical profession is structured: long hours, increasing demands and poor work–life balance are leading to increasing interest in opportunities for more flexible and part-time work (BMA, 2003). EU directives on working hours may ultimately have an impact on reducing doctors' hours.

5.4   Challenges to the health policy community: a shift to multi-level governance?

We have seen throughout our discussion so far that there have been a number of challenges to the established ways of conducting policy making. Can we say therefore that the health policy community is functioning more like an issue network as part of a wider context of multi-level governance in public policy making? We have shown how governments have attempted to increase public participation in policy processes. This has taken the form of acknowledging their rights and responsibilities and also in putting 'the patient' at the core of policies and services. There have been attempts to make policy making more inclusive – for example, at the local level, new forums have been established in England in order to provide greater input from patients and local people into the operation of local health trusts. We have also seen how complex this is, given the existing nature and extent of health inequalities and the gap between needs and services. Furthermore, bringing other groups into the policy process does not necessarily mean their input will be respected or even acknowledged: it could just be construed as tokenistic. For real change to ensue, there needs to be a dual process of increasing power for some groups and *decreasing* it for others. Doctors, in particular, have traditionally enjoyed a prominent role. There have been attempts, both direct and indirect, to reduce their power (as we shall see below, for instance through new contracts, the increasing importance of hospital managers, and through regulation and inspection regimes set up by NICE). But it is not clear that such measures have removed the dominant power of doctors in the structure of the health service.

We can ask, therefore, whether such changes are significant enough to suggest a new model of policy based on multi-level governance and networks. Figure 2.6 illustrates the hierarchical approach to policy making (more like the centre–periphery model). **Thompson (2005)** refers to two types of multi-level governance model – one where policy-making authority is dispersed to a limited number of non-overlapping jurisdictions, and one where governance takes place through a fluid network of overlapping jurisdictions. When we think about health policy making, the first of these types could be represented in Figure 2.7 by amending Figure 2.6. Regional devolution would be the key policy-making level, and the role of local implementation would be strengthened. Figure 2.7 would be accurate if there was evidence of real devolved power to make policy, not just to implement it, at regional and local levels. In Chapter 3, Freeman points to the devolution of some welfare policy making to Scotland, but we have seen both the crucial role that central government continues to play in this area, and the power traditionally exercised by doctors. So if Figure 2.7 looks unlikely to portray the extent to which we have moved from hierarchical to multi-level governance, what about Figure 2.8? Figure 2.8 represents the second type of multi-level governance – a flatter and more fluid model. If there is evidence of a significant shift towards issue networks in health policy making and away from the policy community, then it might be the case that Figure 2.8 has become a more precise depiction of the policy-making process on health.

There are several ways in which the role and power of the medical profession in health policy making *has* been challenged. First, the emphasis on public management awarded greater power to managers in local policy making. This posed a challenge to doctors' autonomy but has often been criticized for creating an equally problematic situation of managerialist concerns over clinical ones. Second, doctors' pay and working conditions have been subject to change in recent years which, while not directly affecting their role in policy

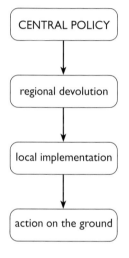

FIGURE 2.6
Hierarchical policy design
Source: Mackian *et al.*, 2003, p.224

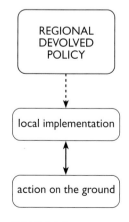

FIGURE 2.7   Devolved-power policy design

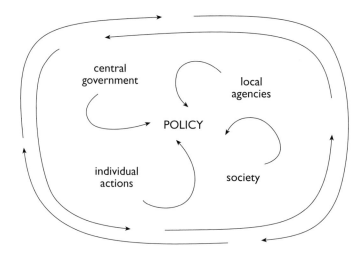

FIGURE 2.8 Fluid policy design
Source: Mackian et al., 2003, p.224

making, does contribute to a reduction in their autonomy. In 2003, hospital doctors and GPs were offered new contracts. Their response was divided: hospital doctors were against the proposals offered to them, with some threatening to take industrial action, and in disagreement with the BMA (their professional organization and trade union). However, GPs overwhelmingly supported their new contracts, which allow them to offer some services traditionally provided by hospitals. If there is a move towards local pay deals, the BMA will be sidelined. The third challenge to the medical profession emanates from increased regulation of their work through clinical governance, which sets standards that doctors are expected to meet. There was already an increasing trend towards setting and improving standards in care. But the well publicized cases of incompetence or worse (which we explored earlier, see Box 2.1) have provided a 'policy window' for consumerist groups and the media to exploit, in order to force change on the medical profession and other health and social care professionals (Salter, 2003).

The growing importance of the idea of 'partnership' also challenges the key role that dominant actors traditionally played in health policy making. 'Partnership' promises increased participation for more groups and actors, and lies at the heart of the model of multi-level governance. Partnership describes collaboration among different organizations, teams and professionals, and its rationale is that more can be achieved by working together and sharing resources. Examples of partnership in the health service are a small informal meeting to discuss a specific project or a case meeting on an individual patient, bringing together all the relevant professionals and other players. On a larger scale, partnership may involve substantial sums of money and a variety of organizations working together perhaps in order to restructure services, develop new infrastructure (for example through the Private Finance Initiative), or as a means of obtaining government or EU funding. Developing trust and an understanding of different professional and organizational cultures and ways of working are key to the success or failure of partnership meetings. At an individual level, the idea of partnership has gained considerable importance as a means of meeting the needs of patients and improving their 'journey' through care services. The impetus towards partnership working has arisen in part from the evidence of health inquiries that, as we saw earlier in the chapter, often reveal a lack of communication and inadequate sharing of information among teams and organizations as factors in cases of negligence.

Emphasis on partnership and multi-professional working has the potential to alter the balance of power relations in the health service, especially through reducing the traditional role of the clinician as the natural leader of teams (Figure 2.9). In some initiatives, nurses are encouraged to take on this role, particularly within local primary care trusts. This is potentially a serious challenge to established ways of working in health care: it has implications for the traditional boundaries between the roles of different professionals, and inevitably issues of gender, class and ethnicity come into play here.

FIGURE 2.9   Health policy inputs: (left) the depiction of hierarchy in medical care in the post-war UK and (right) a health professionals case team in the 1990s

Newman usefully points to a range of external influences that shape and constrain how partnerships operate:

- the need for accountability (having proper structures, formalised roles and transparent procedures)
- pragmatism (getting things done, meeting targets)
- flexibility (adapting fast to changing conditions, expansion)
- sustainability (fostering participation, building consensus and embedding networks to ensure long-term development)

(Newman, 2001, p.113)

It is clear that there is a trend towards partnership in working practices in the health service, along with other changes in health service policy making. But do these reforms warrant a shift from the explanatory model of hierarchical centre–periphery relations to the more fluid and flatter model of multi-level governance? The answer is that some of the evidence suggests such a shift, but the reality is inevitably complex and remnants of the old ways of working continue alongside the new because the groups traditionally holding power are unlikely to relinquish it completely.

In terms of Newman's model, for example, the flexibility and sustainability forms of influence clearly demonstrate a move away from hierarchical and rigid ways of working. But the question of accountability poses a problem in the multi-level governance model as structures of governance become more fragmented and dispersed. By accountability, we mean how the needs of different 'stakeholders' (such as patients, communities, government, different professions) are being met. It is important to ensure that performance of health care is measured and standards safeguarded. If dispersal of power is occurring, it is not desirable for it to have a negative impact on accountability. Loss of accountability could lead to poorer services and lack of understanding of what service users need. With moves away from central control to semi-autonomous trusts and a greater involvement of private sector agencies, there is a need for new structures of accountability to be put into place.

On the other hand, the Labour Government has increased centralization through demands for performance measurement under the auspices of accountability. A variety of frameworks, guidelines, regulation and inspection exist with results of organizational performance published in league tables. Thus, it is not clear how much dispersal of power is really occurring when organizations are still required to operate within tight centrally determined frameworks and targets. In addition, working in partnership is a complex and difficult business, and there can still be a power imbalance between insider and outsider groups. It is not always clear who decides which groups can join the partnership and what influence they can have. Thus, partnerships and networks can still in practice be hierarchical. These points help to illustrate the complexities in explaining how health policy making and delivery occur, and to the continuing explanatory power of both the centre–periphery relations and multi-level governance models.

SUMMARY

- The degree of influence of different actors over policy making has shifted over time.
- Health policy making has historically operated through a tight policy community but there is evidence of a shift towards a looser structure of issue networks, which forms part of a wider set of relations of multi-level governance.
- Challenges continue to the traditional source of power of the medical profession in the health policy community.
- Policy making at international, national and local levels has shifted towards partnership, but this is still problematic and often remains hierarchical and exclusive.
- While devolving power may create problems of accountability, the need to meet government targets has increased central control.

6 CONCLUSION

The discussion in this chapter has focused on a case study of the changing face of policy making in the health service in order to assess the applicability of the models of centre–periphery relations and multi-level governance. We have shown how it is difficult to say that there has been a clear transition from centre–periphery relations to multi-level governance: both are complex and the reality is that different systems may co-exist. While the centre–periphery model of explanation still accords with key aspects of health policy making and the structure of the health service, the explanatory value of the multi-level governance model has some resonance in evaluating changes to the health service.

There are many dimensions and layers to health policy, illustrating its 'embeddedness' within the state. One example is the degree of state intervention in the provision and governance of health care and the rights and responsibilities of citizens in relation to their needs and expectations. We have also seen how geography (or spatial relations) and cultural identities interweave with the nature of the political process in health policy. First, this occurs through understanding where (and why) different factors cause spatial concentrations of power in particular places, whether at national or local level, together with international influences. Second, we provided examples of how where you live affects your access to health care, not only in terms of where care is actually provided but also how the determinants of ill health relate to social, economic and spatial inequalities. These factors in turn impact on people's opportunities to participate in policy making.

Alongside the differential development of national health care systems in the different parts of the UK, it is clear that there are external influences on UK health policy due to the need to collaborate and legislate on major diseases, social inequalities and access to health care.

It is clear that attempts at different levels to increase participation are making inroads into concentrations of power in a strong policy community towards (supposedly) more inclusive issue networks, which are considered a feature of multi-level governance. However, whether these changes amount to a reformulation of centre–periphery relations (with some concessions to other groups) rather than a move towards multi-level governance, as partnerships can still be hierarchical and exclusive, remains to be seen. At the local level the complaint is also made that less powerful voluntary and community groups still struggle to have a qualitative input into policy making. Furthermore, despite some elements of decentralization of power to regional and local levels, concerns persist about the amount of central government control over auditing and monitoring the performance of organizations.

This again illustrates the continuing complexities in understanding the politics of health policy and the co-existence of both models of explanation: a multi-level governance system may itself create new, or exacerbate existing, patterns of centre–periphery relations.

REFERENCES

Barker, C. (1996) *The Health Care Policy Process*, London, Sage.

Blank, R.H. and Burau, V. (2004) *Comparative Health Policy*, Basingstoke, Palgrave Macmillan.

BMA (2003) *BMA Cohort Study of 1995 Medical Graduates*, Eighth Report, London, British Medical Association.

Bristol Royal Infirmary Inquiry (2001) www.bristol-inquiry.org.uk (accessed 30 April 2004).

Cooke, L., Halford, S. and Leonard, P. (2003) *Racism in the Medical Profession: the Experience of UK Graduates*, London, British Medical Association.

Department of Health (1999) *Saving Lives: Our Healthier Nation*, London, The Stationery Office.

Department of Health (2000) *The NHS Plan*, London, The Stationery Office.

Department of Health (2003a) *Tackling Health Inequalities: Programme for Action*, London, The Stationery Office.

Department of Health (2003b) *Equalities and Diversity in the NHS: Progress and Priorities*, London, The Stationery Office.

Department of Health and Social Security (1980) *Inequalities in Health* (Black Report), London, The Stationery Office.

Doyal, L. (1998) 'Introduction' in Doyal, L. (ed.) *Women and Health Services*, Buckingham, Open University Press.

European Commission (2001) *The Internal Market and Health Services*, Report of the High Level Committee on Health, Health and Consumer Protection Directorate-General.

The Guardian (2001) 'Inflexible NHS holds back women doctors', www.society.guardian.co.uk (accessed 7 December 2004).

The Guardian (2003) 'Cancer fund urged to end postcode lottery', 29 October, p.11.

Guibernau, M. (2005) 'Centre–periphery relations: government beyond Westminster' in Heffernan, R. and Thompson, G. (eds).

Ham, C (1999) *Health Policy in Britain. The Politics and Organization of the National Health Service*, London, Macmillan.

Heffernan, R. and Thompson, G. (eds) (2005) *Politics and Power in the UK*, Edinburgh, Edinburgh University Press/The Open University.

Hogg, C. (1999) *Patients, Power and Politics. From Patients to Citizens*, London, Sage.

London Health Observatory (2003) *Diversity Counts: Ethnic Health Intelligence in London. The Story So Far*, London Health Observatory, ww.tho.org.uk (accessed 7 December 2004).

Mackian, S., Elliott, H., Busby, H. and Popay, J. (2003) 'Everywhere and nowhere: locating and understanding the "new" public health', *Health and Place*, no.9, pp.219–29.

McSherry, R. and Pearce, P. (2002) *Clinical Governance. A Guide to Implementation for Healthcare Professionals*, Oxford, Blackwell.

Mossialos, E. and Dixon, A. (2002) 'Funding health care: an introduction' in Mossialos, E., Dixon, A., Figueras, J. and Kutzin, J. (eds) *Funding Health Care: Options for Europe*, Buckingham, Open University Press.

Newman, J. (2001) *Modernising Governance: New Labour, Policy and Society*, London, Sage.

Petersen, A. and Lupton, D. (1996) *The New Public Health. Health and Self in the Age of Risk*, London, Sage.

Royal Liverpool Children's Inquiry (2001) www.rlcinquiry.org.uk (accessed 30 April 2004).

Salter, B. (2003) 'Patients and doctors: reformulating the UK health policy community?', *Social Science and Medicine*, no.57, pp.927–36.

Shipman Inquiry (2003) www.shipman-inquiry.org.uk (accessed 30 April 2004).

Smith, M.J. (1993) *Pressure, Power and Policy: State Autonomy and Policy Networks in Britain and the United States*, Hemel Hempstead, Harvester Wheatsheaf.

Thompson, G. (2005) 'Policy networks and interest representation' in Heffernan, R. and Thompson, G. (eds).

FURTHER READING

Blank, R.H. and Burau, V. (2004) *Comparative Health Policy*, Basingstoke, Palgrave Macmillan.

Newman, J. (2001) *Modernising Governance. New Labour, Policy and Society*, London, Sage.

Salter, B. (2003) 'Patients and doctors: reformulating the UK health policy community?', *Social Science and Medicine*, no.57, pp.927–36.

Welfare, participation and dissent in public policy

Richard Freeman

Contents

1	Introduction	80
2	Forms of participation in welfare policy	81
3	Different kinds of welfare state	87
4	Welfare states and public opinion	90
5	Pressure and change	93
6	Local participation	97
7	Exit, voice and loyalty	103
8	Participation, inclusion and exclusion	105
9	Conclusion	109
	References	110
	Further reading	111

Participation & dissent

1 INTRODUCTION

The provision of welfare is a defining feature of the modern, industrialized state. Where the state has historically developed in a particular way – where it has separated from the church and from the personalized rule of a monarch, where it's accompanied by a national identity, an industrial economy and representative democracy, where it operates through a permanent bureaucracy and independent, often science-based professions such as medicine, engineering and law – there is public welfare too. In eighteenth-century Europe, for example, states undertook only what may be described as essential activities, such as those concerned with security (defence, foreign affairs, law enforcement) and the taxation required to pay for them. In the nineteenth century, more emphasis was put on economic development, on transport and communications, and support for industry. In the twentieth century, social programmes such as those for housing, education, health, social security and personal social services became a prime concern.

By the same token, entitlement to welfare (as well as certain kinds of tax obligation) has come to be a defining feature of citizenship. Social rights now complement legal or civil and political ones. Almost all European countries guarantee minimum (and sometimes generous) protection to almost all of their populations against the risks of, among other conditions, ill health, homelessness and poverty.

In turn, relationships between states and citizens are defined at least in part through respective obligations and entitlements to welfare. Harold Lasswell's 'Who gets what, when, how?' is as good a definition of welfare as of politics: welfare is both source and target of a high proportion of political conflict in advanced industrial societies (Lasswell, 1958). For this reason, the study of welfare policy making is an effective way in which the nature of political participation, as well as its changing form and extent, may be analysed and assessed.

What follows here is an account of different kinds of participation and dissent in welfare policy and provision, illustrated with examples from a variety of countries. The chapter begins with a survey of what participation and dissent mean in the welfare context, and the various forms it takes (Section 2). It suggests that participation can be either positive or negative, direct or indirect and undertaken by individuals or groups, and that these different forms and purposes often interact. Section 3 outlines the variety of welfare states, suggesting that patterns of participation in the policy process are at least partly a function of the different interests and opportunities that diverse institutional arrangements both create and allow.

Section 4 connects the discussion of the welfare state to public opinion, highlighting its importance in democratic politics and in shaping large-scale system policy change. Section 5 considers the recent politics of welfare, pointing to the pressures placed on welfare states across countries and the divergent ways in which they have responded to them. Section 6 looks at issues where participation can be said to be more immediate and direct, examining different kinds of political and organizational activity in, by and on behalf of local communities.

Section 7 introduces Albert Hirschman's modelling of participation and dissent in terms of exit, voice and loyalty. This serves as a summary of the different kinds of response to policy that may be made to any given issue in any given context. Finally, section 8 draws on the life stories of individuals to ask questions about the limits and ambiguities of participation and dissent in welfare politics.

2 FORMS OF PARTICIPATION IN WELFARE POLICY

Participation in welfare aims to shape the services people receive, by sharing in or otherwise influencing decisions about the terms and conditions under which welfare is provided, paid for and used. Participation is political action, and in this context the term refers to actions taken by those without formal political responsibilities, the 'ordinary people'. Participation does not always succeed in shaping policy making, but we are going to look at some of the forms that it can take. One important factor that influences the degree and kind of participation is the type of welfare state one lives in: the welfare state varies in whether it contains targeted or universal-type programmes, in the conditions of eligibility, in the quality of benefits and services, and in whether the right to employment is included or excluded from the definition of citizen rights.

Participation in welfare policy takes many different forms including voting, responding to a questionnaire, writing to a councillor or MP, forming a local pressure group or self-help organization and taking part in a national demonstration or strike. In the previous chapter, Charlesworth and Humphreys detailed the opportunities for participation in health policy forums. Participation may be undertaken positively or negatively, which is to say that it may express assent or dissent. In this chapter, participation and dissent are considered as operating on a single continuum, rather than as two quite separate things. They include action undertaken to express approval, as when a government is returned to office, or disapproval, as when policy changes are resisted by lobbying and letter-writing campaigns. In practice, different forms of participation are often used to complement each other in some common purpose. By the same token, people participate in different ways to different degrees.

Participation can be thought of as political because it articulates some opinion or expresses a conflict of interest: it is an assertion or exercise of power and influence, however small. It is political, too, in the sense that it is often addressed to some part or representative of the state, such as a head teacher, social worker, housing officer, magistrate or elected politician. This implies that a political claim may be made at different levels of political organization, for example at local, regional or national and indeed supranational level. Following equal opportunities and human rights legislation, for example, action against national governments may be pursued through the European Court of Justice.

In so far as consumers express preferences about the services they use and the goods they buy (such as which school their children attend or what kind of pension arrangements they make), they can also be said to participate in decisions made about welfare. Just as significantly, they may, for example, volunteer to help in a day centre for older people run by their local church. So, much of what goes on in economic markets and in communities might also be thought of as participation in welfare provision. In addition, participation is political precisely because it influences who gets what, when, and how. Put another way, markets and communities are constituted through political (and sometimes participatory) processes just as much as the state is.

Participation may be undertaken by individuals or by groups. Where their needs are not met, users of welfare services (claimants, tenants, clients, patients, students) may seek individual redress of grievances through complaints procedures or by a process of litigation such as an employment tribunal. Sometimes they use the larger organizational structures and processes of community organizations or trade unions. Sometimes they turn away from existing provision to form self-help groups: housing co-operatives are a good example. Almost self-evidently, however, sustained, effective participation is more easily undertaken by groups that are well organized and resourced, than by isolated individuals. Also, those who pay for welfare (governments, taxpayers, employers and employees) and those who provide it (doctors, teachers, social workers, administrators and other officials) tend to be better organized and resourced, and so more influential than those who receive and use it.

The most obvious form of participation in welfare policy in liberal democracies – obvious because most widely shared and discussed – is voting. However, because votes are for parties and the principal function of parties is to aggregate interests, a vote for any party or politician can be only indirectly or very generally an expression of concern about welfare. Nevertheless, because responsibilities for welfare administration are widely devolved to sub-central levels, regional and local elections have the propensity to be much more issue-specific (though turnout may be lower, and dominant issues may still be shaped by national concerns). In many European countries, including Italy, Spain and Sweden, for example, health care systems fall within the remit of regional rather than national governments. In Scotland, similarly, the disjuncture between the consistent return of an overwhelming majority of Labour MPs and the public sector reform programmes of successive national Conservative administrations in the 1980s and 1990s was an important factor in the demand for devolution. Furthermore, because the larger part of the new Scottish Executive's responsibilities, particularly in relation to public spending, has to do with welfare (for example, the NHS in Scotland accounts for one third of the Scottish government's budget), its standing is more than usually shaped by public perceptions of its social policy.

Very often, influence on the welfare policy-making process as a whole ('winding back' and 'winding forward' from the key decision-making phase, as Mabbett put it in Chapter 1) falls not to politicians alone but is negotiated with representatives of economic and other societal interests, such as organized labour, farmers, or business and industry. It is in this way that social policies come to be shaped not solely or even principally by politicians, but also by and on behalf of those who pay for and benefit from them. In the UK, for example, a wide range of organizations represent the interests of their members and lobby on their behalf; they include business associations and trade unions, churches, professional associations and campaigning groups. Groups tend to compete with each other for influence, and some achieve greater success than others by virtue of the greater organizational resources at their disposal. There is relatively little merging of groups into larger, more powerful associations. Nevertheless, decision making remains dominated by government.

The government can dominate welfare policy making in different ways. France is a good example of a country where the state dominates economic and social planning. Parties are relatively weak and the party system fragmented, and there is an enduring sense that sectional interests are somehow illegitimate, their influence potentially leading to decision making which may be biased or corrupt. Organizations of both capital and labour are much weaker than in France's north European counterparts, though there is a regular movement of personnel between the management of large organizations and a pre-eminent, technocratic bureaucracy.

Other European countries have a tradition of what is known as corporatism (see Box 3.1). These include Austria, Germany and the Benelux countries (Belgium, the Netherlands and Luxembourg) as well as Denmark, Sweden and Norway. In Germany, the Confederation of German Employers' Associations (BDA) has 400 affiliated organizations and specializes in influencing public policy, while the Federation of German Industry (BDI) specializes in collective bargaining with labour. The German Confederation of Trade Unions (DGB) is composed of seventeen industrial unions and has a membership of eight million workers. A separate civil service union (DBB) represents professional employees in public service and administration. Employers and employees are thought of as 'social partners' in Germany's 'social market' economy.

Corporatism

Corporatism is a system in which interest groups tend to be aggregated into 'peak associations', of employers and employees for example. These then maintain a continuing dialogue with each other and with government in a pattern of negotiated, consensual policy making. Because they effectively monopolize the representation of interests in a given field, peak associations can provide information to government and simplify the process of consultation with it; they can also take responsibility for the implementation of agreements which result.

The case study of the introduction of care insurance in Germany
(Case Study 3.1) typifies the process of policy making in the corporatist welfare state.

Care insurance in Germany

In Germany, legislation was agreed in 1994 to introduce a new insurance scheme for long-term care. It was to be financed by an initial one per cent levy on earnings, funded jointly by employers and employees, for example.

The German political system is a federal, parliamentary one in which (from 1982 to 1998) the government was led by the Christian Democrats (CDU), in coalition with their Bavarian sister-party (the Christian Socialists, CSU) and the liberal Free Democrats (FDP). The upper house was controlled by the opposition Social Democrats (SPD), owing to their leadership of a majority of the governments of the regional states.

The CDU is a mass or 'people's' party, which is in itself a coalition of conservatives, nationalists and liberals, entrepreneurs and Catholic workers, Catholic social reformers and conservative protestants. Within the party, a rift between the Christian Democrat governments of some regional states, seeking to unburden themselves of social assistance payments, and the federal government, concerned to limit public spending, was a source of some tension. In the run-up to the 1990 general election Norbert Blüm, Minister of Labour and Social Affairs, put forward a proposal for a new social insurance scheme to cover the costs of long-term care. In so doing, he was appealing to an older population which was, of course, becoming increasingly significant in electoral terms. The idea gained the support of the party's labourist wing and of its coalition partner the CSU, which in essence represented the government of one of the most powerful regional states (Bavaria). The CDU's business wing, meanwhile, expressed a preference for a private insurance alternative.

The government's coalition partner, the FDP, favoured the status quo, suggesting tax breaks to encourage individuals to take out private insurance. For the SPD, the issue was whether or not to campaign for a social insurance scheme or a more redistributive one funded through taxation. The employers' interest lay in denying the issue, preferring to frame it as one of individual rather than collective risk. Though a sense of responsibility incumbent upon them as social partners made it difficult to obstruct reform, the employers sought to minimize their share of its costs. The unions, meanwhile, were trying to represent both their working and their retired members – those likely to pay contributions and those who might receive benefits – as well as those working in the care sector. A tax-based scheme was preferable in so far as it would minimize the burden on the currently employed, though a social insurance solution was also better than the status quo. Other groups supported a tax-financed scheme, too, for reasons of economic efficiency as much as social justice. These included the sickness funds, some doctors, a white collar union and representatives of disabled people, as well as the Greens.

Following Blüm's initiative and the re-election of the CDU-CSU/FDP, it was clear that the long-running debate over whether or not to confront the problem of finance for long-term care had been resolved. What was still at issue was how – the essential choice being between insurance-based and tax-based alternatives. This choice was made, or perhaps avoided, as successive compromises between principal interests were reached. A first gambit involved the abolition of one or more days of statutory (paid) public holiday, which was to compensate employers for their contribution to the scheme and represented a means of buying off business opposition in the CDU and FDP. A second entailed a phased implementation of the new scheme: one public holiday would be lost when home care benefits were introduced in 1995, and a second for nursing home care a year later. This was the basis of agreement on the legislation passed in 1994.

(adapted from Götting et al., 1994)

In Germany, social policy is formulated and negotiated in parliament, in the parties, in trade unions and in employers associations, and in interested organizations such as the sickness funds and campaigning groups. It is widely debated in the press and broadcast media. In important instances, as here within the CDU and among the members of a governing coalition, there is as much difficulty in establishing internal consensus as agreement with opposing or competing interests. A critical factor in the ultimate passage of this reform was the emergent consensus between dominant elements in the two main parties.

FIGURE 3.1   Norbert Blüm, Minister of Labour and Social Affairs, in debate at the Bundestag, Bonn

SUMMARY

- This section has established that participation and dissent in welfare take a variety of forms. Because these different forms are not always easy to distinguish, and because the way in which resources are mobilized inevitably varies according to issue and circumstance, we should think of it as multidimensional, flexible and contingent rather than as a discrete set of actions or activities.

- Different political and economic systems serve to structure participation in different countries in different ways. The German example testifies to the participation of an array of actors in the decision-making process, the complex negotiations in which they engage and the incremental, consensual policy making that results.

3 DIFFERENT KINDS OF WELFARE STATE

Across countries, the politics of welfare is both varied and changing. Different countries exhibit a diversity of welfare states, established according to divergent principles. They have differing histories: they were created at different times in contrasting ways. They express differing patterns of interest, as described above, and they make for different opportunities for participation and dissent. All these differences strongly affect the style and content of policy making. Box 3.2 summarizes the variety of welfare states.

The notion of a 'world' of welfare, or 'welfare regime' emphasizes the way in which the welfare state is born of, and embedded in, particular relations between political, economic and social structures. Different welfare arrangements are produced by and continue to shape different kinds of interaction between classes and groups. Those interactions are both mediated by and reproduce particular social norms. Patterns of employment, political organization and social stratification are especially important, and are expressed in different kinds of accommodation between the state, the market, and the family.

Empirical data strongly suggest that these models have real-world counterparts: measures of social expenditure reveal three clusters of countries as described here. But it is important to recognize that these are types, and that in practice no country will fit any given model perfectly. Interestingly, one of the most difficult countries to place is the UK: while its arrangements for income support are avowedly liberal, those for health care are much more social democratic.

For our discussion, the real significance of Esping-Andersen's typology is to help connect patterns of employment, stratification and political organization with those of participation and dissent. What cross-national comparison like this tells us is that different kinds of welfare state have differing ways of doing politics and policy making, or contrasting political logics. They are both produced by and make possible a range of ways of participating in politics, as well as varying reasons for doing so.

The conservative model has its origins in an authoritarian politics designed to buttress empires headed by monarchs. In much of Europe, nineteenth-century welfare legislation was designed as a counterweight to democratization. It was meant to ameliorate the conditions of an urban working class tempted by socialism without damaging the interests of farmers. Similarly, and in many of the same countries, church-based parties presented a different, non-socialist version of welfare, providing the foundations of post-war Christian democracy in Italy, Germany and the Netherlands. The Catholic principle of subsidiarity (see Box 3.3), according to which local, family and community-based sources of social support are to be protected and supported rather than replaced by the state, continues to inform social policy in the European Union (EU).

BOX 3.2   **The three worlds of welfare capitalism**

There are three main types of welfare capitalism found in advanced industrial democracies.

Liberal welfare states provide modest and often means-tested benefits to low-income dependants. Entitlement rules are both strict and restrictive, often meaning that a degree of stigma is attached to making a claim. The intention is to support and protect a work ethic by ensuring that the standard of living attainable on welfare is less desirable than one derived from paid employment. The system encourages a strong independent or commercial sector, providing pensions, health and unemployment insurance as well as health and other services to those who can afford them. This fosters a characteristic dualism, or 'two-tier welfare'. The best examples of this kind of regime are found not in Europe but in the USA, Canada and Australia.

The dominant European model of welfare is described as *conservative*, and is exemplified by Austria, France, Germany, and Italy. Here, an array of programmes, usually financed by compulsory insurance schemes, provides social security to different occupational and social groups. Contribution levels are calculated according to income, and benefit levels according to income and length of employment. Civil servants often acquire privileged entitlements. In this system, the state displaces the market in the provision of welfare, but upholds pre-existing status differentials (hence the name 'conservative'). Similarly, benefits encourage women into marriage and motherhood rather than work, while substitutes for family responsibilities, such as day care for children, remain underdeveloped.

Social democratic regimes, such as those characteristic of Scandinavian countries, provide benefits which are both universal and equitable. They cater to optimal rather than minimal conceptions of need, seeking to erode class distinctions in entitlement. They express a unitary system of rights, usually in a single scheme, though benefits are normally related to earnings. Public provision predominates over family as well as market alternatives. An extensive public sector provides for the care of children, older people and others, as well as for a large proportion of women's employment. The social democratic regime is further distinguished from liberal and conservative models by its underlying commitment to full employment.

(adapted from Esping-Andersen, 1990, pp.26–9)

BOX 3.3   **Subsidiarity**

The concept of subsidiarity originates historically in Catholic social teaching and is a principle of social policy in many European countries, especially in those where religious-conservative (Christian Democrat) parties are or have been influential. The idea is that responsibilities of all kinds, including those for welfare, should be held at the lowest level at which they can be realized. 'Lower' and 'higher' levels are distinguished by the closeness of the relationships they entail. First comes the family, because relationships are assumed to be closest there, then the community (neighbourhood, church, workplace), then larger organizations based in the economy and civil society such as unions and charities, and only then successive tiers of government. 'The appropriate basis for provision is the least remote alternative which works.'

(adapted from Spicker, 1991, pp.3–6)

There is a strong case for concluding that when subsidiarity is the driving principle of policy making, the process allows for a greater scope and intensity of participation than other ways of delivering public welfare (for example by the state). Indeed, subsidiarity assumes and takes as significant that societies consist in complex arrangements of networks and associations of various kinds, in family structure and civil society – below the state level.

SUMMARY

- This section has used cross-national comparison not only to identify different kinds of welfare state but also to prompt us to new thinking about both welfare and participation.

- The range of welfare states both reflects and reproduces differing issues, interests and ways of thinking about them. The politics and purposes of participation – who seeks to influence the political process and to what ends – will vary in consequence.

- By looking at a number of countries, we begin to discern typical patterns of activity. These form the categories that in turn become the building blocks of new theory. But comparison also serves to make the familiar strange. Our understanding of welfare politics in other countries forces us to think about UK experience in more general and abstract terms. On both counts, we begin to think more imaginatively and more critically about what we take for granted.

4 WELFARE STATES AND PUBLIC OPINION

We have seen that different models represent distinct trajectories of welfare policy making. This pattern holds not only for their emergence and consolidation but also for their adaptation to (and shaping of) post-industrial economic and social patterns. If the post-war period of welfare state development 1945–75 can be characterized as the 'politics of expansion', that following the end of the long boom in the mid 1970s can be described as a 'new politics' of programme maintenance in conditions of 'permanent austerity' (Pierson, 2001). Across advanced industrial countries the welfare state has been put under pressure of various kinds but has been sustained, again in a variety of ways, by political support for it. These pressures and responses to them are discussed in section 5, below. The present section describes patterns of public support for welfare.

Elected governments have powerful incentives to respond to what voters want, or at least to work to the limits of what they will tolerate. This implies that perhaps the most important mechanism of participation in welfare policy is the most ordinary, however indirect a means of expressing preferences it may be. For the majority of voters, their attachment to the welfare state is immediate: they may well work in it, receive or expect to receive benefits from it, or live with someone who does. In this context, governments seeking majorities have problems doing so on a platform of curtailment of what electorates see as an earned and entrenched system of rights. For the politician, a corollary argument also holds: the political benefits of cutbacks are at best diffuse, uncertain and prospective, while their immediate adverse implications are obvious.

Across Europe, a high level of general support for collective programmes of social protection has remained largely unaffected by economic difficulty (Ferrera, 1993; Taylor-Gooby, 2001). A Eurobarometer survey conducted in 1992 found that, in a majority of the then 12 member countries of the EU, the statement that, 'Social security is a major achievement of modern society. The government should make sure that nobody is left deprived when unemployed, poor, disabled', received more than 90 per cent agreement. In no country was this figure less than 85 per cent.

Over time, however, this support has become more discriminating. Support is strongest in those areas most people might expect to use, such as pensions and health care. It is weaker for others such as unemployment benefits and social assistance, which are used by fewer people and associated with a greater degree of stigma. In addition, there is a widespread perception that welfare arrangements are unduly bureaucratic and complex.

Cross-national public opinion about welfare is structured in two ways. The first is by major social divisions of income, age and gender. Across countries, there is evidence that the rich show less support for state welfare than the poor, and those in full-time employment (and especially the self-employed) demonstrate less support than those who are not. The most recent studies emphasize the continuing significance of this finding. The second way is by regime (see Table 3.1): public attitudes are shaped by the core values expressed in different institutional arrangements for welfare.

TABLE 3.1   Support for state welfare, 1996, percentage population

Type of welfare state	Liberal United Kingdom		Conservative Germany		Social democratic Sweden	
It is the state's responsibility:	Definitely	Probably	Definitely	Probably	Definitely	Probably
to provide a decent standard of living for the old	71	26	53	44	69	29
to provide health care for the sick	82	17	56	42	71	25
to provide a decent standard of living for the unemployed	28	49	24	60	52	38
to reduce income differences between rich and poor	35	33	32	37	43	28

Source: adapted from Taylor-Gooby, 2001, p.139, Table 2

Table 3.1 shows the level of support for state welfare in three countries. The United Kingdom (with the reservations noted above), Germany and Sweden are representative examples of Esping-Andersen's three 'worlds' of welfare. They are liberal, conservative or corporatist, and social democratic, respectively. This kind of data is always problematic, not least because it assumes that complex ideas and assumptions can be assessed by simple and standardized questionnaires. Similarly, individual or personal opinions do not necessarily add up to something we can call 'public opinion' in any straightforward way. Finally, of course, attitudes change over time: measured opinion may reflect immediate context and experience as much as anything more enduring. What we think about welfare may reflect some momentary judgment about our own or our country's position as well as our underlying values.

Nevertheless, the information available here and in other studies suggests some things with some clarity. We should begin by stating the obvious. Across countries, there is majority support for the state welfare (adding 'definitely' and 'probably' columns for each programme in each country always gives a figure higher than 60 and often nearer 80 or 90 per cent). At the same time, however, support is stronger for some programmes than for others. What is significant here is that *across countries* support for public provision for the old and sick is higher than for the unemployed or for the poor. Support is higher for those benefits and services everybody can expect to use. This is largely a matter of self-interest, and reflects social divisions of class, age and gender. Middle-class support for benefits for the unemployed, for example, tends to be lower than for other programmes.

Remember that each regime or world of welfare makes particular assumptions about the relationship between welfare and work. In the liberal regime, welfare is meant as a last resort in the event of the failure of paid work to otherwise meet need; in the conservative regime, entitlement is earned through employment; in the social democratic model, the citizen is taken to be normally in paid employment. This helps to explain why there is more commitment to social protection for the unemployed in Sweden than in either the UK or Germany. But note that work legitimates entitlement everywhere; political participation reflects assumptions about economic participation. This is also why, across countries, there is more support for policies of 'activation' – for connecting entitlement to some kind of obligation to work – than there is for simple retrenchment or cutbacks.

What Table 3.1 also shows, of course, is that there is more conviction about the role of the state in health care in the UK than in Germany, perhaps reflecting the high status of the NHS in national public opinion. Yet, as Charlesworth and Humphreys made clear in the previous chapter, it seems likely that the NHS not only reflects but also reproduces and reinforces such attitudes. Sometimes, voters seem to want what they get. In Germany, for example, the state is no less a guarantor of access to health care than in the UK. But health care there is financed and provided for by independent institutions such as the sickness funds, which are in fact mandated in public law. In Table 3.1 the question of whether the state should provide health care for the sick may well mean different things in different countries.

Attitudes change over time, seemingly as a result of a combination of interest and experience. In western Europe, the greatest dissatisfaction with the extent of social protection is felt in Spain, Portugal, Italy and Greece. Much higher levels of satisfaction are reported in longer established and more generous welfare states in the north, and especially in Denmark, the Netherlands and Luxemburg. The UK comes somewhere in between, and there, where spending was most severely constrained in the 1980s and 1990s, there was some increase in the support for social welfare. In Italy, an expansionist enthusiasm for its late developing welfare programmes has slowly been checked. Support for state schemes is lower in Germany, where the established pattern is one of quasi-autonomous insurance funds managed by the social partners, and where their independence and autonomy are seen to have been threatened by a state seeking to adapt to the economic burden of the unification of West and East Germany after the fall of the Berlin Wall. In many countries, a degree of hesitancy about state welfare became perceptible in the course of the 1990s.

S U M M A R Y

- Across countries, public support for welfare is high and sustained. This support is stronger for pensions and health care than for social assistance.

- Variations among countries reflect the values inherent in different institutional arrangements.

5 PRESSURE AND CHANGE

Pressure on policy making about welfare has come from low economic growth, from a shift in patterns of employment from industrial to service sectors, from ageing populations, from an accumulated burden of commitment to existing provision, and from neo-liberal ideology. Each of these pressures may have been intensified by globalization, though that is not their origin. For almost all European countries, the convergence criteria set for entry to the Economic and Monetary Union (EMU) have provided a source of much more direct and immediate constraint. Economic and other pressures have been similar across countries, but they have not been the same, whether in substance, timing or effect. This is at least in part because the very existence of the welfare state has shaped the social and economic environment to which it belongs, and different schemes and sets of schemes have done so in necessarily contrasting ways.

So how have different states responded to these constraints on welfare policy? Different countries have adopted divergent strategies in dissimilar combinations:

- One is to commodify or recommodify welfare, which means strengthening the market principles according to which work – and the income and other benefits that accrue from it – is allocated. In many instances it amounts to withdrawing support for ways of living outside the market.

- A second strategy is that of cost containment, usually by limiting increases in spending and/or changing the threshold of entitlement.

- A third is modernization, which includes managing programmes in new ways, sometimes by consolidation and sometimes by adapting to new needs.

It is policy making in the liberal welfare state – represented by the USA, as well as New Zealand, Australia, Canada and to some extent the UK – which has placed most emphasis on commodification. Unemployment insurance and social assistance have been cut back: eligibility has been restricted and benefit levels reduced. Levels of poverty have increased in consequence. Significantly, these changes have been made in political systems that offer least opportunity for resistance to them. In the UK, welfare reforms were undertaken by a single-party, majority government returned in a single member plurality (or 'first past the post') electoral system. Weak mechanisms for consultation either with or within business and industry presented little obstacle to its commitment to 'rolling back' the state. And precisely because social security entitlement in the UK is less extensive, popular support for it is less than elsewhere.

Policy makers in conservative and corporatist welfare states have sought to contain the costs of some of their particularly expensive social insurance schemes. Paying for pensions becomes especially difficult when the ratio of workers to retired beneficiaries begins to dip. Increasing contributions from a diminishing workforce increases the cost of labour, which in turn threatens employment and growth. Meanwhile, attempts to limit or retract entitlement have tended to be met with vigorous protest, as evidenced by a newly conflictual negotiation of pensions reform in Germany in the mid–late 1990s and by recent experience in France. Case Study 3.2 demonstrates this point.

FIGURE 3.2   Public demonstration in May against the proposed pension reforms, Strasbourg, France, 2003

Despite the strong public resistance to reform, articulated in key forms of dissent such as public demonstrations and strikes, overall there has been an increasing general acknowledgement in conservative and corporatist countries that the status quo is no longer viable. Politicians such as Gerhard Schröder in Germany have tried to forge a new centrist coalition for reform.

In the Netherlands and Italy, too, incremental reform has been promoted by similar coalitions, attempting to remove obvious sources of inefficiency without overly damaging entitlement or equity.

CASE STUDY 3.2　　　**Pensions reform in France**

In Europe, people have fewer children but live longer than they did when state-regulated pension schemes were first established. This means that the money earned by those in work is increasingly insufficient to pay the pensions of those who have retired. In response to this demographic 'threat' to the financial viability of the schemes, most European countries, guided by EC proposals, are planning to raise the statutory retirement age. The effect of this is to extend the period in which employers and employees make contributions, and correspondingly (if implicitly) to reduce the period in which retirees draw benefit. In political terms, governments are asking employees to work longer for a benefit to which many have assumed they are or would be already entitled.

In France, the conservative government elected in 2002 set about pensions reform soon after it came to power. Its initial proposals were met by public demonstrations in October 2002 and again in February 2003, which forced it to abandon the idea of supplementing general schemes with personal, individual plans. Further proposals were presented in talks with the social partners (the peak organizations of employers and employees) in April, and a bill presented to cabinet in early May. The government's key commitment was to raising the contribution period of public sector workers from 37.5 to 40 years, bringing it in line with that for the private sector.

The major union confederations called a strike for 13 May. They were joined by the civil servants' associations and supported by other organizations too, such as those representing surviving spouses and French families. Between one and two million people were involved, in over 100 cities across the country (Figure 3.2).

The government met the unions the next day, though some withdrew almost immediately. Nineteen amendments to the reform plan were agreed – including a government commitment to negotiating pension increases with business, unions and civil servants every three years – but without affecting the key proposal. Public protest continued, but gradually weakened, undermined by divisions among the labour organizations.

A revised bill was agreed in cabinet at the end of May and presented to Parliament. Debating its 80 clauses lasted more than a month: several thousand amendments were proposed by opposition parties (notably the communists), of which a few hundred were accepted, again without involving major concession. The bill passed at the end of July represented some degree of success for the government, though workers in special schemes – including those run by publicly owned gas, electricity and railway companies – remained exempt from its provisions. A number of public sector unions, now including teachers, made a commitment to continue to protest through the autumn.

Social democratic regimes have looked for means of cost containment, too, in order to contain in turn a sharp rise in unemployment (because increasing taxes and social insurance contributions makes workers more expensive to hire). Unemployment, of course, is the single biggest threat to the viability of the model as a whole. But adjustments have been agreed through a normal practice of intensive dialogue with both sides of industry. Union membership is high, and unions are closely connected with social democratic parties. Women are mobilized in defence of welfare, often finding in the welfare state either an immediate source of employment or the means by which they participate elsewhere in the labour market.

What is interesting about recent change is that the most vigorous assaults on welfare in the 1980s and 1990s came to be made in policy reform in countries where welfare provision was least extensive, such as the UK and the USA. This is at least in part because the key constituency of welfare politics is not the poor and underprivileged, but the middle class. In the liberal world of welfare, its interests are identified with the allocation of social goods – such as insurance and welfare services – by the market as much as by the state. Although the middle class is motivated to support education and health care, it is less inclined to defend state pensions and other benefits it pays for (through taxation) but does not expect to use. In the conservative regime, middle-class interests are identified more closely with social insurance schemes, and in the social democratic regime with the protection of public employment and universal, high-quality services. Thus, in conservative/ corporatist and social democratic countries in Europe, those who pay for welfare also expect to benefit from it. The adaptation by welfare states to a changing environment has been and is being shaped in different ways by the interests those states have themselves constructed.

That said, and as suggested by Table 3.1, there is little support anywhere for cuts in entitlement or provision. But nor is there much willingness to pay more for welfare through taxes and contributions. Given the natural growth in demand for resources associated with ageing populations and some sector-specific requirements such as the development of new health-care technologies, this makes for continued and increasing pressure on welfare state policy making. The general picture is one of the resilience of the welfare state, buttressed as it is by patterns of positive public opinion.

At the same time, of course, the institutional workings of liberal democracy make change of any kind difficult to achieve, and the more significant the more difficult. In most continental European countries, decision-making power is shared: among parties in a governing coalition, with judiciaries, with other tiers of government above and below, and sometimes – through referendums – directly with voters. Implementation is often dependent on the agreement and support of employers and employees, and some key occupational groups such as teachers and care workers.

SUMMARY

- In advanced industrial democracies, policy making is shaped at least in part by what voters want. This is best thought of as a kind of implicit participation in decision making.

- Where participation is more immediate or explicit, different patterns of interest-representation mean that in some countries reform is negotiated and consensual, while in others it is more adversarial and contested.

- The case of French pensions reform shows that effective participation is related to organizational strength and political and economic power, such as is held by some trade unions, professional associations and other interest groups.

6 LOCAL PARTICIPATION

Sections 4 and 5 were largely concerned with national politics and policy making, and described a world in which it is ministers and civil servants, elected politicians and representatives of interest groups who take part in the policy-making process. Public participation largely appears secondary, informing decision-making through voting, the expression of popular opinion and sometimes more immediate protest. But if participation and dissent refer to the political activity of ordinary people, as suggested in section 2, then we are most likely to find it at the local level, in organizations and communities and the services they provide. At this local level, too, types and patterns of participation and dissent vary across countries. They also vary among sectors, that is between governmental, commercial and charitable organizations.

Compared to other industrial democracies, a more limited conception of the role and responsibility of the state for the welfare of its citizens prevails in the USA. In his classic *Democracy in America*, published as long ago as 1835, Alexis de Tocqueville remarked on how many Americans joined associations to discuss and address local issues and public affairs. Though the quality and vigour of US civil society has come to be questioned, a tradition of philanthropy, self-help and community organizing endures, as illustrated by Case Study 3.3.

<table>
<tr><td>CASE STUDY 3.3</td><td>**Youth service in the USA**</td></tr>
</table>

What is called youth service, meaning voluntary activity of all kinds (including participation in welfare), is a key part of the curriculum of most US high schools. Young people serve as members of grant-giving boards, take part in delivering services and running organizations, and get engaged in wider political processes, such as voter registration. Many states run Youth As Resources (YAR) programmes, in which boards of young people award grants to young people to develop projects addressing social issues such as literacy, drug use and gang problems, as well as other health, educational and environmental topics. Different projects include debate and discussion groups, mentoring programmes for peers and younger children, after school sports leagues and hotlines, counselling and resource workshops. Here, participation expresses a strong sense of individuality coupled with responsibility to the community. Self-realization is as important a principle as welfare, as shown by the investment in leadership and personal development.

(adapted from Cutler, 2002)

FIGURE 3.3   One of ONCE's lottery ticket offices in Spain

Meanwhile, private (commercial) and non-governmental (charitable or voluntary) organizations (see Case Study 3.4) have always been essential mechanisms of welfare provision in most democratic countries. They preceded public schemes and have not been eroded by them. Indeed, it is arguable that increasing public provision has stimulated rather than replaced alternative modes of social service organization. In Italy, for example, until the 1970s, non-governmental organizations (NGOs) were best characterized by a traditional 'charity model', often based in the Catholic church or in religious teaching, and representing a philanthropic concern with the needy. As the proportion of lay activity of this kind increased, it took on a more critical or political function, born of the protest movements of the 1960s and 1970s. New, independent organizations began to confront social issues of poverty and marginalization, forming new projects such as housing associations and communities, and recreation centres.

NGOs such as ONCE tend to have two purposes or functions. Some are concerned primarily with advocacy by or on behalf of a particular group. Others are more concerned with providing services to such groups, while some develop a combination of the two. They differ greatly in the degree to which

| CASE STUDY 3.4 | **ONCE, the National Organization of the Blind in Spain** |

In Spain, almost all blind people are in paid employment; their rates of employment are much higher than for blind people in other countries, and higher even than for the non-blind in Spain. Almost all work for ONCE, the National Organization of the Blind.

In the early twentieth century, blind people typically survived by begging, though there was some special school provision for primary education and vocational training. In 1906, an advisory board was set up to campaign and work with government. In many cities, blind people had established mutual aid societies, funded from begging, musical performances, and the resale of state lottery tickets. They provided some welfare benefits for those unable to beg – a kind of sick pay – as well as death benefits. Some societies started up their own lotteries, in illegal competition with the state monopoly. There was some reservation about the low status of the non-productive work involved – selling lottery tickets on the street could be almost equivalent to begging. A new pressure group promoted sheltered workshops.

At the end of 1938, after the civil war, a national federation was formed and awarded a lottery monopoly. Its proceeds were to be invested in residential schools, in creating employment opportunities and in promoting other kinds of social integration. It developed a strong 'family' ethic of independence and autonomy, of the blind 'looking after their own'. It provided medical benefits, pensions and other allowances, free primary, secondary and further education and housing loans, as well as lottery employment (Figure 3.3), whether selling tickets or in administration. In the 1960s it began to sponsor training schools for switchboard operators and physiotherapists. The lottery business was restructured in the 1980s to incorporate new competition from a scheme started by the physically disabled. By 1990, it had also begun to diversify, holding investment interests in the financial and media sectors in particular.

(adapted from Garvia, 1992)

they are staffed by volunteers or depend on salaried professional and administrative expertise. The problem many face is that, as they develop over time, they tend to become more professional or more bureaucratic. Often, too, the boundary between charitable and commercial activity becomes very blurred. These developments may help the organizations serve their primary functions, but they may also undermine an ethos of participation and self-determination on the part of their client groups.

Meanwhile, demands for welfare change in all sorts of ways, just as the composition and dynamics of a local community change. A new service, such as a community centre for an immigrant population, may reflect the emergence of a new need. Some needs are simply newly recognized as public responsibilities, such as support for the victims of domestic violence. Both may be provided only after an often extended period of campaigning by those affected or concerned.

In a different way, increasingly affluent individuals in increasingly prosperous societies look for ways to exercise greater freedom of choice in welfare, as patterns of consumption learned in other domains such as travel, for example, are sought in social services, too. New demand is met by the reconfiguring of existing services and the introduction of new ones. These may be financial services (such as life insurance) or material ones (such as child care). Many of them operate outside the public sector, in markets and communities. Case Study 3.5 demonstrates a change in policy making in maternity care in Sweden in order to be more responsive to women's needs.

CASE STUDY 3.5   **Maternity care in Sweden**

In Sweden in the early 1970s, pregnant women were required to stay in the vicinity of their closest hospital for four weeks before the expected birth date of their child (a principle called 'municipal arrest'). If they were to give birth anywhere else, they could be made to pay for the care they received. Maternity services were controlled by professional midwives, according to a strict regimen: confinements took place sometimes in shared rooms, women were sedated with chloroform during delivery, and had no access to the room where newborns slept.

One midwife, Signe Jansson, began to develop a different model of maternity care in Malmö, based on what she had learned on a visit to Paris. Its purpose was to enable women to give birth on their own terms, and involved teaching women ways of taking control of their own deliveries, making them easier and more humane. This, of course, entailed redefining the relationship between women and professional staff, and met with resistance on the part of other midwives. A pilot project, though much sought after by users, was closed down. A second attempt in a different town, Ystad, took hold, and the effect of demand for it caused the principle of municipal arrest to break down.

By the end of the 1980s, almost half of women having babies at Ystad were from elsewhere. Importantly, too, the service was achieving good clinical results. Its new ways of working began to be taken up elsewhere; where they weren't, demand for a service dropped to a degree which threatened it with closure. Now, in Sweden, women seek to give birth in conditions which they help to determine, and choose between different clinics in order to do so.

(adapted from Rothstein, 1998, pp.188–92)

In the example in Case Study 3.5, participation is realized in a kind of partnership between the provider and the user of services. In this instance, too, it appears progressive, improving the quality of service for the user or patient, and perhaps also the work satisfaction of the provider, the midwife. Participation doesn't mean that demands are made and either met or not met, but more often amounts to a process of active negotiation. In many instances, too, that process of negotiation between provider and user may be more or less continuous rather than episodic. We might think of government, payers, providers, and users of services as taking part in a continuing dialogue about the nature and level of benefits and services that should be provided.

However, there is reason for more critical reflection, too. Participation is not necessarily always what it appears to be. It may be token, as we saw in Chapter 2, undertaken by those in power (governments, service providers and others) as a way of constructing approval for what they do, or legitimating decisions that might otherwise be contentious. Often, consultations, consumer satisfaction surveys, and citizens' forums may be more symbolic than substantial. Participation is sometimes encouraged because subsequent decisions seem more legitimate where it has taken place, whether or not it has influenced (or been allowed to influence) those decisions.

One of the principal difficulties is that, because community interests are many and varied, the outcome of such consultations is not always clear. And even when messages are clear, it will still fall to the authorities to judge whether the action it implies is either appropriate or feasible. This is to say that participation is ultimately limited or constrained: it is about taking *part in* decisions rather than taking decisions as such, and how great or small a part often lies at the discretion of the payers or providers of a service rather than its users. Of course, this applies as much to decisions made about national programmes as about local services.

There are particular problems about participation in welfare politics. Generally speaking, the recipients of benefits and the users of services are almost by definition those with the least resources in society. And where they might want to make more radical claims for different kinds of welfare organization they may be thwarted by the standard ways of doing things in established systems and services. The Claimant Unions in Case Study 3.6 are an interesting illustration of both kinds of problem.

CASE STUDY 3.6 **Claimants' Unions**

Claimants' Unions were a radical attempt to develop an alternative, participatory and democratic form of organization for poor people which emerged in Britain in the 1970s (Figure 3.4). They point to some of the dilemmas and contradictions of participation in social policy. Union members were determined to discuss cases collectively, in group meetings, replacing the individualized relationships typical of social work, counselling and law. Nevertheless, groups tended to be formed and led by student activists and experienced former workers. In the end it was always individual cases which had to be represented at appeals, often by another member who had acquired a particular, superior expertise. And many claimants, of course, were 'active only for a few weeks or months, because to some extent participation is participation in crisis, and eventually all but the most dedicated are reclaimed by the demands of their life situation'.

(adapted from Rose, 1977)

FIGURE 3.4   The Claimant Unions' logo, UK, 1970s

SUMMARY

- Local examples have been used to extend what we mean by participation in welfare policy making and delivery, and to modify the way we think about it.

- As in previous sections, the evidence suggests that different countries have divergent cultures of local or community participation.

- Participation may be about giving or providing services, as much as about advocacy. It may mean negotiating service delivery and may include forms of self-help.

- Participation may take the form of a partnership or dialogue between service-users and service-providers.

- However, the rhetoric of participation may be used as an instrument of those in positions of power.

- Meanwhile, there are specific and fundamental reasons why participation in welfare is constrained.

These dilemmas are explored further in the sections below.

7   EXIT, VOICE AND LOYALTY

So far, this chapter has conveyed a sense of the multidimensional nature of participation and dissent. Individuals and groups in a range of countries engage with different issues in contrasting ways. One conclusion we might draw from our wide-ranging, cross-national approach is that participation and dissent are indeed always issue-specific and context-specific. Drawing on our comparative analysis, however, we can also begin to distinguish categories, models and patterns of participation, noting what we might call systematic differences between types of country, types of issue and types of actor. Corporatism, for example, is a distinctive style of policy making, and subsidiarity a particular way of thinking about it. The issues raised by participation and dissent in the public sector overlap with, but are also distinct from, those in civil society or the community. But is there a more general theory or model of participatory behaviour that might usefully hold across countries, sectors and issues?

According to Albert Hirschman, the politics of participation – of assent and dissent, of engagement in public issues – can be conceived as the politics of exit, voice and loyalty (see Box 3.4). Hirschman's framework was developed as a way of understanding, as his subtitle has it, 'responses to decline in firms, organizations and states'. This is not to suggest that social policy and social services are somehow in decline; rather, it is the degree of change to which welfare has been subjected over the last decade or so which makes Hirschman's work applicable here. Its combined understanding of political, economic and social processes – realized in states, markets and communities – gives it a special merit.

BOX 3.4   **Exit, voice and loyalty**

Voice stands for 'any attempt at all to change rather than to escape from an objectionable state of affairs', whether by individual or collective action – including voting or making a complaint, expressing and mobilizing opinion, by representation and lobbying, or by more elaborate organizational means.

Exit refers simply to the search for and selection of alternatives to a current supplier, that is to 'shopping around'.

Loyalty, meanwhile, has to do with the circumstances and ways of thinking according to which people adopt one strategy or the other.

(adapted from Hirschman, 1970)

Voice is what most immediately corresponds to participation and dissent in welfare politics, and it has been the predominant concern of this chapter (it is interesting to note that in European languages such as French and German, the words for 'voice' and 'vote' are the same). There is an alternative to political engagement, however, which amounts to 'voting with one's feet' or what Hirschman calls 'exit'. It is an essentially economic mechanism, the way in which 'market forces' are expressed. There are various levels of exit open to the user of welfare. For example, the user may move: from one provider to another within a public system, as when choosing or changing a doctor; from one form or sector of provision to another, as when moving from a state-run to an occupational or commercial pension scheme; or from one national system to another, as when a student moves from one country to another for higher education.

Exit is expensive, however. In order to exercise choice, users often need detailed and sophisticated information about the options before them and usually significant material resources, such as money, time and transport. Cross-national, comparative evidence is inevitably fragmented, but suggests that mobility of this kind is limited. Relations between providers and users (teachers and pupils, doctors and patients) are built on trust, which in turn often assumes a degree of familiarity. Patients tend to stay with doctors they know. Precisely because welfare is a function of existential concerns – where to live, which school to go to, how to budget for retirement – the stakes are high. Experimentation – shopping around – is not just expensive but risky.

At the same time, of course, exit generates a systemic problem, for it may threaten the collective principles on which much welfare provision is founded. There is a risk that the ability of some to 'opt out' leads to a two-tier system. Those able to purchase high quality services in the market resent being taxed in order to fund public schemes they don't use, and which in consequence become progressively under-funded.

Loyalty is a complex and problematic idea. Hirschman used the term in a specific sense, to help explain why some take exit options and some use voice. As a rule, he says, loyalty 'holds exit at bay and activates voice'. The propensity to 'exit' or 'voice' will also vary with the cultural traditions of a country. In the UK, for example, loyalty to the principles underlying the National Health Service or comprehensive schooling means that many will seek to protect and improve them by using different forms of voice before exiting to private education and private health care.

Nevertheless, for complex reasons as we have seen, welfare reform strategies in Europe have sought to reduce cost (to the taxpayer or contributor) and increase choice (for the user or consumer). Without denying – or being able to deny – the use of different forms of voice, policy reforms have sought to give new emphasis to opportunities for exit. Meanwhile, for other reasons, some of the more powerful forms of voice, such as trade unionism, are those which are in decline. Similarly, as more inputs into the policy process with implications for welfare come to be made at European level, citizens' engagement with the political process becomes the more difficult the further removed it is from their daily lives.

SUMMARY

- Hirschman's theory of participatory behaviour, using the concepts of exit, voice, and loyalty, provides insights into the welfare policy-making processes of different countries.
- 'Voice' corresponds to a wide range of forms of participation and dissent in welfare policy making. 'Exit' relates to individual decisions on how to pay for welfare services such as schooling and health care. 'Loyalty' helps to explain the commitment to either voice or exit.

8 PARTICIPATION, INCLUSION AND EXCLUSION

So far we've focused on the means of participation and dissent in welfare policy making, but it is also worth reflecting on the processes and effects of participation by asking about its limits – that is, about *non-participation* in social policy making. Some people, many perhaps, have no reason or wish to engage in political activity of this kind: non-participation may be a by-product of successful or at least satisfactory institutions, including public welfare. On the other hand, as we have seen, it is in the nature of social need (such as poverty, ill-health or homelessness) that those who experience it are also those least likely and able to participate in (or dissent from) what for others are quite ordinary social and political processes. They are excluded.

Some people make active decisions about their welfare, while others are more passive. Some think in terms of their individual interests, while others are more collective. These two axes can be combined to give a matrix of four different approaches to participation and non-participation. Table 3.2, setting out this model, is based on an English study of stroke patients discharged from hospital. It draws on ideas about what Tocqueville described as 'habits of the heart': beliefs, attitudes and opinions, moral and intellectual dispositions, as well as ordinary patterns of participation in religious, political and economic life.

TABLE 3.2   Approaches to participation in welfare

	Individualist expectations	Collectivist expectations
High participation	The *consumerist* approach to welfare denotes an active use of market, family and household resources, in the context of minimal expectations of the state and some uncertainty about the loss of autonomy which the use of voluntary or public services might bring.	A *welfarist* position reflects a committed belief in public services and the right to use them, usually supported by a high level of awareness of the range of services on offer and the ability to exploit it actively.
Low participation	*Privatist* attitudes are similarly individualistic and independent, but much more passive in the way they are realized, often resulting in an inability to capture goods not advertised or made available in familiar ways.	*Clientalism* describes the passive receipt of public sector services.

Source: adapted from Baldock and Ungerson, 1996, pp.179–84 and Figure 9.1

What is valuable about this framework is its specification of a variety of relationships between users and given constellations of services. It amplifies and enriches the range of behaviours that might be covered by ideas about exit and voice in such a way as to include all users of welfare.

Other forms of inclusion in and exclusion from participation in welfare can be seen in examples of personal care, and of lives disrupted in a world in transition. Caring is an intensely demanding combination of love and work, and it is difficult to imagine a more committed kind of participation in welfare. But very different experiences of caring are exemplified by the very different cases of Mr Merton (Case Study 3.7) and Mrs Rushton (Case Study 3.8).

CASE STUDY 3.7   **Mr Merton**

Mr Merton looks after his wife. He used to work in the merchant navy, subsequently as a lifeguard, and then as care assistant. He developed epilepsy in his late twenties, and met his wife in a residential hospital. Both are registered disabled, though Mrs Merton needs more help, and also uses a wheelchair. It was she who introduced him to disability rights work. Both are active local campaigners, and are valued sources of advice and information to others. Mr Merton also cares for a number of people in his neighbourhood, doing errands and odd jobs and basic but essential care tasks.

(adapted from Chamberlayne and King, 2000, pp.106–10)

CASE STUDY 3.8   **Mrs Rushton**

Mrs Rushton looks after her husband, who has multiple sclerosis. Her caring helps him carry on an independent life outside the home, though the commitment she makes is effectively at the cost of her own independence. She uses nursing services reluctantly, because she experiences them as an intrusion. She is often tired, and gets out little, other than to carer group meetings which offer her a vital social support.

(adapted from Chamberlayne and King, 2000, p.113–15)

Since the 1970s and the end of the long boom, welfare states have been made to adjust to an 'age of austerity' (sections 4 and 5, above). Individuals, families and communities have been disrupted and dislocated by economic, social and political change. Life transitions such as leaving home, finding work and somewhere to live, forming meaningful relationships and having children, growing up and growing old – however ordinary – are characteristically difficult at any time. But they have been made more difficult in the context of a whole world in transition, in which relationships between those with and without work, between generations, between men and women and between ethnic groups, have become insecure. In this context, basic social identities, roles and responsibilities have been made newly uncertain.

Such change both generates new kinds of need and obviates previously existing patterns and possibilities of participation and inclusion, as illustrated by Djamillah's story in Case Study 3.9.

Djamillah's participation (not just in welfare) is multidimensional, and is expressed in the politics of her family, her education, her relationship with her husband and his family, and her career. In each dimension, she appears to balance resistance with support. Her family, for example, is a source of personal conflict but also a resource which seems to give her a sense of security and identity. Her educational success was achieved only by overcoming discrimination at school. She is married to someone who lives in another country, with the result that kinship and caring networks extend across continents. She exchanges professional prestige for a more engaged, committed legal practice.

For Djamillah, voice and exit are both constructed and constrained by complicated loyalties. Participation, for her, means continually translating between insider and outsider positions across dominant and minority cultures. It entails compromise, which seems to mean for her not simply a middle way between one position and another, but a reconstruction of traditional interests and obligations in new circumstances. Each of her decisions has political significance, though none is made in the domain of formal politics.

<table>
<tr><td>CASE STUDY 3.9</td><td>**Djamillah**</td></tr>
</table>

Djamillah was born in Luton in 1971. Her father had been a major in the Pakistan army, but was injured in the 1950s. He came to England to join his brother in a bakery, and his wife followed two years later, in 1969. An older child had been born already, in Pakistan, and then came three younger brothers. Djamillah's family lived with her uncle in an extended household until she was 12, when her father also stopped work because of illness.

The family, and especially her father, attached great importance to education. 'All the time he was on our back to study, study, study,' she says, though she also openly recognizes that he has always been there for her when she needed his support. The children all attended Koranic school, and all became doctors, lawyers or scientists. Djamillah studied law, becoming a barrister, though she fought with her father over a white boyfriend, and about living in a mixed hall of residence.

She also resisted her parents' choice of husband for her, marrying instead a wealthy but uneducated Muslim man from her family's area of Pakistan. She later found out that he has a wife and family in Pakistan but stays with him, in part to protect her own family from the shame of having allowed a free marriage that didn't work. Her husband lives partly in Pakistan, where she enjoys visiting him. Two of his children now live with them in London, as does one of her brothers.

She left the bar to join a community law centre, in an area where she also faces racial harassment on her way to work. She is studying part-time for a degree in the humanities.

(adapted from Chamberlayne et al., 2002, pp.232–6)

Djamillah's story is part of a recent study based on biographical interviews of the socially excluded in seven European countries. Extensive case studies of unqualified young people and unemployed graduates, lone parents, ethnic minorities, migrant workers and early retired people 'showed individuals struggling personally, without any sense of social support, in what were actually collective situations' (Chamberlayne et al., 2002, p.15). At the same time, too, many manage to manipulate the opportunities and constraints that face them, combining their resources and aspirations in different ways.

SUMMARY

- At the level of the individual, participation in welfare stands for the way in which people negotiate their relationships with those around them. Our examples support the widely cited claim of the women's movement that 'the personal is political'.

- Here, too, types and patterns emerge. Different individuals seem to hold different dispositions to welfare, leading them to participate in decisions about the services they receive in different ways and to a greater or lesser extent.

- Individuals take part in the policy-making process in several different arenas, including the home and the workplace as well as an array of local agencies and organizations. Decisions reached in one setting may well impact on others. As Djamillah's story shows, the family is a crucial site of political activity, with implications for welfare policy.

- The experience of social exclusion and dislocation appears to make participation both more necessary and more difficult. Indeed, we might almost define exclusion as the inability to participate.

9 CONCLUSION

Political participation and dissent are as varied as the individuals and groups who engage in them, and as diverse as the issues and circumstances with which they are concerned. Indeed, they constitute much of what we recognize as political life and, as such, form the backdrop to policy making of all kinds.

Our cross-national study of welfare policy suggests a number of more specific things. Different political systems present contrasting opportunities for and constraints on participation and dissent. This makes for a variety of kinds of policy making and, indeed, sometimes for different decisions. But it is also true that many of the pressures individuals face they share with others: they must be addressed and resolved in some way, if by different routes. Public support for welfare across countries has largely meant that governments have sought to manage pressures on welfare states by programmes of modernization or restructuring rather than dismantling. In pluralist democracies, in which a number of different groups take part in the policy-making process, policy change is often complex and incremental, and for the most part this holds for welfare reform, too.

Meanwhile, it is clear that important avenues and arenas of participation and dissent in welfare lie outside the state and the formal political system, in the organizations and institutions of civil society. Examples from different countries also suggest that local participation may sometimes be concerned to change the terms and conditions on which existing services are provided, and sometimes to develop new ones.

Further reflection reveals a deeper ambiguity inherent in participation in welfare. Defining the terms and conditions under which it takes place is as significant as political participation itself. The effects of participation may be conservative as well as progressive: it is part of the more general process by which broader prevailing systems (including states, organizations and families) are preserved as well as adapted, changed or even discarded.

Examples of individual experience further emphasize that there is no one way to engage in politics, and certainly no one right way. The problems of exclusion and dependency that are intrinsic to social policy serve to remind us that participation may be most difficult when it is most necessary.

Cross-national comparison of the kind developed in this chapter serves a number of purposes. Perhaps the simplest is that it provides a richer range of experience and example for discussion than we would otherwise have to hand. The effect of this is often to make our own experience relative in some way, to place it in a broader context, making us think differently about it. Sometimes, as with any sort of comparison, different cases can be categorized and re-categorized into distinctive and typical ways of doing things. This is one of the ways in which we build and deploy new theory, such as Hirschman's model of exit, voice and loyalty, or Baldock and Ungerson's account of approaches to understanding welfare policy. It also forces us to think more critically about what we mean by participation as such.

REFERENCES

Baldock, J. and Ungerson, C. (1996) 'Money, care and consumption: families in the new mixed economy of social care' in Jones, H. and Millar, J. (eds) *The Politics of the Family*, Avebury, Aldershot.

Chamberlayne, P. and King, A. (2000) *Cultures of Care. Biographies of Carers in Britain and the Two Germanies*, Bristol, Policy Press.

Chamberlayne, P., Rustin, M. and Wengraf, T. (eds) (2002) *Biography and Social Exclusion in Europe. Experiences and Life Journeys*, Bristol, Policy Press.

Cutler, D. (2002) *Taking the Initiative – Promoting Young People's Involvement in Public Decision Making in the USA*, London, Carnegie Young People Initiative.

Esping-Andersen, G. (1990) *The Three Worlds of Welfare Capitalism*, Cambridge, Polity.

Ferrera, M. (1993) *EC Citizens and Social Protection: Main Results from a Eurobarometer Survey*, Brussels, Commission of the European Communities.

Garvia, R. (1992) 'Mutual dependence between government and private service monopoly: the case of the Spanish blind' in Kuhnle, S. and Selle, P. (eds) *Government and Voluntary Organisations. A Relational Perspective*, Aldershot, Avebury.

Götting, U., Haug, K. and Hinrichs, K. (1994) 'The long road to long-term care insurance in Germany', *Journal of Public Policy*, vol.14, no.3, pp.285–309.

Hirschman, A.O. (1970) *Exit, Voice, and Loyalty: Responses to Decline in Firms, Organisations, and States*, Cambridge, Mass, Harvard University Press.

Lasswell, H.D. (1958) *Politics: Who Gets What, When, How*, Cleveland, Ohio, Meridian Books.

Pierson, P. (ed.) (2001) *The New Politics of the Welfare State*, Oxford, Oxford University Press.

Rose, H. (1977) 'Up against the welfare state: the Claimants' Unions' in Fitzgerald, M., Halmos, P., Muncie, J. and Zeldin, D. (eds) *Welfare in Action*, London, Routledge and Kegan Paul.

Rothstein, B. (1998) *Just Institutions Matter. The Moral and Political Logic of the Universal Welfare State*, Cambridge, Cambridge University Press.

Spicker, P. (1991) 'The principle of subsidiarity and the social policy of the European Community', *Journal of European Social Policy*, vol.1, no.1, pp.3–14.

Taylor-Gooby, P. (2001) 'Sustaining welfare in hard times: who will foot the bill?', *Journal of European Social Policy*, vol.11, no.2, pp.133–47.

FURTHER READING

Esping-Andersen, G. (1990) *The Three Worlds of Welfare Capitalism*, Cambridge, Polity.

Hirschman, A.O. (1970) *Exit, Voice, and Loyalty: Responses to Decline in Firms, Organisations, and States*, Cambridge, Mass, Harvard University Press.

Taylor-Gooby, P. (2001) 'Sustaining welfare in hard times: who will foot the bill?', *Journal of European Social Policy*, vol.11, no.2, pp.133–47.

Fair policy or special treatment? Disability politics

Nick Watson

Contents

1   Introduction: what is disability politics, and why is disability
    a political issue?   114

2   The social model of disability   117

3   How does disability involve disadvantage?   121

4   How are disabled people a minority grouping?   123

5   Critics of the social model   131

6   Identity politics   134

7   Civil rights for disabled people and anti-discrimination legislation   136

8   Conclusion   139

    References   141

    Further reading   144

1   INTRODUCTION: WHAT IS DISABILITY POLITICS, AND WHY IS DISABILITY A POLITICAL ISSUE?

To many people, disability and the needs of disabled people might appear far from the political arena. Surely, it could be argued, these are medical issues and if there is a political dimension to the issue of disability it is related to how, say, policy making in the health care system is funded and how much a government gives to fund health care in that country. Yet, in the second half of the twentieth century, disability and the needs of disabled people emerged as the basis of a distinct political movement with a policy agenda in its own right, and demanded that disability be viewed as separate from medicine. Disability politics drew its inspiration from new social movements that developed in the 1960s and 1970s from previously excluded groups such as African Americans in the USA, black and other minority ethnic groupings elsewhere, women, and lesbians and gay men. All of these groups emerged in the sixties to challenge their social exclusion and to bring the needs of their constituencies to the attention of governments and industry. These organizations learnt from each other, and the disabled people's movement, one of the last to emerge, clearly modelled itself on the actions of those that had gone before.

FIGURE 4.1   ADAPT (American Disabled for Accessible Public Transportation) campaigned for disabled people to be able to use buses

In the USA, for example, members of American Disabled for Accessible Public Transportation (ADAPT; see Figure 4.1) campaigned in the 1980s for lifts on public buses. Public transport was chosen for the campaign because of its centrality to the lives of disabled people. Without public transport people could not operate as part of the community – they could not go to work, to school or to college, and neither could they go out socially. Without access to public transport, disabled people were clearly situated as second class citizens. This mirrored campaigns by the early civil rights movement in the Southern states of the USA for the right of black people to travel on unsegregated buses. In one memorable campaign, demonstrators wore badges saying 'I am Rosa Parkes', referring to the black woman who, in 1955, refused to give up her seat on a bus in Montgomery, Alabama, when a white person got on, as she was compelled to do under the law. This sparked the boycott of buses by the Montgomery Improvement Association and began one of the most visible phases of the black civil rights movement. 'I can't even get on the bus' was another campaign slogan used by activists.

In the UK, while there was a long tradition of campaigning and demonstrating for better services, it wasn't until the late 1980s that disabled people started to use civil disobedience, a tactic learnt from the peace movement. The Direct Action Network (DAN; see Figure 4.2) used civil disobedience to bring city centres to a standstill as they campaigned for accessible public transport. They had found that asking politely did not lead to change and reform of policy. Using non-violent direct action, they presented a direct challenge to mainstream politics. Through these tactics they brought their message to the attention of the public, something that they, as a group without economic leverage, would otherwise have been unable to do (see Chapters 2 and 3). However, what was perhaps most important about these demonstrations is not only that they challenged the structural exclusion experienced by disabled people but that they created a positive political identity for disabled people (Campbell and Oliver, 1996). These actions challenged the prevailing view of disabled people, showing that they had power and agency and were not tragic and passive victims to be pitied.

This chapter explores the emergence of disability as a political issue in the later part of the twentieth century. It will examine the meaning of the concept of disability politics. It will also explore how politics and policy making are linked to how the 'problem' of disability and disablement are categorized. Shakespeare and Watson (2001) identify three key elements that determine what disability politics is, how it came about, and what sort of political claim is being made in the name of disability politics, and these three elements set the agenda for this chapter.

The most important of these three elements has been the emergence of what is called the social model of disability (described in Section 2; the other two key elements are discussed in Section 4). In this approach, disability is regarded as a *social* rather than a *medical* problem; disability comes to be seen in terms of discrimination and prejudice rather than in terms of individual medical conditions. There were two important developments that had to be in place for this model to emerge: disabled people had to be seen and to see themselves, as a marginalized and disadvantaged constituency; and disabled people had to be seen as forming a minority group. The organizations that emerged as a consequence of these developments demanded the redefinition of disability – from a personal, medical problem to a political one with policy consequences. Being seen and being recognized as a minority group has reinforced the social model of disability. These three elements together have established modern-day disability politics.

In exploring these three elements, we are examining the meaning of equality and difference in politics and policy making in general and in disability politics in particular. The chapter also deals with how that meaning has been challenged and redefined, and how the relationship between equality and difference has been reconstituted. Equality is based on a notion of equal inclusion and treatment. It is about the integration of disabled people into the mainstream (Figure 4.2). The politics of difference is a relatively new concept, emerging through feminism in the 1970s and 1980s. It argues that, for example, the category 'woman' needs to recognize the important differences *among* women – both in terms of how they are positioned in different societies, and in the light of their own self-identities. If the women's movement (and society) is to truly acknowledge the differences among women then it must acknowledge that there are differences of class, ethnicity, sexuality, age, ability and culture. The same arguments can be applied to disabled people.

FIGURE 4.2   Direct Action Network (DAN) engaged in a civil disobedience campaign

Organizations of disabled people have, then, demanded the redefinition of disability from a personal, medical problem to a political one and as such have established modern-day disability politics. Central to this has been the development of what is called the social model of disability, which we now need to consider in detail.

2 THE SOCIAL MODEL OF DISABILITY

As I have indicated, one of the most important developments to emerge for the politicization of disability and disabled people was the rejection of the definition of disability in traditional medical terms. A new definition emerged as a result of disabled people organizing themselves. Radical groups demanded that disability be defined in terms of how well or badly society deals with disabled people. Disability, they argued, is not the result of having an impairment as such, but arises as a result of discrimination and prejudice.

The disabled people's movement, made up of disabled people, was essential to the development of this approach. Academics, many of them disabled themselves, developed the social model and gave it what may be termed 'academic credibility'. The work of Mike Oliver (1983, 1990, 1996) has been most influential, indeed he coined the phrase 'social model of disability'. His work develops the ideas of activists that sought to dislodge the association of disability with mental or physical incapacity. It looked at the wider cultural construction of disabled people. The Union of the Physically Impaired Against Segregation (UPIAS) were responsible, as Oliver (1983, 1996) makes clear, for sowing the seeds of this theorizing of disability in their groundbreaking manifesto *The Fundamental Principles of Disability* (1976). In this document UPIAS clearly locates the cause of disability in society:

> In our view it is society which disables physically impaired people [Figure 4.3]. Disability is something imposed on top of our impairments by the way we are unnecessarily isolated and excluded from full participation in society. Disabled people are therefore an oppressed group in society. To understand this it is necessary to grasp the distinction between the physical impairment and the social situation, called 'disability' of people with such impairment. Thus we define impairment as lacking part of or all of a limb, or having a defective limb, organ or part of the body; and disability as the disadvantage or restriction of activity caused by a contemporary social organisation which takes little or no account of people who have physical impairments and thus excludes them from the mainstream of social activities. Physical disability is therefore a particular form of social oppression.

> (UPIAS, 1976, pp.3–4)

From these fundamental principles came two centrally important definitions, distinguishing clearly between impairment and disability (Box 4.1). These definitions were later adopted, with slight modifications to include all people with impairments, by Disabled People's International.

| BOX 4.1 | **Distinction between impairment and disability** |

Impairment ... lacking part or all of a limb, or having a defective limb, organ or part of the body.

Disability ... the disadvantage or restriction of activity caused by a contemporary social organisation which takes no or little account of people who have physical impairments and thus excludes them from the mainstream of social activities.

(UPIAS, 1976, pp.3–4)

FIGURE 4.3   An example of how society disables physically impaired people

This approach to disability is comparable to a key distinction in second wave feminism. Where feminists distinguish sex as biological from gender as cultural and social (Oakley, 1972), the social model separates impairment and disability, the former physical and the latter social and cultural. The social model, by locating disability in society, makes it impossible to reduce the cause of disability to the individual or to the biological. It shifts the focus away from the individual and on to the disabling barriers and attitudes, and makes the political approach adopted by the disabled people's movement plausible. The emphasis is no longer one of changing the individual, but of changing society. However, it is important to note that there is a key distinction to be made between the sex/gender and impairment/disablement analysis. Gender is a social role and does not necessarily imply oppression; disability, by its very definition, implies that those who are defined as disabled are oppressed.

The social model contains a 'materialist' or 'structuralist' explanation. It locates disability in social structures, that is, in social, political and economic processes that are beyond the control of individuals. These processes are wide-ranging and include, for example: the built environment that is often organized in such a way as to exclude disabled people; and problems of isolation that occur because of inaccessible transport and poor education and training for disabled people, as a result of a lack of resources. The materialist analysis starts from the assumption that humans exist in a society in which structures shape the lives of individuals. These structures can either limit or enable individuals in their pursuit of their goals. While not all structuralists or materialists are Marxist, there is a very strong Marxist element within this tradition. The social model suggests that the inequality experienced by disabled people connects with the Marxist analysis of economic-based class divisions. The social model aims for the large-scale transformation of society. It asserts the interlocking relationship of economy, class and disablement.

Oliver (1990) provides the clearest explanation of this model in his influential monograph, *The Politics of Disablement*. He supports the main elements of UPIAS's *Fundamental Principles* and suggests that the single biggest cause of disablement in society is the exclusion of disabled people from work. This exclusion, he suggests, is a consequence of changes in the mode of production that accompanied industrialization and the growth of an industrial society. With the advent of manufacturing industries and the creation of factories, disabled people became regarded as a social and educational problem. Disabled people were no longer included in the labour force and they were seen as a social burden. Institutions had to be built to accommodate them and this period saw the birth of asylums, special schools, workhouses and a whole range of other exclusionary practices.

In addition, Oliver also draws attention to the emerging ideology of individualism that accompanied the rise of capitalism. In capitalism, people are judged on their ability to contribute to the labour force, with work seen on an individual rather than collective process. Individuals were no longer seen primarily as part of a collective grouping such as the family or the community but as isolated individuals. The notion of 'able-bodiedness' emerged. Able-bodied people were those who were able to control and operate the new machines and were able to submit to the controls enforced by the factory, such as working a full shift. Disabled people, unable to meet the requirements of capitalism – that is, they were seen as unable to meet the demands of individual wage labour – had to be controlled by other means. This was achieved through exclusion, a process facilitated by the emerging medical profession. These factors led to the medicalization of disability. According to this model, then, capitalism and the mode of production that accompanied its rise served to reinforce difference as a basis for exclusion and to mark disabled people out as different and inferior.

Part of the role of the medical profession within capitalism was to decide who was and who was not disabled. This differentiation was essential to the way society decided whom to support and whom not to support. The legacy of the ideas of the 'deserving' versus the 'undeserving' poor still map on to ideas about social welfare in policy making. Forms of such categorization have been in existence since at least the fourteenth century and the passing of the early English Poor Law, initially implemented for the regulation of vagrancy. Those people whom society deemed as unfit to work are supported through charity, welfare provision or other forms of disability insurance. It is medicine that has been used to determine who is disabled, and so to decide who has a legitimate claim for social aid. Disability, therefore, has a different meaning to the state and to policy makers. That is, the institutions of government use disability as an administrative category, as a way of determining whether or not an individual has a right to privileges such as financial aid or the right not to work. This obviously sets up other agendas, such as how entitlement to these privileges is assessed, what these privileges should be, and how such privileges should be funded.

As well as marking out and deciding who are and who are not disabled, doctors and other health professionals have become centrally involved in the lives of disabled people. While it is true that there has been an increase in medical power and surveillance for all, especially in the last 50 years, as Zola describes (1972; see Box 4.2), it could be argued that this is even more the case for disabled people. Health and social care professionals, as well as determining who is fit or not fit to work, have the power to decide what sort of work disabled people can do, what school they go to, who can have a baby, who is fit to act as a parent, and who is fit to fly on commercial airlines. Some of these powers, as Oliver (1990, p.48) points out, are entirely appropriate, while some should perhaps be left up to the individual concerned.

BOX 4.2   **Four main ways in which our lives have become medicalized**

Zola (1972) identifies the following ways in which medicine influences our lives:

- by its expansion into our private lives, such as deciding what we should and should not eat, whom we should and should not sleep with and what we should do when we do sleep with them, and how much exercise we should have;
- by its expansion into public life such as the banning of smoking in public places;
- by extending its control over procedures like prescribing drugs and performing surgery, and deciding who receives what treatment and from whom treatment is withheld;
- by gaining dominance of taboo areas such as addictions and sexual practices.

For the social model of disability to be considered as a valid descriptor of the experiences and lives of disabled people it is essential that it can be proved that being a disabled person involves disadvantage. It is to an exploration of this that we now turn.

SUMMARY

This section has reviewed the social model of disability. The social model argues that:

- disability does not arise as a result of having an impairment
- disability is a consequence of the way that society is organized
- society is organized so as to exclude people who have an impairment
- disabled people are marked out as different through the medicalization of their lives.

3   HOW DOES DISABILITY INVOLVE DISADVANTAGE?

Although it is true to say that, in many parts of the world, disability is portrayed as an individual medical problem, increasingly it is being seen as an equal opportunities issue. To a large extent the pairing of disability with equal opportunities has been achieved through disabled people lobbying for the acceptance of the social model, despite the fact that disability as an issue has rarely been on the agenda of mainstream political parties. Disability is now more often being represented as a political issue and examined in the same manner as sexism, racism, heterosexism, ageism and other forms of social exclusion. The establishment of disabled people as a disadvantaged or marginalized group has, to a large extent, been the focus of the politicization of disability by disabled people and their allies throughout the world. It could be argued that the focus of disability politics was initially about establishing disability as a political issue in this sense. This was a necessary step for the establishment of the social model; without awareness of the political dimension of disability, there would be no social model.

The first real attempt to produce evidence of the discrimination faced by disabled people in the UK was by Alf Morris, Minister for the Disabled in the then Labour Government. He set up the Committee on Restrictions Against Disabled People (CORAD) in 1979. This committee was charged with the task of establishing whether or not disabled people encountered discrimination in their everyday lives and if so to make further recommendations on how this could be tackled. The report concluded that discrimination was widespread. Later, Colin Barnes's (1991) comprehensive exploration of discrimination against disabled people added weight to the evidence that disabled people are a marginalized constituency. Barnes clearly showed how disabled people were discriminated against in a wide range of settings, such as employment, housing, schooling and transport. More recent research has merely served to reinforce this view. For instance, Riddell and Banks (2001) provide an overview of disability in Scotland (see Box 4.3).

A recent report by the International Labour Organisation (ILO) provides evidence to suggest that such discrimination is worldwide. In its Report, *Time for Equality in Work* (April, 2003) the ILO suggests that there is an 80 per cent unemployment rate among disabled people worldwide. The ILO states that the denial of opportunities in the job market, education and job training constitutes the most common form of discrimination. Because of this situation, when disabled people find work they tend only to be able to find low-paying, unskilled jobs, without any type of social protection.

This, and other evidence, clearly adds up to a case that disability is a political and public policy issue, and that the solution to the problems faced by

---

BOX 4.3   **Overview of disability in Scotland**

- Disabled people are less likely to be in employment than non-disabled people.
- The unemployment rate for disabled people is almost double that for non-disabled people.
- Disabled people are around eight times as likely as nondisabled people to be out of work and claiming benefits.
- Disabled people are twice as likely as nondisabled people to have no qualifications.
- Disabled people have difficulty in finding suitable housing and are less likely to be owner-occupiers than nondisabled people.
- There are approximately 20,000 households in Scotland where a household member uses a wheelchair but only 5,000 dwellings of full wheelchair standard.
- Only 12 per cent of buses in operation in Scotland have a lowered floor, and less than 50 per cent of bus providers intend to operate low-floor buses in the next three years.
- In Scotland in 2000, disabled people are more likely to be living in poverty than the rest of the population. 33 per cent of households with a disabled person have an income of less than £6,000 per annum compared with 26 per cent of households without a disabled person. Only 6 per cent of households with a disabled person have an income of greater than £20,000 in contrast to 24 per cent without a disabled person.

(adapted from Riddell and Banks, 2001)

---

disabled people lies in the political and not in the medical arena. This has now been widely accepted and documented, for example by the United Nations, which in 1993 adopted the *Standard Rules for the Equalisation of Opportunities for Persons with Disabilities*, and the European Commission, which in 1995 adopted the *Communication of the Commission on Equality of Opportunity for People with Disabilities*.

In addition, the fact that disabled people face discrimination in many aspects of their lives serves to show that they are often viewed negatively by society at large. Arguably, the only way to rectify unfair treatment is to introduce special policy measures that tackle this discrimination. However, to qualify for special treatment, disabled people are, again, marked out as different in the sense of deviating from the norm. If society is to make special provision for disabled people, then there has to be some means of determining who is disabled so as to ensure that this treatment is available to those who qualify. But this logic, as discussed earlier, can have a double-edged effect. It raises the issue of whether attempts to increase equality are likely to result in the reinforcement of a negative sense of difference.

In addition to the provision of evidence that disabled people are an oppressed group, for disability politics to emerge – and for the social model to be given potency and to ensure that rules for the removal of discrimination are adopted – disabled people and their allies had to act to promote their interests. They had to unite and operate as a pressure group. Supporting the view that disabled people have much to unite around, Charlton writes in his analysis of the disabled people's movement worldwide:

> The vast majority of people with disabilities have always been poor, powerless and degraded. Disability oppression is a product of both the past and the present. Some aspects of disability oppression are remnants of ancien régimes of politics and economics, customs and beliefs, and others can be traced to more recent developments. To understand the consequences and implications for people with disabilities an analysis is called for which considers how the overarching structures of society influence this trend.
>
> (Charlton, 1998, p.21)

The chapter moves on to explore these issues, showing the rise of disabled people as a collective group. Without this development there would be no social model, nor would disability be seen as a political issue.

SUMMARY

- Disabled people face disadvantage in almost all aspects of their lives.
- Disabled people have sought to provide evidence of disadvantage.
- The provision of this evidence has been responsible for both laying the foundation of the social model and ensuring that disability is seen as a political rather than a medical issue.

4 HOW ARE DISABLED PEOPLE A MINORITY GROUPING?

The claim that disabled people constitute a distinct minority is the second key element that Shakespeare and Watson (2001) identify as influential in the politicization of disability. This does not imply that having a disability leads to an automatic identification with others who are disabled. There is no organized constituency of disabled people, nor are there powerful voting lobbies as found in, for example, the minority ethnic lobby or the gay and lesbian lobby. This may in part be due to the lower levels of socio-economic power enjoyed by disabled people, which is itself a consequence of their exclusion from the mainstream of society (as described above).

It is also the case that disabled people do not constitute a homogeneous grouping. Just because a person has an impairment, it does not follow that they share a common identity with other people who have an impairment. The diversity among disabled people contrasts with the physical markers for gender and ethnic identities, and the popular 'model' of a disabled person in a wheelchair is inaccurate. Some people may be born with their impairment, others may acquire their impairment at different stages in their lives. Some may have a visual or hearing impairment, others a mobility impairment, a learning difficulty or a mental health problem. The impairment may be progressive, such as multiple sclerosis, or it may be relatively stable, as in cerebral palsy.

In addition, other identities apart from their impairment may be more significant to the disabled person. For example, locality, ethnicity, sexuality, gender or class may be more important in determining what identity someone subscribes to. Also, while there are political and cultural benefits to be gained from claiming an identity premised on, for example, ethnicity, there is little cultural cachet gained from declaring an identity premised on disability. There is, rather, a stigma attached to disability. It is rare for disabled people to embrace their impairment in the same way as, say, a black person embraces their ethnicity.

However, there are occasions when disabled people can mobilize as a collective, displaying a degree of external unity. This can happen in a variety of ways. For example, when disabled people are segregated from the mainstream of society and forced together in special schools and residential homes, they can become a distinct interest group (Barnart *et al.*, 2001). Developments such as this can snowball beyond the immediate group, and political clusters can emerge and have impact beyond the close environment of the group. This has happened since at least the end of the nineteenth century. Organizations of disabled people have emerged on this basis in nearly every country of the world (Charlton, 1998). Disabled People's International, a grassroots, cross-disability network whose purpose is to promote the human rights of disabled people, has member organizations in over 110 countries, the majority in the developing world.

While there was a major growth in the establishment of organizations of disabled people in the 1970s, with the modern-day disabled people's movement having had its origins in this expansion, there has been a small but significant number of organizations of disabled people that can be traced back to the nineteenth century. For example, in the UK the National League of the Blind formed in 1899, and the British Deaf Association was established in 1890. The National League of the Blind was a registered trade union and used its political muscle to lobby political parties and governments, and succeeded in securing legislation such as the Blind (Education, Employment and Maintenance) Act 1920 and the Blind Persons Act 1938 (Pagel, 1988, p.5). Furthermore, protest marches in 1920, 1933 and 1947 highlighted the high levels of unemployment, low wages and poor working conditions of blind people (Humphries and Gordon, 1992; see Figure 4.4). Similarly, in the USA the National Association of the Deaf (NAD) and the National Fraternal Society of the Deaf (NFSD) were founded at the turn of the century (Van Cleve, 1993). (The NFSD excluded African-Americans until as late as 1959 and women as equal members until 1947, and the NAD excluded the former until 1949, though it has always had women members.)

FIGURE 4.4 Blind disabled pensioners march in protest for higher pensions

In Norway, Denmark and Sweden blind and deaf people also organized themselves into single-impairment pressure groups, and as Dreidger (1989) documents, in Denmark people with other impairments started to unite in the 1930s. In 1953, a pan-European confederation of organizations of disabled people, *Fédération Internationale des Mutilés, des Invalides du Travail et des Invalides Civils* (FIMITIC) was founded.

However, despite the political success of these organizations and their popularity with disabled people, organizations of disabled people were an exception until the 1970s. By far the most common organizations were those *for* rather than *of* disabled people – the conventional, philanthropic, charitable organizations run mainly by non-disabled people (Drake, 1994). These organizations dominated the disability field, acting as barriers to the self-development of disabled people (Hurst, 1995). Since the end of the nineteenth century, paternalistic charities have dominated the disability field. These charities have tended to be condition-specific; to see disability as an inevitable consequence of impairment; and to focus their attention on rehabilitation, adaptation or cure (Drake, 1996). Emphasis is placed on incapacity, with the consequence that the more incapable a person is portrayed as being, the greater the funds that that organization stands to gain. Such organizations have failed to address the issues that disabled people themselves see as important. For example Coleridge (1993, p.83) cites a survey in Uganda where disabled people were asked to list their needs in order of priority. Rehabilitation came a distant fifth. Yet, as he states, 'the literature on disability in developing countries is primarily about rehabilitation'. The 1950s and early 1960s, both in the USA and UK, saw a growth in impairment-specific charities, again controlled mainly by non-disabled people, with a focus on raising funds for cure.

Many single-impairment, or single-issue *self-help* groups were also formed after the Second World War. These differ from the political organizations of disabled people in that they tend to be formed around medical conditions. While these are usually initiated by disabled people or their parents or carers, their efforts are placed on support. They allow people to exchange experiences and swap treatments. They may lobby for changes in health care provision (for example, many of the mental health self-help groups have lobbied for health policy change), but they do not seek to challenge the medical profession's power base. They seek to supplement the medical profession and often reinforce the medical profession's position by calling for more money for research into a particular condition. However, self-help groups vary, and some do seek to challenge the services that they receive. Self-help groups are different from political organizations in that they focus on support and sharing rather than social change. As Anspach puts it:

> While the emerging activist groups borrow from the self-help movements the emphasis on indigenous organisation and self-reliance, they are political, rather than therapeutic, in orientation. They seek not to modify their own behaviour in conformance to a pre-existing normative mould, but rather to influence the behaviour of groups, organisations and institutions.
>
> (Anspach, 1979, p.766).

A classification of the spectrum of disability organizations is given in Box 4.4.

There were, however two important developments in the 1960s in both the USA and the UK that led to the founding of the disabled people's movement. In the UK, as Campbell and Oliver (1996) document, groups of disabled people became disillusioned with the welfare state and service provision and dissatisfied with the restricted lives on offer to them. The Disablement Income Group (DIG), formed by two disabled women, was one of the first organizations to directly challenge this situation. The organization consisted of both disabled people and social policy academics and activists and campaigned for a comprehensive disability income. Its stated aim was to campaign 'for the provision of a modest basic income, with special supplementary allowances for all disabled persons ordinarily resident in the United Kingdom, whatever the cause of disablement, and irrespective of previous national insurance contributions' (DIG, 1965, p.1, quoted in Oliver and Barnes, 1998, p.79)

As a registered charity it was prevented from overt political activity. Oliver and Barnes (1998) point out that DIG arose as a response to the improving

> ### BOX 4.4   **Disability organizations**
>
> 1 *Partnership/Patronage*: organisations for disabled people – working for provision of services (often in conjunction with statutory agencies); provide consultative and advisory role for professional agencies – for instance Royal Association for Disablement and Rehabilitation, Royal National Institute for the Blind, Scope, Rehabilitation International.
>
> 2 *Economic/parliamentarian*: primarily organisations for disabled people – focused on single issue; parliamentary lobbying and research; legalistic bodies – for example Disablement Income Group, Disability Alliance, American Foundation for the Blind.
>
> 3 *Consumerist/self help*: organisations of disabled people – engaged in self-help projects; sometimes campaigning groups or working in collaboration with local or voluntary agencies – such as Spinal Injuries Association, Derbyshire Centre for Independent Living, Berkeley Centre for Independent Living.
>
> 4 *Populist/activist*: organisations of disabled people – politically active groups, often antagonistic toward partnership approach; primarily activities focused on 'empowerment', personal and/or political, collective action and consciousness raising – for example Union of the Physically Impaired Against Segregation, British Deaf Association, Americans Disabled for Accessible Public Transport.
>
> (Barnes *et al.*, 1999, p.157)

economic circumstances in the UK at the time, and the fact that disabled people were being left behind and were not sharing in the new affluence. To DIG, a disability income was seen as a means of compensating for disability, an approach that was seen by some to reinforce the stereotype of disabled people as unable to function socially (Finkelstein, 1993). DIG eventually became part of the Disability Alliance, an umbrella body for organizations of and for disabled people.

In 1972 another, more politically active group arose. Paul Hunt, who had been a resident in a Leonard Cheshire home became increasingly disillusioned with both DIG and the Disability Alliance. Leonard Cheshire is a leading UK disability charity which runs residential homes for disabled people. Hunt felt that current disability organizations had failed to address what he saw as the central issue of disability, namely, control. As well as identifying control over his life as the key problem, he was also concerned by the link in current disability groups between impairment and poverty, their anti-democratic nature, and their colonization by non-disabled people. He wrote a letter to *The Guardian* calling for a united struggle by disabled people against discrimination:

> Severely physically handicapped people find themselves in isolated, unsuitable institutions, where their views are ignored and they are subject to authoritarian, often cruel regimes.

> I am proposing the formation of a consumer group to put forward nationally the views of actual and potential residents of these successors to the workhouse.
>
> (*The Guardian*, 20 September 1972, quoted in Campbell and Oliver, 1996, p.65)

Many disabled people responded to his call and two years later the Union of the Physically Impaired Against Segregation (UPIAS) was formed. (For a full discussion on the formation of UPIAS, see Campbell and Oliver, 1996; for a discussion on the Fundamental Principles of Disability, see Oliver, 1996.) The immediate concern of UPIAS was to produce a unified theory of disability, avoiding single-issue campaigns. They criticized current disability groups from a Marxist position and produced the key document for the disabled people's movement in the UK, *The Fundamental Principles of Disability* (1975). This document not only led to the formulation of the social model, but radically challenged the position of 'experts' in the lives of disabled people:

> We reject the whole idea of 'experts' and professionals holding forth on how we should accept our disabilities, or giving learned lectures about the psychology of impairment. We already know what it feels like to be poor, isolated, segregated, done good to, and talked down to – far better than any able-bodied expert. We as a Union are not interested in descriptions of how awful it is to be disabled. What we are interested in is the ways of changing our conditions of life, and thus overcoming the disabilities which are imposed on top of our impairments by the way this society is organised to exclude us ... We look forward to the day when the army of experts on our social and psychological problems can find more productive work to do.
>
> (UPIAS, 1976, pp.4–5)

UPIAS never became a mass movement, but its members were instrumental in setting up many organizations of disabled people, for example the British Council of Organisations of Disabled People (BCODP) and the National Centre for Independent Living, and in establishing Centres for Independent Living throughout the UK. *The Fundamental Principles of Disability* was also influential in setting the agenda for Disabled People's International.

Meanwhile, in the USA, disabled people, coming from a different political direction began the Independent Living Movement (ILM). As Oliver (1990, p.121) argues, the origins of the disabled people's movement in the USA are different from those in the UK.

The disabled people's movement in the USA emerged under the influence of the civil rights movement and in the absence of a history of an organized labour movement, but with a constitutional emphasis on individual rights, coupled with the virtual absence of a developed welfare state. In the USA, under the influence of civil rights and liberation movements such as the black campaign against Southern segregation, disabled people sought to destabilize established institutions that legitimized discrimination against them. Their aim, however, was not to challenge the legitimacy of these institutions, but to demand that the USA live up to the principles of individual rights of equal opportunity for all.

The ILM grew out of student action at Berkeley in the University of California by the Physically Disabled Students Program (PDSP). The PDSP were a group of severely disabled college students who lived together in Cowell hospital on the university campus. On leaving university, ex PDSP members began to form a community-based organization, influenced by the civil rights movement in 1972. As DeJong writes:

> Although original references to independent living rehabilitation go back more than twenty years, legislative, social and philosophical forces finally converged to create the Independent Living Movement in the early 1970s. Throughout the previous decade this country had experienced a growing sensitivity toward the civil rights of minority groups, and people with disabilities began to realize the ways in which they shared a minority status. They also began to recognize themselves as consumers – not merely recipients – of health and rehabilitation services. Furthermore, they began to see more clearly their power to help themselves and each other instead of relying exclusively on professional caregivers.
>
> (DeJong, 1983, p.3).

The ILM, in contrast to UPIAS, did not seek to establish a theory of disability, but focused its attention on service provision, challenging the prevailing orthodoxy operating in organizations for disabled people in the USA at the time. It argued that:

- Those who know best the needs of disabled people and how to meet those needs are disabled people themselves.
- The needs of the disabled can be met most effectively by programmes that provide a variety of services.
- Disabled people should be integrated as fully as possible into the community.

The ILM incorporated a philosophy that worked for self-determination, equal opportunities and self-respect for disabled people. The ILM is located within the US tradition of self-reliance and individual rights. However, in contrast to the British disability movement, which aligned itself with other radical labour movements of the time and agitated against the social status quo, the US movement lacked a unity of purpose and opposition. The disability movement focused on disability issues – in the same way as the black liberation movement, the gay movement and the women's movement were all built around the ideas of a common identity and worked towards their own social visions. The ILM was unified by an assumption of a common disability identity based on a shared experience of being disabled and it spoke for all, and only, disabled people.

The ILM emphasized the importance of public attitudes to disabled people and the laws and legislation that maintained inequalities. Its aim was to integrate disabled people into the mainstream of US life. The American Coalition of Disabled People, formed in 1974 to fight for the passage of the Rehabilitation Act (the first example of anti-discrimination legislation for disabled people), also endorsed this 'consumerist' view (Zola, 1983).

They did not reject the notion of difference between disabled and non-disabled people. UPIAS and the social model on the other hand clearly did.

Through these various movements, disabled people were able to initiate and lead demands in the development of policy reform for disabled people. Charlton (1998) shows, in his aptly titled book, *Nothing About Us Without Us*, the importance of disabled people's demand for control in the development of disability politics worldwide. He draws on the writings of Ed Roberts, one of the leaders of the disabled people's movement in the USA, who argued 'If we have learnt one thing from the Civil Rights Movement in the US, it's that when others speak for you, you lose' (Dreidger, 1989, p.28).

All of the rights-based organizations of disabled people that we have considered have a demand for control at the heart of their movements. This demand can be linked to the emergence of the independent living movement described above. Rights-based disability groups themselves come in different shapes and sizes. The most obvious difference in these groups is between those that are controlled by disabled people, termed organizations *of* disabled people, and those controlled by non-disabled people, called organizations *for* disabled people. The former tend to be more political. These two different groups can be further subdivided and Charlton's (1998) classification of ten different types of disability rights organizations is represented in Box 4.5.

BOX 4.5   Types of disability rights organizations

1   Local self-help groups (for example, Self-Help Association of Paraplegics, Soweto)
2   Local advocacy and programme centres (for example, Centres for Integrated Living)
3   Local single issue advocacy groups (for example, Acesso Libre, Mexico City)
4   Public policy groups (for example, World Institute on Disability, Oakland USA)
5   Single issue national advocacy groups (for example ADAPT – USA)
6   National membership organisations (for example Organisation of Disabled Revolutionaries, Nicaragua; National Council of Disabled Persons Zimbabwe; Women with Disabilities, Australia)
7   National coalitions/federations of groups (for example British Council Of Disabled People)
8   National single impairment organisations (for example National Association of the Blind, India; British Deaf Association)
9   Regional organisations (for example Southern African Federation of the Disabled; Disabled Persons International, Europe)
10 International organisations (for example Disabled Persons International)

(Charlton, 1998, p.136)

SUMMARY

- Disabled people do not constitute a homogeneous grouping.
- Disabled people have, however, come together to act as a single group for political purposes.
- There are various organizations involved in disability; these include organizations of disabled people and for disabled people.
- The tradition of disability groups in the USA is geared towards disability rights, whereas disability activists in the UK focus on the social model and the rejection of being labelled negatively as different.

5   CRITICS OF THE SOCIAL MODEL

The social model has, as stated, been very influential in the development of disability politics and in policy reform. However, it is not without its critics, both from within the disabled people's movement and outside. Disabled feminists such as Jenny Morris (1991), Liz Crow (1996), Sally French (1993) and Carol Thomas (1999) have all expressed disquiet at the disregard of impairment and bodily experience. They directly challenge not only the medical model but also the materialist emphasis of the social model on social structures. Morris (1991; Figure 4.5) has argued that the disability movement needs to move beyond campaigns for better access and include more on the personal experiences of impairment. Unless the movement does this, she contends, it is, itself, contributing to the oppression of disabled people.

FIGURE 4.5   Jenny Morris

Crucially, these writers share the social model's focus on barriers, but argue that to ignore the *experience* of impairment at the expense of disablement fails to fully explain life as a disabled person. There are, they argue, bodily dimensions to both disablement and impairment, and that these have political policy implications. For example, having an impairment can cause pain or incontinence, it can damage sexual function or it can induce fatigue, all of which can be disabling in their own right. Such experiences can become marginalized within the rhetoric associated with the social model. These disabled feminists argue that by focusing on the materialist element of disablement, personal experience is lost. Being disabled is more than being excluded from the world of work or being denied access to buildings – it is more than the presence of social barriers. While issues like work and buildings are important, there is more to the life of a disabled person than the struggle for economic gain and power. Life involves the creation of shared worlds and meanings, solidarity and community and aspirations to social ideals such as justice, self-fulfilment and autonomy.

These disabled feminists also criticize the social model for primarily reflecting the experiences and values of disabled, white, heterosexual males. Disability cannot be isolated from gender or class or ethnic origin or sexuality. However, there is a debate about whether this should be taken to suggest that, say, a black, disabled woman suffers a triple burden. It could be argued that this woman would have to endure the burden of discrimination on the grounds that she was a women existing in a patriarchal society, that she is a black person living in a racist society, and that she is a disabled person living in a disablist society. Others take the view that these three forms of discrimination cannot be separated because they are experienced simultaneously, and that to suggest that they are a triple burden reinforces the ideal of a white, male, non-disabled person as the norm (Stuart, 1993).

These writers, whether they are disabled feminists or black disabled people, do not find their experiences reflected in the writings of social model theorists. Such writers are following the feminist dictum: the personal is political – that is, that aspects of personal identity already carry social values and policy implications, that these can be contested, and that political reform is the way forward. They are not seeking to subvert the social model, but to expand it. These writers are seeking a model that can include the variety of all their experiences, a model that can incorporate their experiences of, for example, the right to have and look after children, the right to form relationships with whom they want, and the right to have their voice heard. This approach follows the positive ideas of the politics of difference discussed in the introduction to this chapter. The social model is seen as reductionist in that it reduces the experience of disability to one aspect – the social context – and fails to examine the complexity of disabled people's lives.

Disabled feminists have sought to expand the representation of disability from one that prioritizes work to one that incorporates a diversity of experiences and, in so doing, expands the legitimate range of identities that disabled people could claim and incorporate on the basis of difference. While this claim multiplies the possible articulations of disabled people's identity, and the political responses, it also raises doubts about a single disabled identity. On the one hand, can disability politics exist without such a unitary identity? But, if disabled people differ by class, age, sexual orientation, gender and impairment, is the disabled people's movement – premised on the unity of disabled people – legitimate? If disabled people's experiences vary so widely, can a unitary disabled identity be assumed? And without such an identity, can the disabled people's movement exist?

Following this line of argument, some disabled feminists such as Mairian Corker have sought to question the very category 'disability' (see Corker, 1999). They argue that the label 'disabled' is normative and political. According to these writers there is no core identity that marks out disabled people from non-disabled people. To be an activist, a person has to apply a label to themselves with which they may not fully identify. But Helen Ligget (1988) argues that in order to be politically active in an effective way, disabled people can only do so by taking on the label of 'disabled person'.

By claiming the disability label, activists give themselves authority to speak for other disabled people. At the same time they are also forced to acknowledge that they are different from non-disabled people.

What we can take from this group of disabled feminist theorists is the understanding that being disabled is contingent rather than necessitated. Disability can be viewed in different ways and it depends on how it is interpreted. Throughout history disabled people have been shunned as 'freaks', loved in spite of their disabilities, and loved with their disabilities. Being 'disabled' has shifting meanings that are conflicting; and being 'disabled' is situated – dependent on circumstances and context. These theorists, rather than appealing to a single identity of disabled people, favour using categories of composite, multiple, selves. The demand is for a collapse of rigid social classification. Such theorists also argue that it is necessary to employ a more subtle and flexible understanding of power and how it operates socially than is found in much of the social model theorizing.

It is hard to disagree with the perspective gained from this analysis – that disabled people do not constitute a unitary group and that, for disabled people, being disabled is but one of the many factors that make up their lives. For some disabled people, other issues such as ethnicity, gender, class or sexuality may be more important, and which is more important and when will vary depending on other factors such as social or geographical location. The result of this analysis is that disability politics is caught in a dilemma. If the rights of disabled people are to be furthered it is necessary to make claims on the basis of the idea of a disabled identity. Yet to do so can have the effect of excluding and disempowering some disabled people. The most effective way forward is probably a micro-approach to the problem of disability. That is, disability politics should focus on local, piecemeal solutions and should abandon appeals to disabled people as a grouping. However, such an appeal could be accused of throwing out the baby with the bath water.

There is little room to doubt the universal nature of disabalism. If disabled people suffer oppression and disability, then politics cannot abandon large-scale theory. However, disability politics must also recognize that overarching theories such as the social model are necessarily incomplete, and that political campaigning and policy proposals must be situated within this knowledge. Any legislation must be focused on the benefit to the community as a whole. Civil rights or anti-discrimination legislation can only be implemented if those whom it is hoped to help are identified.

SUMMARY

- The social model has been criticized because of its materialist focus on social conditions.

- Its materialist focus means that it fails to include all the relevant experiences of disabled people.

- To become a disability activist, people have to identify as disabled. To do so implies a negative difference.

6 IDENTITY POLITICS

The disabled people's movement operates at the boundaries of conventional politics. It is not a mainstream political party, but it is a pressure group that tries to influence politics and win policy reforms that will improve the lot of disabled people. One of the most important trends in disability politics in recent years has been the development of a more radical political grouping. Two of its distinctive features are that it embraces the identity of disability, and that it is sceptical of a politics of seeking to influence governments to produce significant policy reforms. It holds that reforms are unlikely to accord with their wishes, and favours a loosely organized, collective, and more public form of politics. This emergent group has been called a 'new social movement' by Oliver (1990, 1996).

As we saw earlier, the term 'new social movement' has been applied to describe progressive movements such as the women's movement, the peace movement and the Green movement. These movements, typically, differ from more traditional political movements in that they have, to a large extent, eschewed class-based politics. They tend to focus on individual rights, on the users of services in challenging treatments on offer, on campaigns on health and on the environment. Identity politics lies at the heart of much of the work of such movements (Melucci, 1989). Political actions taken by activists in these new social movements operate instrumentally and symbolically as they seek to challenge the social position of the constituent group. The idea is that by challenging structural exclusion and disempowerment, the members of the new social movements become, by that very process, empowered. Such empowerment impacts both on the state and the economy at a macro level, but also at a local level in the creation of positive political identities.

The campaigns by ADAPT and DAN, described at the beginning of this chapter, provide an example of this type of political action. They are not traditional forms of political activity. Through such examples of actions the personal may, in feminist terms, be said to have become political. It is not class-based, but aims to achieve an improved social role for disabled people. New social movements also involve what Iris Marion Young has termed 'a celebration of difference'. 'To promote a politics of inclusion, then, participatory democracy must promote the ideal of a heterogeneous public, in which persons stand forth with their differences acknowledged and respected though perhaps not completely understood by others' (Young, 1990, p.119).

For Young, difference becomes something around which people can mobilize. Disabled people, her theory would contend, have different needs from non-disabled people and they need to form organizations that enable them to determine these needs and through these organizations find a voice to express them.

This notion of difference is, as argued earlier, a double-edged sword. Attractive as it might at first seem, it demands that people must identify as different and deviant. It is also not clear where difference stops. Are all disabled people to be treated as a group, or should the groups subdivide further, for instance in terms of physical and mental impairments? If disabled people are to be encouraged to form a movement based on difference there is a danger that they will start to construct difference within themselves and the movement will be weakened (Shakespeare and Watson, 2001).

There is, however, another take on identity politics that can usefully emerge alongside the new social movements. As argued at the beginning of the chapter, disabled people are traditionally seen as passive and dependent and as a burden. By taking political action they challenge this identity. Rights-based legislation can also impact on identity. In their recently published book on the impact of the American's with Disabilities Act, Engel and Munger (2003) argue that rights can have a positive impact on identity in a number of ways. First, they can change self-perceptions. Rights make people believe that more is possible. If a person believes they have a right to a job or an education then they are more likely attempt to achieve these aspirations. Second, people who interact with disabled people begin to do so within a rights-based agenda. Third, institutions such as schools and universities, as they adopt anti-discrimination practices, can have a dramatic and positive effect on shaping the identities and lives of children and young people who go through them. As they leave these institutions and move on to other workplaces, disabled people expect the same treatment and are more likely to agitate to try to ensure that they get it.

SUMMARY

- Identity politics has been an important influence in the recent development of disability politics.

- Some have described this as an example of a 'new social movement'.

- In identity politics, people organize around the notion of difference.

- This can be a risky strategy as there is a danger that individuals will construct differences themselves and the movement will be weakened.

7 CIVIL RIGHTS FOR DISABLED PEOPLE AND ANTI-DISCRIMINATION LEGISLATION

Campaigns for civil rights for disabled people and anti-discrimination legislation have been the focus of much of the political actions taken by disabled people throughout the world. At the roots of these campaigns has been a demand for basic citizenship rights for disabled people. Citizenship is, as Lister (1997) points out, a contested subject. It is concerned both with the relationship between the individual and the state and among individuals within the state. Citizenship incorporates notions of rights, responsibilities, obligations, needs, actions, virtues and opinions. Perhaps the most influential writer on this topic has been T.H. Marshall (1950). Marshall presented a tripartite conception of citizenship, breaking down the concept into political citizenship, social citizenship and civil citizenship (see **Squires, 2005, pp.110–11**)

Oliver, in work published in 1996 but written prior to the passing of the Disability Discrimination Act 1995 (DDA), has used Marshall's work to demonstrate how disabled people are denied basic citizenship rights and argues that they are not seen as citizens in Marshall's definition of the term,. He argues that disabled people are denied political citizenship because many do not appear on the electoral register; many polling stations are inaccessible; political meetings are held in inaccessible premises; and information about the political process is not always provided in accessible formats. Social citizenship is denied to disabled people as many disabled people live below the official poverty line and face many other disadvantages, as described above. Civil rights are also withheld from many disabled people. They do not have equal access to home loans and life insurance, and those living in residential accommodation are often denied the right to make their own choices about many basic issues.

Central to Marshall's notion of citizenship are the concepts of legal rights and legal obligations. It is these that lie at the heart of the disabled people's movement's response to the denial of full and active citizenship to disabled people. Much effort has been placed on a demand for anti-discrimination legislation – to both implement and set the standard for policy making on disability – and the disabled people's movement campaigned vigorously for such legislation throughout the world.

In the UK the campaigning led eventually to the passing of the DDA in 1995. With the passing of this legislation the UK Government, for the first time, accepted that disabled people were discriminated against. Legislation has ideological as well as legal implications. Prior to the DDA the Chronically Sick and Disabled Person's Act 1970 was the only piece of legislation on the British statute book devoted solely to services for disabled people. Written by the Labour MP Alf Morris, it included sections on the duties of local authorities to identify the needs of disabled people in their area, the provision of services and a duty to provide suitable housing. It also included a section on access to buildings. Section 4, the critical section in terms of access, stated that whenever new buildings were built, or old buildings redesigned or adapted, access must be arranged for disabled people where practicable. The legal effectiveness was dissipated by the inclusion of the clause 'in so far as it is in the circumstances both practicable and reasonable'. When the Bill was drafted, this clause remained. Developers could, and did, flout the Act without threat of penalty. There is only one example of a local authority taking a builder to court over the issue.

The DDA went much further than the earlier Act as it also, for the first time, outlawed discrimination in the fields of employment, services and the sale and rental of property. Subsequent amendments to the Act have outlawed discrimination in education and seen the establishment of a Disability Rights Commission.

While the legislation is to be welcomed, there are many restrictions on the scope of the DDA. Such restrictions do not apply in comparable anti-discrimination legislation on sex and race. For example, the Act only applies to companies that employ more than fifteen employees. The armed forces, firefighters, barristers, prison officers and employees who work wholly or mainly outside the UK are not covered by the DDA. There are also many problems to do with definitions.

To be covered by the DDA an individual has to establish that they are a disabled person in terms that are acceptable to the Act. A disabled person is defined by the Act as somebody who has a disability. The DDA defines disability as 'a physical or mental impairment, which has substantial and long term adverse affect on a person's ability to carry out normal day-to-day activities.' This is a medical model definition, defining the person with the disability according to their impairment and that the impairment prevents them from having a normal life. We have seen earlier in the chapter that a medical definition of disability is problematic from disabled people's point of view, but in addition this definition raises many specific questions. For example, how are physical or mental impairments to be measured? Some, such as cerebral palsy, multiple sclerosis, cancer or spinal cord injury may seem straightforward. But are people with conditions such as repetitive strain injury, chronic fatigue syndrome or other conditions that are not universally recognized in medicine to be covered under the Act? The Act uses the term 'clinically well recognised', yet its meaning is not clear and is open to widely varying interpretation. Should a condition be accepted as an impairment if a significant number of medical practitioners accept it as a legitimate condition? What should that number of practitioners be, and who should these practitioners be? All of these questions are unanswered in the legislation and, because the answer is open to contestation, it is political.

Repetitive strain injury, for example, is a condition that has been recognized only relatively recently. When it first emerged there was much debate about its existence. In a court case brought in 1992, *Mughal* v. *Reuters Ltd*, a maverick ruling by a judge, Judge Prosser, declared that the condition did not exist. While the term is now accepted, there was a period when the condition would not fit within the definition.

In addition, what is meant by 'substantial', in the phrase 'substantial and long-term adverse affect'? The Act merely defines it as not trivial or minor, making this another area open to debate. While 'adverse' may be fairly easy to define, what is covered by 'normal' day-to-day activities? The Act carries a list of 'normal' activities including mobility, dexterity, co-ordination, ability to lift, continence, the ability to learn, memory, sensory abilities and perception of risk. The list is very broad-ranging and, again, open to interpretation. The implementation of the Act and delivery of services under the Act hang on these definitions. It is therefore very important to have clearly understood definitions. The outcome of the ambiguity and wide scope for interpretation under the Act has been that many employers have sought to challenge a claimant's status as a disabled person when taken to a tribunal under the DDA (Meagar *et al.*, 1999).

There are also other problems with the Act. Discrimination, as defined by the Act, refers to both treating a disabled person less favourably, and failing to provide what are described as 'reasonable adjustments' to the environment when disabled people are placed at a 'substantial disadvantage' compared to other people and being unable to justify these actions. It must also be proved that this discrimination occurred solely because the person was disabled, which places a difficult burden on the disabled person to prove discrimination. Furthermore, one of the main differences between the DDA and legislation against discrimination on the grounds of race or sex is that discrimination against disabled people, provided it can be justified, is not illegal. Justification, moreover, can only be upheld if the reason is 'material and substantive' – that is, if it is an employer who is discriminating against a member of their workforce or a service user. Disabled people contest the wide scope for 'legal' discrimination allowed by the Act.

Finally, another problem arises from the emphasis placed on rights in this Act, and the corresponding Americans with Disabilities Act (ADA). Such legislation talks about, for example, the right of disabled people not to be discriminated against in employment, in the provision of goods and services, and in access to facilities. Although this opens the way for individual actions through the legal system, there is a danger that such an approach will weaken collective political struggles (Barnes and Mercer, 2003). The effective fight for political rights needs to be more than a matter of individual fights as individual cases of discrimination are fought through the courts.

In addition, Jones and Marks identify a set of problems with rights-based action:

> A rights based approach to legal developments has been rejected by many modern critical legal scholars. They raise a number of concerns about rights. These include a misuse and abuse of the concept of rights, the indeterminism of rights; the fact that rights are unstable and context bound; the fact that rights cannot determine consequences; and the fact that rights formalise relationships and thereby separate us from each other.
>
> (Jones and Marks 1999, quoted in Barnes and Mercer, 2003, p.123).

SUMMARY

- The DDA represents the first time that the Government has officially acknowledged that disabled people are a discriminated-against group.
- The DDA outlaws discrimination in the fields of employment, services and the sale and rental of property. Subsequent amendments to the Act have outlawed discrimination in education and seen the establishment of a Disability Rights Commission.
- The disabled people's movement campaigned vigorously for this legislation.
- There are problems with the DDA, one of which is a danger that the individualized nature of rights claims under the DDA will lead to a weakening of the disability movement.

8   CONCLUSION

This chapter has sought to provide an overview of disability politics and policy making. The discussion highlights the influence of disabled people on the wider policy process, and shows the importance of other stages of the policy process as well as the decision-making phase. We have surveyed the different strategies adopted by different disability groups (the key organizations discussed are listed in Box 4.6 below) – through the social model, disability rights, the emphasis on experience, and through identity politics. In particular we have examined the benefits and disadvantages of the social model of disability. We have also explored the advantages and problems in constituting disabled people as a political minority. In addition the chapter has considered a policy-making initiative in anti-discrimination legislation in the form of the DDA. These concerns have shown how social attitudes shape lives, and how disability politics is shaping legislation.

The theme running through the chapter has been about what equality and difference mean in the context of disability politics and policy making. Disabled people certainly seek equal opportunities with those of non-disabled people, based ultimately on the principle that disabled people deserve equal respect and dignity as human beings. But disabled people also demand that sometimes special measures need to be implemented to allow them access to equal opportunities, for instance in the workplace, education and housing. Disability politics has also wrestled with the benefits and problems in casting disabled people as 'different' from a norm of the mainstream. On the one hand, the idea of difference can encourage a 'ghetto' mentality and play down the similarities between disabled and non-disabled people. On the other hand, it can highlight the issues of discrimination faced by disabled people as a group. In the course of the chapter we have discussed the claims of disabled people to be equal rather than (negatively) different; equal as well as different (in the sense of special provision); and to be recognized in their (positive) self-identified differences. If negative difference casts disabled people as 'other', disability politics seeks a difference that does away with dominance rather than reinforcing it. The complexity of the relations between equality and difference in disability politics and policy making demonstrates the complexity of our relationships to the social and political worlds.

The history of disabled people being defined, first, in terms of a medical model and then through a social model, intersects and resonates with these various perspectives on equality and difference. The history of disability politics tracks the move from organizations *for* disabled people to organizations *of* disabled people, and this move is mirrored in the view that effective policy reforms need to incorporate the experiences of disabled people more fully.

Despite changes in policy such as the DDA and the emergence of a more radical form of disability politics as a new social movement, the question still remains – are disabled people equal citizens yet? Many within the disabled people's movement would argue that the answer is no. Disabled people are still denied access to mainstream schooling and the opportunities that that offers. Disabled people are more likely to be unemployed and to live in poverty. Different laws are applied on abortion if there is a risk that the child would be seriously disabled. There are many other examples of unequal treatment faced by disabled people. Disadvantage and discrimination are entrenched in our society and it will take a long time before they will be eradicated. That is not to say that such a wish should not be the aim.

BOX 4.6	**Key organizations**

American Coalition of Disabled People

American Disabled for Accessible Public Transportation (ADAPT)

British Council of Organisations of Disabled People (BCODP)

British Deaf Association

Centres for Independent Living

Committee on Restrictions Against Disabled People (CORAD)

Direct Action Network (DAN)

Disability Alliance

Disablement Income Group (DIG)

Disabled People's International

Fédération Internationale des Mutilés, des Invalides du Travail et des Invalides Civils (FIMITIC)

Independent Living Movement (ILM)

National Association of the Deaf (NAD)

National Fraternal Society of the Deaf (NFSD)

National League of the Blind

Physically Disabled Students Program (PDSP)

Spinal Injuries Association

Union of the Physically Impaired Against Segregation (UPIAS)

REFERENCES

Anspach, R. (1979) 'From "stigma" to identity politics', *Social Science and Medicine*, no.13A, pp.765–73.

Barnart, S., Schriner, K. and Scotch, R. (2001) 'Advocacy and political action' in Albrecht, G., Seelman, K. and Bury M. (eds) *Handbook of Disability Studies*, London, Sage.

Barnes, C. (1991) *Disabled People in Britain and Discrimination*, London, Hurst and Co.

Barnes, C. and Mercer, G. (2003) *Disability*, Cambridge, Polity Press.

Barnes, C., Mercer, G. and Shakespeare, T. (1999) *Exploring Disability: a Sociological Explanation*, Cambridge, Polity Press.

Campbell, J. and Oliver, M. (1996) *Disability Politics: Understanding Our Past, Changing Our Future*, London, Routledge.

Charlton, J. (1998) *Nothing About Us Without Us: Disability, Oppression and Empowerment*, Berkeley, University of California Press.

Coleridge, P. (1993) *Disability, Discrimination and Development*, Oxford, Oxfam.

Corker, M. (1999) 'Differences, conflations and foundations: the limits to "accessible" representations of disabled people's experiences', *Disability and Society*, vol.14, pp.624–42.

Crow, L. (1996) 'Including all of our lives' in Barnes, C. and Mercer, G. (eds) *Exploring the Divide: Illness and Disability*, Leeds, Disability Press.

DeJong, G. (1983) 'Defining and implementing the independent living concept' in Crewe, N. and Zola, I. (eds).

Drake, R. (1994) 'The exclusion of disabled people from positions of power in British voluntary organisations', *Disability and Society*, vol.9, no.4, pp.461–80.

Drake, R. (1996) 'A critique of the role of traditional charities' in Barton, L. (ed.) *Disability and Society: Emerging Issues and Insights*, London, Longman.

Dreidger, D. (1989) *The Last Civil Rights Movement*, London, Hurst and Co.

Engel, D. and Munger, F. (2003) *Rights of Inclusion: Law and Identity in the Life Stories of Americans with Disabilities (Chicago Series in Law and Society)*, Chicago, University of Chicago Press.

Finkelstein, V. (1993) 'Disability: a social challenge or an administrative responsibility' in Swain, J. *et al.* (eds).

French, S. (1993) 'Disability, impairment or something in between' in Swain, J. *et al.* (eds).

Humphries, S. and Gordon, P. (1992) *Out of Sight: The Experience of Disability 1900–1950*, London, Northcote House Educational Publishers.

Hurst, R. (1995) 'Choice and empowerment – lessons from Europe', *Disability and Society*, vol.10, no.4, pp.529–34.

Ligget, H. (1988) 'Stars are not born; an interpretive approach to the politics of disability', *Disability, Handicap and Society*, vol.3, no.3, pp.263–76.

Lister, R. (1997) *Citizenship; Feminist Perspectives*, Basingstoke, Macmillan.

Marshall, T.H. (1950) *Citizenship and Social Class*, Cambridge, Cambridge University Press.

Meagar, N., Doyle, B., Evans, C., Kersley, B., Williams, M., O'Regan, S. and NiiDjan, T. (1999) *Monitoring the Disability Discrimination Act 1995*, London, Department for Education and Employment.

Melucci, A. (1989) *Nomads of the Present*, London, Radius.

Morris, J. (1991) *Pride Against Prejudice*, London, Women's Press.

Oakley, A. (1972) *Sex, Gender and Society*, London, Maurice Temple Smith.

Oliver, M. (1983) *Social Work with Disabled People*, Basingstoke, Macmillan.

Oliver, M. (1990) *The Politics of Disablement*, Basingstoke, Macmillan.

Oliver, M. (1996) *Understanding Disability: From Theory to Practice*, Basingstoke, Macmillan.

Oliver, M. and Barnes, C. (1998) *Disabled People and Social Policy*, London, Longman.

Pagel, M. (1988) *On Our Own Behalf: An Introduction to the Self-Organisation of Disabled People*, Manchester, Manchester Coalition of Disable People.

Riddell, S. and Banks, P. (2001) *Disability in Scotland: A Baseline Study*, Report for the Disability Rights Commission, Strathclyde Centre for Disability Research, Glasgow, University of Glasgow.

Shakespeare, T. and Watson, N. (2001) 'Making the difference: disability, politics and recognition' in Albrecht, G., Seelman, K. and Bury, M. (eds) *Handbook of Disability Studies*, London, Sage.

Squires, J. (2005) 'Common citizenship and plural identities: the politics of social difference' in Lewis, P. (ed.) *Exploring Political Worlds*, Edinburgh, Edinburgh University Press/The Open University.

Stuart, O. (1993) 'Double oppression: an alternative starting point' in Swain, J. *et al.* (eds).

Swain, J., Finkelstein, V., French, S. and Oliver, M. (1993) (eds) *Disabling Barriers – Enabling Environments*, London, Sage.

Thomas, C. (1999) *Female Forms: Experiencing and Understanding Disability*, Buckingham, Open University Press.

UPIAS (1976) *The Fundamental Principles of Disability*, London, Union of the Physically Impaired Against Segregation.

Van Cleve, J. (1993) *Deaf History Unveiled*, Washington, Gallaudet University Press.

Young, I.M. (1990) *Justice and the Politics of Difference*, Princeton, Princeton University Press.

Zola, I. (1972) 'Medicine as an institution of social control', *Sociological Review*, vol.20, pp.487–504.

Zola, I. (1983) 'Developing new self images and interdependence' in Crew, N.M. and Zola, I. (eds) *Interdependent Living for Physically Disabled People*, San Francisco, Jossey-Bass.

FURTHER READING

Barnes, C. and Mercer, G. (2003) *Disability*, Cambridge, Polity Press.

Barnes, C., Mercer, G. and Shakespeare, T. (1999) *Exploring Disability: A Sociological Explanation*, Cambridge, Polity Press.

Shakespeare, T. and Watson, N. (2001) 'Making the difference: disability, politics and recognition' in Albrecht, G., Seelman, K. and Bury M. (eds) *Handbook of Disability Studies*, London, Sage.

Talking about policy

Raia Prokhovnik

Evidence &
argument

Contents

1	Introduction	146
2	Political science	147
	2.1 Shifts in political science	148
	2.2 Changing perspectives on evidence	150
	2.3 Are case studies representative?	155
3	The importance of values	158
	3.1 The role of values	158
	3.2 The role of ideas	166
	3.3 The construction of the recipients of policy	169
4	The use of models	171
5	What is 'thinkable' and what is 'doable'	174
6	Conclusion	181

1   INTRODUCTION

Vicki quickened her step. She was late for her meeting with Jasmin and Ewen. They had arranged to meet before the tutorial on the first four policy-making chapters. They had been given four headings for the discussion in the tutorial. Today they were going to discuss aspects of studying political science as they apply to public policy, and the role of values in the policy-making process.

Vicki was keen to find out what the others thought about *studying* political science and why *values* might be important. They were going to meet a second time before the tutorial as well to talk about the use of models in policy making, and the curious business of the difference between what is 'thinkable' and what is 'doable' in the process of policy making. Vicki wasn't sure what all the headings were all about: hopefully talking with her friends would help. She had agreed to bring some newspaper cuttings along that she hoped illustrated some of the points. Jasmin was bringing summaries of some of the points, and Ewen had promised to bring some political cartoons. Vicki reached the coffee bar and as she collected her latte she heard Jasmin's voice.

Jasmin   OK, I can see that the previous chapters have explored four case studies in policy making. The first chapter examined the relation between powers and structures with reference to the EU '1992 initiative' policy-making process that led to the Single European Market. Chapter 2 looked at whether the centre–periphery model or multi-level governance model was most apt in describing the making of health policy.

Ewen   (Flicking through the book) Yep, and the next chapter discussed opportunities for participation and dissent in policy making about the welfare state. Chapter 4 looked at how ideas about equality and difference in disability policy making have changed. I'm hoping there's an exam question on Chapter 4.

Vicki   (Pulling up a chair, trying to dig her notes out of her bag) Yeah, but I'm not sure I am! One thing I'm hanging on to is that we were told we didn't have to become experts on particular policy issues. The point was to 'make vivid' to us questions of public policy making in the real world. It's not the details of the case studies that are at issue but the more general points about the policy-making process.

Jasmin   That's right. And the tutorial isn't going to involve a new case study. Remember we're supposed to 'reflect back' on the use of evidence and argument in those chapters, right?

Ewen   (Eyebrows raised) Well, fine, but what do you two think 'reflect back' means?

Jasmin   [Pause] Well, remember in the Introduction – hang on, I've got it here – we're going to revisit particular examples of evidence, unpack some of the issues they contain, and consider some of the methods used and the implicit methodological assumptions they contain ... things like that.

Vicki   Yeah, I think the plan is really to step back from the actual case studies and not get too tangled up in their details. So I think each of the four headings takes up one part of this 'process of reflection' about evidence and argument in policy making. OK, so maybe we know roughly what we need to think about. Sounds interesting.

Jasmin   (Enthusiastically) I hope there's lots about the 'argument' side of this 'evidence and argument' theme – that's what I like about politics, a good argument, and seeing people squirm a bit when they have to defend their arguments! Do you watch *Prime Minister's Question Time* on the TV? Pretty lively really. And did you hear the transport minister having to defend the train fare rises on the radio the other morning? He really did get a grilling! I like TV programmes like *Newsnight* too. Did you see that feminist writer take on the government's record on equal pay last week? It was really good, even dramatic.

Vicki   (Gesticulating) I see what you mean, but I think it's more interesting to dig into the *evidence* politicians and campaigners use, and to listen to them when they attack each other's evidence. Maybe that's because I like to see some facts and figures – they always make me feel I'm on safe ground.

Ewen   Maybe. I think I'd rather just do a question on the fourth chapter.

Jasmin   (Catching Vicki's and Ewen's eyes, briskly) But anyway, what's the first thing we're looking at – yes, aspects of what's involved in studying 'political science' when doing policy studies. Let's see where we can get to on that ....

2   POLITICAL SCIENCE

Ewen   Where do we start with this one? We're not political scientists.

Jasmin   No, but we *are* studying politics, and political scientists are very important in the study of politics. We take our bearings from them. Remember in Chapter 3? Look at how significant political scientists are there. Esping-Andersen's theory of different welfare regimes was great in helping us understand the material on welfare states. And Albert

Hirschman's theory of exit, voice and loyalty really added to what Freeman meant by participation.

Ewen   (Nodding) Yes, I remember that.

2.1   Shifts in political science

Jasmin   (Businesslike) So the first thing we're looking at here is 'shifts in political science'. I guess this refers to how political science theories develop over time. There's a whole tradition of studying politics that goes back to Plato and Aristotle, isn't there? All those thinkers say different things so I guess those are 'shifts' over time … .

Vicki   (Holding up one hand) That's if you take 'political science' to go back to the ancient Greeks. Some books I've read see 'political science' as starting in the mid-twentieth century, particularly with the attempts of some American academics to study politics 'scientifically'.

Jasmin   Fair enough. But either way it directs our attention to how political science theories develop over time. And we can set up a kind of *argument* between them – Plato thought democracy was rubbish but Aristotle had a lot of time for it – things like that.

Vicki   (Thoughtfully) I guess this 'shifts in political science' could also refer to the way political scientists working at any one time put forward different explanations from one another.

Ewen   (Shaking his head) Now my father would hate the idea that political scientists don't always agree with each other. He'd say, if that's the case, doesn't it just mean that one is right and the rest are wrong? What's the point of all that expertise if they can't even agree on the basics?

Jasmin   (Carefully) Well, maybe sometimes you could say one is right and the others are wrong. But I don't think that's always the case. I reckon 'truth' is a pretty complicated business when it comes to dealing with something as complex as political society. One thing I understood is that different political scientists may highlight equally valid but different aspects of political society and how to study it. [pauses] Like in Chapter 1 – do you remember? Deborah Mabbett talked about political scientists disagreeing amongst themselves about which actors were most influential in the Single Market initiative. She pointed out that Sandholtz and Zysman argued that multinational businesses would be influential, while Moravcsik regarded intergovernmental negotiations as primarily important.

Vicki   That's right. It's not a matter here of one being right and the other being wrong, is it? Both obviously have something to offer in the discussion of the Single Market. Now, let's find some more evidence in public policy for 'shifts in political science'!

Jasmin   (Finding her place in the book) OK, well I think Mabbett gives another good example of a shift among political scientists. She talks about the move from the 'iron triangle' explanation to the 'issue networks' explanation. Political scientists studying US politics in the 1960s discerned an 'iron triangle' involved in policy making, made up of government agencies, special interest lobbies, and members of relevant Congressional committees. This 'iron triangle' theory seemed to give them a good grip on what was going on in policy making in America. Then, more recently, the idea of 'issue networks' has been used to describe how the interest lobbies have become more diverse and the policy process more open. The 'issue networks' theory seems to explain more than the 'iron triangle' did or to explain recent developments – like a more fragmented policy-making process – better.

Ewen   From 'iron triangle' to 'issue networks' – that certainly sounds like a big shift in political scientists' explanations. I guess an 'iron triangle' approach would be like if the three of us go to the tutorial and dominate the discussion and stitch up the outcomes between us. You can be the government agencies Jasmin, I think that suits you. Vicki can be the Congressional committees. And I'll represent the interest lobbies.

Jasmin   (Laughing) You're getting carried away!

Ewen   (Smiling) No I'm not, I'm 'making it vivid' like Vicki said! Anyway, to continue – in an 'issue networks' approach we don't try to control the group. We each go to the tutorial with our own interest predominant but each of us is more open to forming networks in the tutorial with other people, to build on our separate interests.

Vicki   You've certainly illustrated the shift graphically, Ewen, that makes sense to me. But can we get back to the chapters? I've found some more evidence in Chapter 1 as well. Do you remember how Dahl set up a new way of explaining the decision-making phase of the policy-making process in terms of the *behaviour* of the actors involved? Mabbett describes how this was quite a departure from some earlier accounts. That's another kind of 'shift' in political science, I guess.

Ewen   (Excited) Yeah, that's right, I noticed that one too. Bachrach and Baratz's *criticism* of Dahl represents a further shift in political science. They reckoned that power is exercised not just in the decision-making phase but also before it, when the agenda is being set and people are influencing how issues are defined.

Vicki   And Mabbett points out that Bachrach and Baratz's contribution shows that some *potential* policies never get to be put on the agenda. I guess that means that some big issues never really get debated publicly, they never quite 'surface' in political argument.

Jasmin   (Chiming in) And then don't forget that Lukes also criticized Dahl. Lukes argued that there was a 'third' dimension of power. As Mabbett puts it, this third dimension of power highlights how the preferences of the actors involved are shaped.

Ewen   (Thinking out loud) Hmmm, all of that shows just how important power is in making policy, doesn't it? And power works in different ways, on different levels.

Vicki   Absolutely right. Now what about some evidence from the other chapters we've read? I can think of another example of shifts in political science thinking – in Chapter 4. Nick Watson talks about the academic work that has had an impact on changing ideas about disability.

Jasmin   (Looking at the other two quickly) That's right. So we've looked at how shifts in political science theories and approaches have occurred in the public policy arena, and how they've led to different descriptions and evaluations of policy within an area. Another aspect of this 'reflecting back' on political science in these four chapters has to do with changing perspectives on evidence. You'll like this one Vicki.

2.2 Changing perspectives on evidence

Ewen   (Smiling) My father would say but why are there 'changing perspectives' on evidence? Surely evidence is evidence and no-one can contest it?

Jasmin   (Slowly) Well let's think of an example. Let me try this on you: say someone came into this café and saw the three of us talking. They've got the evidence of the three of us sitting here, right. But what it means is not at all clear-cut. They might think we were just passing the time of day. Or arranging an end-of-year party. If it was another student from our course who thought the tutorial had already started, they might see us sitting here as evidence that we'd skipped the tutorial. Or they might see it as evidence that they'd been excluded from our meeting. Hmmm, I'm getting in the swing of this now. If it was my father, he'd probably take it as evidence that I was just skiving instead of working in the library. If it was our tutor, she might see this as evidence that we were preparing for the tutorial. If it was the person collecting the cups and wiping the tables in here, they might see us as evidence of people providing used cups to collect.

Ewen   (Smiling) Yeah, actually you are right, I didn't think of it that way, thanks, but what about some evidence from the chapters now!

Vicki   Well, what about where Mabbett highlights that different policy actors regard evidence differently?

Ewen   (Repeating slowly) Different policy actors regard evidence differently?

Vicki (Determined) Yes. Take environmental policy making in Britain. Take the notorious Twyford Down business. The government regarded this hill in Hampshire just as an obstacle to cut through in order to be able to extend the M3 motorway down from London to the south coast. But environmentalists and scientists saw this hill as part of a context of natural beauty and special scientific interest. Same hill, same evidence, completely different views of it.

Ewen Views! I bet there was a good view from that hill. But OK I take the point.

Vicki (Thinking it over) Right. So the general point Mabbett is making is that a range of policy actors will have different interests. They'll interpret 'the facts' differently in the light of those interests. And they'll select different forms of evidence and information as important. Does that make sense?

Jasmin Yeah it does. And the example of policy actors is different from the one I gave about different people seeing us in the coffee bar, isn't it? With the policy actors, they all have different interests. They all wear different hats – their job is to represent a certain interest – whereas the different people noticing us in the coffee bar all have different perspectives, not necessarily only driven by interest.

Vicki Like the picture – you know – that looks like a vase but when you blink it looks like two people's profiles.

Ewen (Keenly) Yes, and I remember now another example of interests from Chapter 1. Mabbett said that different *venues* of policy making can also encourage different views of evidence. She gives the example of how the German representatives at the European Commission tend to be in favour of market liberalization, whereas German representatives in *national* German politics are much less keen. German representatives in both venues – but they have different perspectives.

Jasmin That's a good one, isn't it? Because you'd expect the two lots of representatives to 'sing from the same hymn sheet' whatever 'venue' they were in. But when they get to the European Commission, those representatives start to have a different perspective on policy making. I suspect the same process happens with the other European delegations, to a greater or lesser extent.

Ewen (Smiling) Yeah, it's like I think it's fine when I go out with my friends and stay out late. But if my brother Angus wants to stay out late, I'm suddenly in a different 'venue', that occupied by the older protective brother, and I tell him he has to be home early!

Vicki (Hunting through her book) There's also an interesting example from Chapter 3 on this 'changing perspectives on evidence' thing. It's a different sort of example. Richard Freeman talks about how different evidence leads to changed perspectives – and so to different policy.

Ewen   (Slowly) Different *evidence* leads to changed perspectives ... so the example is the other way round.

Vicki   Yeah, he says that as countries faced the evidence of low economic growth and an ageing population they adapted their policies on welfare. In other words, ideas about the direction a policy should take can change according to hard evidence about what can be afforded.

Ewen   (Thinking it through) So evidence affects predictions about the future. So change the evidence and the perspective on future policy making changes, right? This is like my little brother Douglas.

Jasmin   *Another* brother?

Ewen   Yeah. Doug wants a new skateboard .... Whether or not he gets it is going to depend on our parents' view of their finances. If they think the evidence of their bank account is healthy they might buy it for him. The policy outcome would be the decision to buy it. But if they think the evidence is a bit grimmer, then they're going to say no, aren't they? The evidence has a big say in their decision.

Vicki   That's right. Changing perspectives on *evidence* affect attitudes towards what can be accomplished with a policy.

Jasmin   (Thinking hard) Well, tell me what you think of this example on changing perspectives on evidence. There's a young man that sits outside the bank begging, near where I live. The evidence is there but I never know how to respond. If I thought the values of charity and compassion were most important, I would respond in that light and give him some money. If I had generally liberal values but didn't feel them that strongly, I might give him a few coins if I had any and maybe say something to him about the council's new scheme for homeless people. If the values of self-reliance and hard work were most important to me, I'd tell him to get up, 'get on his bike' and find a job. If my values were confused or complex, I might ignore him.

Ewen   (Looking intently at Jasmin) So depending on the way you perceived him – what you saw him as evidence *of* – would affect your decision or policy towards him.

Jasmin   (Nodding) Right ....

Vicki   Exactly! That's a good example. I guess we're always reading evidence in the light of the values and ideas we have, aren't we? Politicians and policy makers are just the same. There's also an example of this in Chapter 2. Julie Charlesworth and Wendy Humphreys contrast two models of health care and what they show is that the two models contain different interpretations of the evidence.

Ewen   (Thinking out loud) *Different* interpretations of the evidence, right?

Jasmin   Yeah – I saw a debate on TV the other night about this. This guy advocating the new 'public–private partnership' approach to the health service argued that the evidence of waste, mounting costs, and misdirection of funding could only be solved by a whole new approach to health policy by the government. Whereas the woman defending the earlier 'welfare state' model maintained – on the basis of the same evidence – that the health service could be reformed to be more cost-effective, efficient, and would be far more accountable, by remaining under direct state control.

Vicki   (Gesticulating) I saw that too. It was interesting that they both drew on evidence about what had happened over the past thirty years to make their point.

Jasmin   But did you notice the different languages they were using too?

Vicki   That's right. The guy was into this whole public–private partnership thing, the responsibilities of citizens, waste, efficiency ....

Jasmin   And the woman was talking about the tradition of universal and comprehensive provision of services, citizens' entitlements .... It really shows, doesn't it – I've noticed this before – that when you're having an argument with someone, if you can make them use your language then you've half won the argument already.

Vicki   Yeah, controlling the language is a big deal in policy making.

Ewen   (Digging a folder out of his bag) Look, that reminds me. I've got this great set of cartoons. There's one here on the health service that criticizes the effects of restructuring – you'll like it.

'... anyway, that's enough about how we're going to create more empty beds. Now a word about the economy and our foreign policy...'

Vicki   Great, I like that. It reminds me of another example that Charlesworth and Humphreys bring up too. They're talking about inequalities: inequalities between different groups of people in health terms. They look at the impact of different government reports and inquiries into health inequalities. The reports are a kind of evidence aren't they?

Jasmin   Right. And they talk about how Conservative and Labour governments drew very different policy conclusions from the evidence they were presented with.

Vicki   Hey, you're right. [pause] And that shows up a really important point – that evidence is not neutral.

Ewen   (Scoffing) Oh come on! How can evidence not be neutral?

Vicki   Because it's always being read in the light of values and ideas – don't you see? And the meaning of evidence is not self-evident because it depends on what it is being seen as evidence *of* …. When I'm driving and see an orange traffic light I stop but my aunt … [laughs] she sees an orange light as an invitation to put her foot down and get through the intersection! [musing] Actually there's another good example of this in Chapter 4 I've just thought of. Nick Watson discusses how a clear shift in perspective on evidence happened about disabled people. Disabled people used to be regarded simply in terms of them each having individual medical problems. But now the perspective is switching – and disability is increasingly being seen in terms of what *society* needs to do, what we need to do collectively, in order to provide equal opportunities to disabled people.

Ewen   (Leaning forward, cautiously) So you're saying that, given the evidence provided by a group of disabled people, what is taken to be the *meaning* of that evidence is changing, with important policy making consequences?

Vicki   Right, exactly! And Watson also speaks of how disability has become a political issue in a way that it wasn't before. The evidence of our previous treatment of disabled people is now seen as leading to the conclusion that society as a whole – and public policy – is disadvantaging them.

Ewen   I remember. Watson talks about evidence from a range of policy areas – employment, claiming social security, education, housing standards, bus design, poverty – to support his claim that disabled people were treated as second-class citizens.

Vicki   Yeah, and this shows us something else important about the way perspectives on evidence change. Its about values. As values about disabled people changed – shouldn't be treated like second-class citizens any more – so the perception by policy makers on the evidence changed.

Ewen   (Shifting in his chair) So, let me get this straight. Different perspectives on evidence can arise from a number of sources, right? [counting off on his fingers] There were the perspectives of the different people in the café. Then there were the interests through which different policy *actors* interpreted evidence in a variety of ways, and the way different *venues* provide different contexts for interpreting interests and evidence. Thirdly there was the way changes in evidence lead to changes in perspective and policy. And just now we've seen how values and evidence can be linked.

Vicki   (Triumphant) Yep – perspectives, interests, changes in evidence, and values. [pauses, turns to Jasmin] So come on Jasmin, you've been quiet for a bit. Do you reckon values and evidence can be linked?

Jasmin   (Smiling) Actually, yes, I was just thinking of my family. When my mother cooks a big meal my father sees it in terms of the value of family, a family being together, enjoying good food together, enjoying each other's company, celebrating its achievements as a family. But my brother groans. He just sees the evidence of the meal as meaning an obstacle to playing his new computer game. The longer the meal, the more time away from the game.

Vicki   Yeah, so same evidence, different values. And what about you, Jasmin?

Jasmin   Actually that's interesting. Like I had an essay due last week and the night before we had this big family celebration. I really enjoy those occasions but I felt torn. I valued the family dinner but it was in my interests to get away as quickly as possible and finish the essay, so I valued that too.

Vicki   (Happily) Well, I think we've covered the evidence pretty well on how change occurs in perspectives on evidence and the selection of evidence! What's the last aspect of 'political science' we're looking at?

Ewen   Ah, case studies! Good, I like this one.

2.3   Are case studies representative?

Jasmin   (Challengingly) OK, Ewen, you're pretty keen, so what good is a case study? How much can you get out of it? Let's hear it.

Ewen   Well, to kick off, I think using case studies in the four chapters so far, of four public policy areas, *has* made questions of policy making come alive. The EU, health policy, the welfare state, disability policy – I've learned a lot about policy making. The case studies make the policy process mean much more to me than just an abstract set of principles about policy making could have done. I think case studies are an excellent *method* for studying politics and policy making.

Vicki   Yeah, case studies are a big method in comparative politics aren't they? And there are case studies *within* the chapters too, aren't there. Don't you remember that Freeman has a number of case studies taken from welfare state examples? There's the introduction of insurance for long-term care in Germany, pension reform in France, employment rates for blind people in Spain ....

Ewen   (Sitting up) That's right. Each of these case studies was designed to – kind of showcase an aspect of policy making.

Vicki   Yes, they show us, through concrete examples, some of the big points he'd been making in Chapter 3. That first case study about the introduction of long term care insurance in Germany – it showed up really well how policy making is done in the conservative and corporatist kind of welfare state.

Ewen   (Nodding) And the case study on welfare policy toward blind people in Spain – I learned a lot from that about how community participation can affect policy.

Jasmin   (Leaning back) Now, hold on a minute. Before you two get too carried away, Mabbett also raised a *problem* with case studies. She says that each policy presents its own unique set of political issues. So a *single* case study does not raise all the aspects that policy making involves and, naturally enough, a single case study considers issues in the light of that particular policy area. Conversely, because issues and the way they are treated *varies* across policy areas, it is difficult to make generalizations about policy making and to study the policy process in general. When you look at it that way, maybe case studies aren't much use really?

Ewen   (Interrupting) Look, of course we accept that no case study can raise *all* the issues involved in policy making, don't we Vicki?

Vicki   (Nodding) Yeah, and that doesn't invalidate using them.

Ewen   (Warming to his argument) After working our way through the whole book you're not seriously questioning the value of case studies in political science are you, Jasmin? Because we've seen how useful they are.

Vicki   (Softly to Ewen) I think she's just being argumentative – just trying to wind you up!

Ewen   (Muttering) Maybe she's succeeding.

Vicki   (Breaking in) Yes, we've seen that case studies are useful – I guess we just have to be aware if we want to study political science – that there's a balance to be struck between generalizations, on the one hand, and the value of case studies in bringing the material to life, on the other.

Jasmin   (Holding up her hands) Fair enough, OK. I can see that case studies have a place but I just think you shouldn't underestimate the drawbacks. When you're examining a case study you constantly have to have this double focus between the particular – the case study – and the general – what it's a case study of. And it's not easy to maintain that double focus all the time. You can easily get so involved in the case study that you forget what the general point was.

Ewen   Even so, I think it's a terrific method for making an area of politics – namely policy making – 'vivid', in Vicki's phrase again.

Vicki   As I said, there's a balance to be struck between the general and the particular.

Jasmin   (Eyes glinting) OK, but there's another interesting problem about case studies too. It's brought out in Watson's chapter. He talks about disabled people not being a 'homogeneous grouping', not being all the same. Watson is challenging the ... [looking for the right word] unthinking assumption that some people might have, that disabled people form a 'natural' case study. He's uneasy about all disabled people just being lumped together as a case study. Watson is making the good argument here that some of us might see all disabled people primarily through that label of 'disabled'. And it's an important point, because – actually – disabled people might see themselves differently, as *not* belonging to a 'disabled people' case study. To disabled people themselves, Watson says, other identities may well be more significant. He mentions other identities like locality, ethnicity, sexuality, gender and class.

Ewen   So a disabled woman might see herself as a woman first – rather than as disabled?

Vicki   Actually I think you've got a good point there about the problems with case studies.

Ewen   Take the example of my friend Yannis. He's a disabled person who is involved in an anti-pollution campaign. He wouldn't want to be seen as a disabled person, but as someone involved in environmental politics.

Jasmin   (Sitting forward) Exactly. That's one half of Watson's point. Also, he says, disabled people don't form a coherent interest group on the political stage. There's no 'powerful voting lobby' of disabled people, no 'organized constituency' of disabled people. Remember that? This is partly because they haven't been encouraged to form a political lobby and to have their own 'voice'. But it's also partly because there are many kinds of disability. So people with some learning disabilities might want to campaign for more signs with symbols rather than words to help them get around. Whereas blind people might want more computers adapted with speaking equipment. And people in wheelchairs might want low-entry buses as standard, so that when there is train track maintenance and alternative bus services are put in place, people in wheelchairs are not disbarred from travelling.

Ewen   Sure, that's a good point. But, anyway, I liked this stuff on case studies. I could see that it was concerned with what we are doing when we use the case study method. And we also managed to think about how and to what extent a case study is representative.

Jasmin   (Looking at Ewen and Vicki) OK, so we've covered some of the questions of argument, evidence and method in political science that crop up in policy making. I think we've done pretty well. [ticking off her list] We looked at shifts in political science, changing perspectives on evidence and the case study method. Now – after another latte, that'd be lovely, thanks Ewen – the importance of values in public policy. And it looks like the issue of values breaks down into – the role of values, the question of ideas and, hmmm, something called 'the construction of the recipients of policy'.

3   THE IMPORTANCE OF VALUES

3.1   The role of values

Vicki   Well, we've already touched on the role of values when we talked about how values and evidence can be interconnected.

Ewen   (Leaning forward) I'm just playing devil's advocate here, but do we really need to say anything more about values? Politics would be a lot more rational and clearer if people would just stick to the facts, don't you think? Why should personal opinions and values get into politics? Oh I'm starting to sound like my father, but there is something in the argument isn't there? Politics is about solving problems, and the solutions lie in assessing the relevant facts.

Vicki   (Smiling) Quite a devil's advocate Ewen! But we've already seen some answers to your argument. We know that values are implicated in evidence, and that political science explanations are debated and shift over time. It's a bit late in our conversation to start wanting politics and the study of politics to be value-free! I'm all in favour of people having to provide evidence for the claims they make, but that doesn't mean trying to do away with values completely!

Jasmin   (Musing) I guess, in general terms, 'values' in policy making arise from a range of places. 'Values' could refer to social norms and standards, for instance about equality in areas like gender and race. Feminists in Britain argue that women will never be able to enter and remain in the workplace on the same basis as men until government policy making values women's contribution equally with men's, and the problem of child-care places is seriously addressed.

Vicki   And values also crop up in phrases like 'patriotic values', don't they. Some people feel a very strong attachment to their country, or to what

they think their country stands for, and feel strongly about symbols like
the flag, national anthem, etc. All these kinds of values affect government
policy making, and changes in values lead to calls for changes in policy.

Jasmin   (Slowly) So, changes in social values about women led to
recognition of the crime of rape in marriage, didn't they? And changes
in social attitudes towards racial violence after the death of Stephen
Lawrence led to changes in policing procedures and perceptions of
race in the police force.

Ewen   And more questions about policing and how it's conducted.

Jasmin   You're right.

Vicki   (Excited) Hey, 'values' can also be about – coming back to the
example of the young man begging – for instance whether you favour
encouraging self-reliance, or whether you think providing opportunities
for people is the best standard to set, can't they?

Jasmin   We also need to remember that people's values are part of their
identity, and political parties are distinguished from each other partly
by the values they stand for. In one sense politics is about settling
which values should be dominant in a society. Then there's bound
to be on-going debate and periodic contestation of those values.
I suppose that in politics and policy making the 'argument' in 'evidence
and argument' is often about which values should be given priority.

Ewen   (Groaning) Does that mean there's nothing *but* values in politics?

Jasmin   (Thinking) Well, it doesn't mean that *only* values count. But on the
other hand I suppose that values are a dimension of *all* arguments in
politics.

Vicki   (Challengingly) What about this evidence, Ewen? Do you remember
when the Hutton Report came out, about the death of Dr David Kelly
and the BBC report by Andrew Gilligan accusing the government of
'sexing up' the dossier about Iraq's weapons. Well, I thought it was
really interesting that in the period immediately after the report was
published – what were the media going on about the whole time?
Not the substance of the report as such but what it meant in *political*
terms – for the relationship between the BBC and the government –
what it meant for the relations of power between the BBC and the
government, what value should be placed on each.

Jasmin   (Leaning towards Ewen) And look, we've already seen that values
are involved in evidence. But that doesn't mean there's nothing else
but values. Look, Watson gives a good example of the role of values in
politics. We talked about this earlier, in the link between evidence and
values. Disabled people feel passionately about how their disabilities are
perceived in society. The value – or lack of value – attached to them is
very important, and it's partly through campaigning and claiming a voice
that disabled people have contributed to policy reform. The values

expressed in recent policy moves and legislation reflect both anti-discriminatory measures, and attempts at equal opportunities in terms of things like mobility access and employment.

Vicki   (Breaking in) Yes, and we can see from Watson's chapter that the label 'disabled' is normative and political – not value-free. Watson is highlighting that 'values' can also refer to policy areas that people attach strong positive and negative feelings to. He is saying that disability has a stigma attached to it, and that this is being hotly contested.

Jasmin   Exactly. Words matter enormously in an area like this, don't they? … what words you use. And different words can convey different values and prospects for value change.

Vicki   (Animatedly) What's more, we can see from evidence in Freeman's chapter that the role of values goes even deeper than we've discussed so far, don't you think? I really liked that bit about how different kinds of politics, or what he calls different 'political logics' are at work in different welfare states. These different 'political logics' arise from different styles of participating in politics across different countries. But the 'political logics' also make possible different styles of participation.

Ewen   (Putting his hands up in front of him) OK, OK, let me get a word in will you? [slowly] So are you saying that the kind of participation open to me, and the kind of dissent that is likely to be recognized as legitimate, will vary. Under a social democratic form of welfare state like Sweden, the kind of participation available is different from the kind available in a conservative welfare state like Germany. And participation means something different again in a liberal welfare state like Canada?

Jasmin   (Triumphant) Yeah, exactly Freeman's point here. He's saying that the kinds of questions that can be asked in the three forms of welfare state politics will be different, because each form of welfare state carries a different set of values and principles.

Ewen   (Shaking his head) But hang on a moment. When you talk about 'values' here, you aren't just talking about things like personal preferences – or what I like or dislike – are you? You seem to have extended the meaning of 'values'.

Jasmin   You've hit the nail on the head, Ewen. Social values in this broader sense are also involved in different styles of doing politics. In the social democratic form of welfare state there's a premium put on active citizen participation, while in the conservative welfare state top-down decision making is the order of the day.

Ewen   You mean like the left traditionally going for the values of comprehensive welfare and some on the right going for economic liberal market solutions?

Jasmin   (Nodding) Sure, the choice of approach is clearly political.

Vicki   (Interjecting) But wait up – 'values' also means something specific in the public policy discourse too. Remember when Mabbett *distinguished* values from mere preferences or interests?

Jasmin   Hey, I remember that. In the language Mabbett is using, like when she talks about symbols, she's saying that values are supported by symbols, and that arguments based on values/symbols thrive when it is difficult to form preferences or calculate interests.

Vicki   (Digging out a bunch of newspaper cuttings) Yeah, and I've got another example here, whoops! [the cuttings spill on the floor]

Ewen   You all right?

Vicki   (Struggling to pick up the cuttings) Yeah, I'm fine thanks – [to herself] if I can just find the right one – ah here! This is an example of maybe values in a different sense again. It's a newspaper cutting about how the protests of what they call 'some of Italy's poorest and least influential citizens' – in southern Italy – forced a U-turn by the government on the positioning of a nuclear dump in their area. The government's policy decision was going to be determined by certain values – based on geological reports, and not wanting to upset those living in the north. But then they had to bow to other values, as expressed by the protesting southerners.

Southern poor force nuclear dump u-turn

John Hooper in Rome

Silvio Berlusconi's government was hounded into an embarrassing about-turn last night by some of Italy's poorest and least influential citizens.

Faced with protests in southern Italy, ministers withdrew a decree to dump the country's nuclear waste on the town of Scanzano Jonico in the region of Basilicata.

Last night's cabinet meeting was reportedly heated, with the environment minister, Altero Matteoli, under fire.

Mr Berlusconi was quoted as telling his ministers: "We've provoked a popular uprising."

By yesterday, the whole of Matera, the province in which Scanzano Jonico is located, was on strike. Protesters blocked a main rail link and eight roads, including three motorways. The government had intended to store the waste in an underground vault. It said a geological research showed Scanzano Jonico was the safest place in Italy.

But locals said the dump would contaminate their water supplies and risked destroying the area's fledgling tourist industry.

At the root of the anger was a perception that the country's waste was being unloaded in the south because its leaders did not dare find a site in the more prosperous north.

Last night the cabinet approved a decree that ordered that a panel of scientists be set up to find another site within 18 months.

On hearing the news of the decision, hundreds of people rushed into the streets of Scanzano Jonico to celebrate.

Jasmin   (Nodding) Good one! And then again, as Chapter 1 shows, while a government makes thousands of policies during its term of office, only some are 'political' in the sense of having a bearing on the campaign agenda for the following election.

Vicki   Also, some areas of policy are more open to public debate than others.

Jasmin   (Seriously) I think ideological differences are really important as a source of 'values' in policy making too. Ideology comes into how policy is made, doesn't it. Mabbett asks how did the idea of greater economic integration come about. The answer she gives is – through ideology. She points out [Jasmin finds the right section in the chapter] that ideas about the benefits of market liberalization, the reduction of state subsidies, and the extension of competition policy, constitute an ideology, a set of ideas that form the basis of the Single Market initiative.

Ewen   (Grudgingly) OK, I can see how values play a part in politics and policy making through things like social norms, individual values and ideological commitments. I guess I can see how different people are going to have different commitments and perspectives in politics. [thinking] Actually I've got a really good cartoon that demonstrates ideological differences. It's about those for and against the euro. Have a look.

Jasmin   (Smiling) Yeah, nice.

Ewen   Anyway, back to what we were talking about. My friend Yannis has his strong commitment to environmental politics, for instance, and my uncle Donald is just as committed in his life-long membership of the Tory Party. But why can't these differences just be sorted out once and for all? And why are there shifts in values over time?

Vicki   (Thinking) Well, it's precisely because values and policy making are very closely connected, I think. It's often a change of values that leads to policy change. You could chart the evidence to show that there is a connection. A good example in Britain is how changing values about the rights of children has led to policy reform in many areas, including the way children are now given extra legal protections.

Ewen   There are more provisions to protect children, through the vetting of school teachers for instance, aren't there?

Vicki   (Rummaging in her bag) That's right. And I've got a newspaper cutting that gives another example of policy changing under the impact of changing social values. [extends the cutting to the others] It's about the state legislature of Massachusetts changing its policy to allow gay marriages, in line with a change in social values.

US state to allow gay marriage

Massachusetts could become first to allow same-sex union

Gary Younge in New York

Massachusetts is poised to become the only US state to allow gay marriage following a legal ruling yesterday which will have widespread political ramifications ahead of next year's presidential election.

The Massachusetts supreme court gave the state's lawmakers 180 days to work out how to ensure equality at the altar after ruling 4 to 3 that same-sex couples were legally entitled to get married under its constitution.

"Whether and whom to marry, how to express sexual intimacy, and whether and how to establish a family — these are among the most basic of every individual's liberty and due process rights," the majority opinion said. "And central to personal freedom and security is the assurance that the laws will apply equally to persons in similar situations."

The state's Republican governor, Mitt Romney, immediately criticised the ruling, saying: "Marriage is an institution between a man and a woman. I will support an amendment to the Massachusetts constitution that makes that expressly clear. Of course, we must provide basic civil rights and appropriate benefits to non-traditional couples, but marriage is a special institution that should be reserved for a man and a woman."

But Mary Bonauto, the lawyer who represented the seven gay couples who sued the state, said that the legislators would not be able to change the

state constitution within the 180-day timeframe. She insisted that the only task assigned to the legislature was to come up with the legal changes to make gay marriage possible.

"This is a very good day for gay and lesbian families in Massachusetts and throughout the country," Ms Bonauto said.

The court, however, stopped short of allowing marriage licences to be issued to the couples who challenged the law until the legislature had come up with a means of enforcing the ruling.

The decision marks yet another victory for gay rights activists in a tumultuous year that has seen the ordination of the Episcopal church's first openly gay bishop and a United States supreme court judgment which declared anti-sodomy laws unconstitutional, effectively making consensual sex between gay couples legal.

But it is also likely to make the issue of gay rights the central social issue in next year's presidential elections, pitting the Christian right — the bedrock of Republican sup-

port — against gay rights campaigners and civil libertarians.

Gay rights groups are now braced for a backlash.

When the Hawaii supreme court ruled that the denial of gay marriages was unconstitutional in 1993, the legislature quickly intervened with legislation banning gay marriage. Dozens of other states moved pre-emptively to ward off a similar development, while Congress moved to deny federal recognition of homosexual marriage and allowed unions licensed elsewhere.

Polls show American public opinion is in flux on the issue. Attitudes towards homosexuality have softened in recent years. In a USA Today poll in July nearly one third said they had become more accepting of gay people in recent years, compared to just 8% who had become less accepting. Almost 90% said gay people should have equal rights in terms of job opportunities.

However, while the nation may have become more tolerant it is divided when it comes to granting gay couples full equality. According to a poll

released yesterday, most Americans, 55%, say they felt that homosexuality was a sin, while 33% did not. And while 32% favoured gay marriage, 59% opposed it.

The gulf between the court rulings and a rapidly shifting public opinion has provided the space for an intense cultural and political clash. The gay advocacy group the Human Rights Campaign has launched a $1m advertising campaign to put gay marriage in a positive light.

> 'Whether and whom to marry, how to express sexual intimacy — these are among the most basic of every individual's liberty'
> **Court ruling**

> 'Marriage is a special institution that should be reserved for man and woman'
> **State governor**

> 'This is a very good day for gay and lesbian families'
> **Gays' lawyer**

Gary Chalmers and Rich Linnell, one of the couples who took their right to marry to court
Photograph: Steven Senne/AP

Jasmin (Handing the cutting back to Vicki) Yeah, it's a good example. There's also evidence in Chapter 4, isn't there? The changes in social values associated with disability, and the changes in policy making that follow from that. Public opinion and public values are now strongly behind the idea that disabled people should be regarded as having equal rights with able-bodied people.

Ewen   (Breaking in) Yeah, Chapter 4 shows how there's been a big shift in public perception – from when disabled people used to be regarded as somehow sub-human and marginal in society. There were even 'freak shows' at travelling circuses of disabled people. We've come a long way since that. At least we have policies now that try to integrate disabled people into the community more.

Vicki   (Thinking hard) Those are changes in *progressive* values, emancipatory values, driving policy change, aren't they? You also get changes in policy due to changes in *circumstances* or conditions. For instance, there's this newspaper cutting about China's communist government introducing a constitutional protection of private property – for the first time since the 1949 revolution. I guess circumstances had changed in a big way – the country had been transformed by market forces over recent years. See?

China takes steps to protect private ownership of land

Jonathan Watts in Beijing

China's communist legislators looked certain to adopt a key capitalist principle yesterday as they began debating the first constitutional protection of private property since the 1949 revolution.

The historic move — along with a proposal to enshrine the entrepreneur-friendly theories of the former president Jiang Zemin — are among the most significant steps yet taken to bring the legal framework into line with reality in a country that is being transformed by market forces.

In another sign of change, the UN world food programme announced that China no longer required the international food aid it has been receiving for 25 years. Instead it will be asked to become a donor and to share its experience of lifting 400 million people out of poverty.

Yesterday the standing committee of the Chinese parliament, the national people's congress, considered a constitutional amendment that would take the country further from its centrally planned and publicly owned economy.

"Private property obtained legally shall not be violated," said the proposal, quoted in the Xinhua news agency. "Private property should be on an equal footing with public property."

The amendment is certain to be approved in March by the national people's congress.

Millions of Chinese people have been applying the principle of private ownership for a long time. Although the government owns the land and has a controlling stake in many industries, more and more members of the rising middle class are buying homes and company shares.

Entrepreneurs say they need legal protection so they can invest with confidence. Homeowners are demanding assurances that their flats and houses will not suddenly be demolished by developers.

They have good reason to be concerned about the lack of safeguards. The explosive development of Beijing and other cities has been mired in corruption scandals involving property speculators and Communist party officials who control land usage rights.

President Hu Jintao has been reminded of the political risks of failing to protect the property-owning classes and to improve regulation of the developers. In recent months several people who have lost their homes have set fire to themselves in Tiananmen Square.

But the acceptance of property rights is also part of a long-term strategy to create a legal framework for the market forces that were introduced 25 years ago by Deng Xiaoping.

Rather more difficult has been finding a political rationale for the Communist party. This was the subject of the second amendment tabled yesterday — the constitutional enshrinement of the "Three Represents" capitalist-style theory of Mr Jiang. It takes its place alongside Marxism, Leninism and the theories of Mao Zedong and Deng Xiaoping.

Under the doctrine, the party is supposed to represent "advanced forces of production, advanced culture, and the interests of the majority of the people". It was the basis for allowing the party to accept business tycoons as members.

Although President Hu has promised a government that is more responsive to the people, democracy was notably absent from the proposed reforms.

The party argues that it has improved the standard of living of the vast majority of China's 1.2 billion people over the past 20 years. This was given a boost on Saturday by the head of the world food programme, who said China had graduated from its aid dependence.

The programme's executive director, James Morris, announced a new partnership with the government in Beijing that will see China start to provide rather than receive support from the international community.

"China has lifted as many as 400 million of its own people out of poverty in less than a generation," he said. "That is an extraordinary achievement."

Jasmin   (Handing the cutting back) Yep, I see. Also, in the 1970s there was the oil crisis that led to huge public policy changes in so many countries – as governments made choices to tighten their belts.

Ewen   (Grudgingly again) All right, I can see how shifts in values – through public opinion and government circumstances – can affect policy making. [pause] But I can see a problem with the discussion of values we've had up to now. So far, you two have talked about values as if they are always a 'good thing'. Values can't always be warm and positive can they?

Jasmin   You're right Ewen – good argument. I can think of values that exclude people, discriminate against them, want to isolate them and set them apart from the benefits that the rest of us have from being citizens. Vicki just mentioned how this other side of the role of values in policy making is brought out in something in Chapter 4. That label 'disabled' is both 'normative' – that is, implying a value, not just a scientific description – and 'political' – not neutral, not agreed on by all, highly-charged.

Vicki   (Shifting in her seat) OK, so let's just recap on the importance of values before we move on. We've seen that policy making is not a neutral business. Values have a major impact on the process of public policy, through the role of ideologies and norms, through the contested nature of commitments and perspectives in politics, and in shifts over time in what is taken as desirable.

Ewen   (Rubbing his hands) Ah, now we come to another aspect of values, the 'role of ideas' in policy making. What have ideas got to do with it? Jasmin, are you going to start us off on this one?

3.2   The role of ideas

Jasmin   (Thinking out loud) Well, I guess ideas are closely linked to the importance of values, actually. 'Ideas' is another aspect of the 'argument' side of the 'evidence and argument' theme, don't you think? And for starters [passing over a sheet of paper to Vicki and Ewen] I've made a list of the roles that I think ideas play in policy making – what do you think?

The role of ideas

1   Particular policies and the policy-making process are affected by ideas and theories. Policies don't just emerge out of thin air but in part from ideas – and debates between different ideas. For instance, when Thatcher and Reagan introduced their neo-liberal policies in the 1980s, they drew heavily on the ideas put forward by political and economic advisors.

2   Governments may listen to ideas from a <u>number</u> of sources. Governments might take account of ideas not just from civil servants and interest groups, but also from think tanks, intellectuals and big business. So governments don't just know automatically what policies to make. They don't just have a kind of default position and make policy on a sort of auto-pilot.

3   Policies are always framed in <u>language</u>, and language expresses ideas. Academic literature and other kinds of 'reflective' formulations of ideas about what politics, society and culture are, and should be, are expressed in specific choices of vocabulary. All of them inform the way policy options are discussed and debated.

4   Watson looked at different ideas of what disability means. To radical groups of disabled people, he says, disability is not the outcome of having an impairment. The idea of disability, in their view, is also the result of prejudice and discrimination. To radical groups the onus is on society, not the individual disabled person. So there is a very important policy consequence that follows from this perspective. As Watson says, the emphasis is switched from changing the individual to changing society.

5   The role of ideas is also clear in the shift that Charlesworth and Humphreys chart in the restructuring of health policy. That restructuring occurred, in part, under the impact of ideas about privatization, internal markets, managerialism and so on. <u>Ideas matter</u>. It wasn't just that the evidence dictated the changes. The meaning of the evidence wasn't self-evident. These new ideas about internal markets and privatization were seen by the government of the day to be salient. They seemed to offer something new and effective.

6   Another example is the very question that frames the first chapter, 'How is policy made?' As well as being about values, 'How is policy made?' also indicates that policy does not follow 'naturally' from a set of given inert facts. Policy making is shaped by the interaction between <u>ideas</u> about policy making ....

Ewen   (Frowning) Well, I disagree on point 5 to some extent, Jasmin. The change in policy was at least partly a response to evidence about the mounting costs of public services. But I agree that it *was* ideas that spearheaded the policy change. That's my interpretation anyway.

Vicki   (Looking at the sheet) It's a good list, but maybe you could add holding people accountable for the ideas they use. Also locating who's accountable is a pretty important aspect of policy making, don't you think? And the meaning of an idea like 'accountability' can change quite radically. Charlesworth and Humphreys ask what accountability means within this new model of multi-level governance.

Ewen   (Sitting forward) Yeah, I remember that. The line of accountability in the old hierarchical relationship between central government and the regional health trusts was much clearer than it is with a more complex centre–periphery relationship involving semi-privatized agencies as well as government bodies.

Vicki   Right, that's my point. Accountability is much less clear in the new system. Precisely who is accountable to whom, and how? And how can parts of the system be held accountable to the people?

Ewen   Hey, that reminds me of when I rang the customer services number for my insurance company yesterday. They give you a whole range of options and tell you they value your call, but make you wait for ages before answering. From the customer's, citizen's, or consumer's point of view, it's awful – it's really hard to talk to someone who's accountable.

Vicki   (Agreeing) Yeah, that's really frustrating. I've been thinking – another thing your list doesn't take into account, Jasmin, is the *limits* of ideas in policy making. Mabbett talks about this, doesn't she? In a way she sees ideas coming up against power considerations. She distinguishes between different forms of 'policy actor': those who can 'advocate' a policy but have little influence, and those who have the power to influence the shape the policy takes. She relates this to the difference between 'consultation processes' and 'the real business of policy making'.

Jasmin   Well, you're right that there are constraints on the role of ideas in policy making. I remember another example from Chapter 1 too. Mabbett points out that the scope of citizen involvement varies radically across policy areas. Take a highly technical area of policy making like pensions. The economic complexity of the issues, and the lack of time and expertise of the general public to gather information and engage in debate, is inhibiting. On top of that, an area like pensions is already 'colonized by experts and technocrats'. All of this leads to the conclusion that the 'policy space' on pensions is largely left clear for the experts. In the pensions policy field, the ideas of experts dominate and there's very little room for the ideas of individual pensioners.

Vicki   (Getting up) That's good. Now, I'm going to get another coffee – anyone want anything?

Jasmin   Ah, coffee. Good idea! I'd love a decaf cappuccino with one brown sugar, thanks.

Ewen   And I'll have another Americano – with cream not milk.

Vicki   (Pretending exasperation) Whoever had the *idea* of introducing all these different coffees has a lot to answer for!

Ewen   (Turning to Jasmin) Now this seemed a tricky heading. But actually it was pretty straightforward to see how ideas and norms shape public policy in different contexts. And how public policy shapes ideas, too. What've we got left on 'values'?

Jasmin (Reading) 'The construction of the recipients of policy'. Curious way of putting it, don't you think? I guess the 'recipients' are those affected by the policy. The 'recipients' of unemployment benefit policy would be unemployed people.

Ewen And the 'recipients' of health policy would be patients.

[Ewen and Jasmin look through the chapters to find some examples]

3.3 The construction of the recipients of policy

Vicki (Returning with the coffees, slightly breathless) Slow queue – have I missed anything? This is an interesting one, isn't it? I can think of an example I read in the paper the other day – about how the recipients of policy are constructed. It was about the impact of values about race on the identity of recipients of policy. Remember those statistics in the newspaper on the disproportionate number of young black men subject to police 'stop and search' policies? These young men were being 'constructed' by the police as more likely to be involved in criminal behaviour.

Ewen (Raising his hands) Now wait a minute! OK, fine, I can see the point about the 'stop and search' policy. But the rest I disagree with you about. I've accepted that values and evidence are intertwined, and I've more or less taken on board what you two said about the importance of values in policy making. But as far as I can see, unemployed people and patients aren't 'constructed', they just are that way. It's a fact. I'm not sure how far I can go with this 'constructed' business.

Vicki (Gesticulating) Well, think of the evidence in other examples. Something else that popped into my head about the 'construction of the recipients of policy' was something Watson said in Chapter 4. He talks quite a lot about how disabled people are constructed in terms of being recipients of policies of different kinds. For instance, he refers to paternalistic charities where the emphasis was 'placed on incapacity'. Disabled people were being constructed as in need of rehabilitation and so policy was made that prioritized rehabilitation.

Jasmin Yeah, I remember now. Watson said that, by contrast, in one survey disabled people put rehabilitation as only 'a distant fifth' on their list of their needs. So we can see that there can be quite a gap between what policy makers think of the recipients of policy, and how those recipients actually see themselves!

Vicki And reading about health policy in Chapter 2 that we talked about earlier, it seems to me that there's a clear difference in the way recipients are 'constructed'. Under the comprehensive welfare state idea, patients and citizens were 'constructed' as having a universal right or entitlement to health care. Under the public–private partnership framework, patients and citizens become 'claimants' who may or may not get what they want from state health care – even though there's more rhetoric about empowering patients. You could get evidence to back this up quite easily.

Jasmin   I think that's right, and Charlesworth and Humphreys have another good example too, don't they? They also talk about the shift from a 'medical model' of health to a 'social model' of health. These models describe different views of the patient.

Vicki   Right. Charlesworth and Humphreys say that the social model of health emphasises *health* rather than *sickness*. The social model also sees people's well-being holistically.

Jasmin   And Watson talks a lot about the move from the medical to the social model of disability too.

Ewen   (Slowly) I see what you mean. So instead of the doctor only seeing me in terms of the illness I present her with, I'm regarded in terms of my whole health status. *That's* why she told me to give up smoking last time I saw her, even though what I went to see her about was back pain that had nothing to do with cigarettes or my lungs or anything. And it's interesting to think that when you go and see your doctor, there's more to the relationship than I'd realized. It looks like the doctor is encouraged by health policy makers to regard you as a certain kind of 'construction'.

Jasmin   That's a good point, Ewen. And look, I've just noticed an interesting connection – there's clearly a link between the section on ideas and this one on the recipients of policy. Ideas obviously had a big impact on the change in health policy, from the paternalistic idea that the professional knows best to the notion of 'empowering' the patient.

Vicki   (Looking at her watch) Great, now – oh I'm so late! – I've got to rush, but, ah, we're meeting again next week to talk about – what was it?

Jasmin   I've got it here: model building and the 'thinkable' and 'doable' in policy making, right? And then it's the tutorial?

Vicki   OK guys, thanks, that was great, see you next week.

[Vicki dashes off, and Jasmin and Ewen collect up their stuff and leave]

A week later, in the same café.

Jasmin   (Settling herself on a chair next to Ewen) Hi, have you seen Vicki yet?

Ewen   (Grinning and stirring his coffee) Not yet!

Vicki   (Arriving breathlessly) OK, what's the next heading? Oh, sorry, Hi! So, what's the next heading? Ah, the use of models in explaining the policy-making process. This is a bit like case studies, isn't it?

Jasmin   Yeah, its about the method used to develop policy formulations.

4   THE USE OF MODELS

Ewen   (Stirring his coffee thoughtfully) You know, the classic case of models that I can remember in these chapters is Freeman's discussion of three major types of welfare capitalism in advanced industrial countries. There were the liberal welfare states as in the US, Canada and Australia, the dominant European conservative model of France and Germany, and the social democratic regimes of the Scandinavian countries.

Vicki   (Struggling out of her coat, and getting out her book and notes) And I liked the way his models of the welfare state are not just narrowly defined, but are underpinned by 'different models of economic, social and political organization'. I guess that means that they run pretty deep in those societies, they tap into basic features of those societies?

Ewen   Yeah, I think that's the idea too. But it's not like those models are fixed and can't change. The way Freeman talks about them, they come across as pretty dynamic, don't they? I must admit I think of models as being like an architect's model – where everyone's wearing suits and they show the beautiful scale model of the building to the investors before its built. [pause] In fact, I guess models are especially useful to policy makers as well, aren't they? Actually, policy makers are a bit *like* architects aren't they? Because policy making is looking towards the future, isn't it, and trying to think of how it will work out.

Vicki   That's right, I guess a model is what my old methods textbook calls a 'heuristic device'. Policy makers can't just set up a whole policy and see if it delivers what they want it to, so they model it first and try and iron out the unwanted consequences. The model helps gain some understanding. And it highlights some features while reducing the significance of others.

Ewen   Yeah, and when political scientists use models?

Vicki   It's a kind of selective rewriting of a complex idea, isn't it? To pick out what's most important.

Ewen   (Energized) Absolutely. I liked the way Freeman talked about the role of evidence to back up these three models of the welfare state.

He said that empirical data could be advanced, that suggested that these models of the welfare state have 'real-world counterparts'.

Vicki   Like how social expenditure levels show clearly the three clusters of countries that the models describe. Good use of evidence too.

Ewen   Yeah. [pause] And Watson's discussion of the 'social model of disability' is another clear example of using a collection of features formed into a model – to clarify a situation or position or perspective on a policy area – isn't it?

Vicki   You're right. He discusses how, as a result of using the social model, we can see how disabled people are marginalized, excluded from the world of work, and experience social barriers. Yeah. [thoughtfully] So the use of the model helps you to see general trends and structural factors, above and beyond the experience of individuals. Is that how you see it Ewen?

Ewen   (Sitting forward) Yeah. You could even say simply that models help you to see what you're dealing with. And there's clearly an exercise in model-building going on in Charlesworth and Humphreys' diagrams on policy design – look here – on hierarchical and fluid policy design. The diagrams each indicate a different approach to policy making.

Vicki   (Smiling) It's just like my family actually. My father represents the hierarchy model – keen on structures, roles, procedures and top-down decisions. While my mother follows the fluid policy design model! Gathering inputs from all of us and trying to come up with something sensible.

Ewen   Ah. Quite some family! [rubbing his hands] Well, I think the strengths of model building are clear. When you have a model of policy making like the policy communities one or the issue networks one, you don't have to reinvent the wheel every time you want to study another area of policy. You transfer it over and see what's there. Political scientists can take some of the features for granted and make predictions.

Vicki   Actually Ewen, this thing about prediction is weird, isn't it? Freeman notes that models of welfare become embedded in how we see the world, and then affect future policy making. I think that's a really interesting effect models can have.

Ewen   (Leafing through the book) Yeah, that *is* interesting. Let me find it – right, I've got it here – he says that different models represent 'distinct trajectories of welfare'. These apply to the emergence and consolidation of the model, but also to how they adapt to change. The models hold true in the post-industrial economic and social era.

Vicki   That's a really intriguing idea, that models cease to be an 'added-on' way of understanding something, and something you can externally predict from, and actually become part of how we see and interpret the world.

Jasmin   (Agitated) Well. OK guys, but I think this is all a bit too positive about models and what they can do. I think I disagree with you two on models! I've tried to jot down why – what do you make of it?

The weaknesses of models

1   Models simplify our account of a problem or situation by making assumptions. Assumptions are never completely true, but they may be true enough for what we want to explain. When problems or situations change, we may find that the assumptions are no longer adequate to explain what is happening and we need a new model.

2   Another problem has an example in Freeman's chapter. The social democratic model of the welfare state remains a valid model even if the world changes so that there are no actual social democratic welfare states of the original type left. For instance, the model gives a good account of Sweden, 1932–86. However, the model contains a theory of how social democratic welfare states are sustained, and that theory relies on the idea of a state's ability to prevent long-term high unemployment. In a situation of rapidly increasing unemployment the model doesn't fit any longer.

3   It's very difficult to test models to see if they are right, or how robust they are. Economists build models using quantitative and/or qualitative data. Some models (especially quantitative ones) can be used to make predictions about how policies will work, and sometimes it might be possible to check these predictions against actual outcomes. However, usually it isn't possible, because the effect of the policy is difficult to disentangle from other events taking place at the same time. This is a problem for all models.

Vicki   (Restless) Well, I'm not sure. These are important points, Jasmin, but I can see advantages as well as disadvantages in using models. The main advantages seem to be that models can account for a range of factors and enable prediction. Certainly in the field of policy making, as well as in the study of the policy process, using models seems to be a popular way of accounting for a range of evidence – hanging on in your head to a collection of points that are clustered together in a certain way. And it's an aid to envisaging policy consequences. On the other hand, the major disadvantages are that the model may make inaccurate assumptions, fail to take account of crucial evidence, and be difficult to test.

Ewen   (Holding out his arms to the sides) Good points on both sides then?

Jasmin   (Briskly) Right. Let's look at the final heading, the differences between what is 'thinkable' and what is 'doable' in public policy.

5 WHAT IS 'THINKABLE' AND WHAT IS 'DOABLE'

Ewen   Now my father ....

[Vicki and Jasmin groan]

Ewen   Well, anyway, my father would say here – what's the problem? As prime minister or whatever, you think about what's best and then you just do it.

Jasmin   (Laughing) Come on Ewen! We've seen that the whole policy process goes through a long set of stages – [ticking them off her list] debates over ideas, listening to experts and others, thinking about the likely consequences, thinking through the options and actually making a decision, then implementing the policy, evaluating its effects and thinking about what to do then.

Vicki   So [pause] I think what this heading points up is the importance of thinking about all the things that can go wrong, [pause] of attending to all the kinds of *constraints* on what policy making can achieve.

Ewen   What, you mean things like how much the government can afford to spend at any one time, and whether there's money for education because so much as been allocated to health etc?

Vicki   (Nodding) Right, financial constraints are certainly part of it. Government plans and aspirations and intentions are always restrained by things like competing demands on their budget, whether they'll get value for money.

Ewen   One new prison, or ten thousand prisoners tagged? Something like that?

Vicki   Yeah that's right, and also with one eye on whether that policy will be successful, and with the other eye on whether the 'thinkable' will make them popular with the electorate.

Jasmin   (Leaning forward) But there are some other kinds of constraints too, aren't there? One is about – like take a thing like unemployment. It can be around for a long time and at one time it might be seen as a phenomenon that nothing can be done about, and at another time as a problem that requires a new policy to solve it.

Vicki   (Digging through a bunch of newspaper cuttings) Hey, I've got a really good example of that here. Hang on, where's the right one? It's about how domestic violence in Britain isn't seen as a problem whereas street crime is, even though the evidence shows that street crime only accounts for 2 per cent of all violent crime, while domestic violence accounts for 25 per cent. Now where's it gone?

Jasmin   (Pointing) That's it on top isn't it?

Vicki   Right! [passes over the newspaper cutting]

Reform at heart of Women's Aid mission

Campaigners call for joined-up thinking on domestic violence

Martin Wainwright

When Joseph Rowntree set down his memorandum in 1904 explaining why he had set up — uniquely at the time — a non-charitable trust to further social reform, he made hard-headed points about what he called the "charity of emotion, the charity which takes the place of justice".

Here was a man who did more practical good than almost any of his British contemporaries, but he never believed in soup kitchens, sticking plaster and "shroudwaving tactics" to tap the kind-hearted public's purse.

What he wanted was to tackle the underlying causes of poverty and injustice, campaigning for change in the law which was banned for charities in his day. Hence his non-charitable Reform Trust which paid (and still pays) tax in return for the freedom to support the boldest campaigners. Had Women's Aid been around in 1904, you can be sure they would have got a grant.

The "charity of emotion" has a place in Women's Aid work, helping to galvanise volunteers and meet the cost of refuges which take in threatened women and children. But the eyes of the group are on a future where it is victims rather than abusers who can stay safely in the family home. A visit to the group's headquarters leaves no doubt that fighting for change is the core.

You are not there long before damning figures ring round your head: street violence, about which we make so much fuss, accounts for 2% of violent crime; domestic violence for a quarter. Mental cruelty in a relationship is hard to tackle, but who can equivocate about punches, kicks and worse? It is a question Nicola Harwin, the director of Women's Aid, has been asking for 30 years since a meeting in a Bristol basement of a group of victims determined to get something done.

"There was nothing in those days," she says. "It was a time when police talked dismissively about 'just a domestic'. Victims and survivors had no voice whatever."

A long, hard road followed, past milestones like Jo Richardson's private member's bill, the first government legislation and — as recently as 1990 — the first Home Office circular to chief constables advising that domestic violence should be treated as a crime.

But the journey has been marked by other milestones such as Women's Aid's publication, Not Worth the Paper, which took apart 10 years of the 1976 Domestic Violence Act. Campaigners still besiege bastions of the law where, Nicola says, "judges still believe that an Englishman's home is his castle". They still have to press for joined-up thinking in the agencies involved with victims of violence at home.

Passion

Attitudes are changing and the pending bill on domestic violence takes practical measures further than ever. But the passion for reform is needed as much as ever, along with the money to make it work.

As Nicola talks, the phones go non-stop at the national women's helpline, 0808 2000 247, manned by volunteers and staff such as Sue, who want to put something back in gratitude for what Women's Aid did for them. Sue remembers when her husband brought her tea on a tray in bed — not to drink but to throw at her and their small daughter. Her friend Shell took eight years to rebuild her confidence after the betrayal of a partner who beat her up.

Almost as bad as those memories is recalling trying to contact the helpline and finding it repeatedly engaged. Three weeks ago the service was enlarged with the help of Comic Relief, but the funding shortfall is still chronic.

Sue, Shell, and the others deal with victims of every income and age, calmly directing them towards help with the authority of women who have been there too. They have helped the partner of a police domestic violence officer; an 82-year-old who got in touch through the internet; and women and their partners speaking to them simultaneously, using different extensions and trying to keep violence at bay.

Back in her office, Nicola returns to the reform agenda and gives a take on the Women's Aid version of the 12 days of Christmas:

1. A national framework to tackle the issue.
2. Stronger legislation to protect victims.
3. Safe child contact arrangements after separation.
4. Equal treatment for all victims, regardless of gender and including those with insecure immigration status.
5. Powerful government media campaigns on domestic abuse.
6. Education and information for the young.
7. A legal system which relocates and re-educates perpetrators.
8. National standards, training and reporting systems for all agencies.
9. Personnel policies on domestic violence in all workplaces.
10. Safe rehousing priority for victims who have to leave home.
11. A national taskforce of statutory and voluntary agencies to oversee longer term strategy.
12. Funding — your gifts to make all this possible.

Jasmin   (Passing the cutting back) That *is* a good example. And another kind of constraint is about the tensions and conflicts between what is 'thinkable' and what is 'doable' between two stages in the policy process – policy *making* and policy *implementation.*

Ewen   (Looking baffled) And you mean by that ...?

Vicki   Well, *I* can think of an example – do you remember how Chapter 1 talks about policy implementation. It outlines the problems with actually delivering a policy and the constraints on putting policies into practice.

Jasmin   And earlier in the chapter, remember when Mabbett is talking about the usefulness of Dahl's, Bachrach and Baratz's, and Lukes' theories of how power is exercised in the policy-making process? She makes a good argument for the importance of 'winding forward' to the implementation phase, as well as 'winding back' to events before the formal decision-making stage.

Ewen   To make sure your policy ideas aren't just wildly unrealistic?

Vicki   (Nodding) Right. But she also argues that implementation and delivery 'is also a domain in which power is exercised'. That's important, isn't it – 'also a domain of power'.

Ewen   Oh yes, I do remember that. I also remember an example of this in Chapter 2 when Charlesworth and Humphreys are talking about the introduction of the idea of the rights and responsibilities of patients. There's a question mark over how well the wider language of rights and responsibilities 'translates' into the relationship between individual patients and professionals. Other factors can intervene and play a part.

Vicki   (Sitting forward) Yes, such as that patients have been given expectations of their rights within the health service. But competition for funding within the health service, at both national and local levels, can affect the availability of services, despite the rhetoric of extending patient choice.

Ewen   (Listening hard) So there can easily be a gap between what has been thought or set up, and what is currently deliverable under the system as it stands.

Jasmin   (Interjecting) Freeman also has an example of the gap between what is thinkable and what is doable in practice, doesn't he? He makes it clear that the political system of liberal democracy in particular can represent a constraint on policy making and policy reform. Decision making, in most European countries, is shared between a range of political parties in a governing coalition.

Ewen   (Leaning forward) That's right, I've got it here – he says that courts and judges can also be involved, along with other tiers of government both above – like a prime minister or president – and below – at regional and local levels.

Jasmin   So, in liberal democracies voters can sometimes also be directly involved, say through referendums. As a result, implementation can be a matter of bargaining between different interests. Implementation can also depend on the support and agreement of representatives of both employers and employees, along with the consent of key professional groups like doctors.

Ewen   (Shifting in his seat) So let me see if I've got this right. Liberal democracy works with inputs from lots of directions, and a process of bargaining and prioritization goes on before the final output stage of the policy, the implementation. I guess this means that implementation is difficult at the best of times. But it also makes changes in policy or reforms pretty daunting.

Jasmin   Yes, and the more important the reform, the harder it's going to be to accomplish.

Vicki   (Gesticulating) And remember back to our discussion about the interplay between values and evidence? Well, Freeman identifies the strategies followed by different welfare regimes in the light of constraints on them, right? This is another example of how the 'doable' may be less, a lot less, than the purely 'thinkable'. He talks about the strategy of 'recommodifying', the strengthening of market principles, undertaken by liberal welfare states, and the strategy of 'cost containment' followed by conservative and corporatist welfare states.

Ewen   (Delving in his papers) I've got another cartoon here. I reckon it shows up the difference between the 'thinkable' and the 'doable' in another sense too. Look, the left-hand image shows Beveridge's solid construction of the welfare state in Britain, that was thinkable in 1945. By contrast the image on the right shows the creaky structure that the government says is the only 'doable' version of the welfare state at the end of the twentieth century.

Jasmin   That's a good one, Ewen.

Vicki   (Thoughtfully) I guess the gap between 'thinkable' and 'doable' could also refer to a policy that was *unsuccessful*. There's a good example of this in Chapter 2 on public health campaigns I remember. Charlesworth and Humphreys talk about how health professionals give loads of information about risk – from things like smoking, non-safe sex, etc. – to the public and then expect them to simply comply with what they've been alerted to. But the translation from giving out the information to people acting on it tends to be a difficult one.

Jasmin   (Ticking off on her fingers) Yeah, Charlesworth and Humphreys noted three reasons why this gap emerged with public health campaigns, between the 'thinkable' and the 'doable', didn't they? The first thing that gets in the way between the information and putting it into practice is the sheer complexity of health education messages.

Vicki   (Breaking in) You mean like the message being too abstract to take account of ordinary people's lives?

Ewen   Like my great uncle Duncan lived to 103 – smoked 60 a day!

Vicki   Yeah, but that's not a typical example, is it?

Jasmin   (Still ticking off on her fingers) Secondly there was the neglect by health policy makers of risks that come from society rather than from the individual, like pollution. Individuals are certainly susceptible to pollution risks, say from lead pollution from a busy road, but individuals can't overcome pollution risks like those just by individually being told to do so.

Ewen   And the third thing was that health policy makers underestimated the way young people are more prepared to undertake risk.

Jasmin (Smiling) Funny. That's the opposite to your aunt, isn't it Vicki? She seems to like risk.

Vicki (Laughing) My aunt that puts her foot down when she sees an orange traffic light? Yeah, she likes a challenge. But she's the exception for her age I guess.

Ewen Yeah, mostly it's young people that are more likely to take risks.

Vicki I've got another newspaper cutting here, about an unsuccessful policy. Apparently convictions for rape in the UK stand at just 6 per cent, down from 33 per cent in 1977. The writer argues that, given that only a small proportion of rapes are reported, the policy leaves it 'increasingly easy to rape with impunity'. The intention behind the policy just hasn't been put into practice, in the way the policy operates.

Institutional sexism

Shona Bettany's claim that only 7% of reported rapes result in conviction (Letters, December 20) is not quite accurate. In fact the conviction rate is just under 6%, down from 33% in 1977. Given that informed estimates suggest only a small proportion of victims report rape, should the conviction rate drop much lower, it really will be more than mere rhetoric to invoke a "right to rape". As it is, subject to stupidity or sheer bad luck, it appears increasingly easy to rape with impunity.

The reality of a society in which rape as a crime for the most part goes unpunished has been horribly highlighted in the Soham case. It is simply not adequate to respond to the seriousness by trotting out the usual excuse, "Rape is a particularly difficult offence to prove for the best of reasons: a man wrongly accused and convicted loses everything ..." (Letters, December 22). We need to take seriously the dramatic drop in the rape conviction rate, and consider its causes and its troubling consequences. The fact is men are not being wrongfully convicted of rape. Indeed, the statistics suggest the opposite: namely, that the guilty are escaping justice in growing numbers.

A mature society should be able to tackle this appalling situation *and* avoid the wrongful conviction of innocent men. How hard can this be? In any case, it is salutary to reflect on a criminal justice system which places an insurmountable evidentiary burden in the way of women who have been raped, while at the same time allowing flimsy evidence to convict innocent women of the murder of their small children. Bettany's claim of institutional sexism does not seem misdirected to me.
Prof Joanne Conaghan
University of Kent

Jasmin (Flicking through her book assiduously) Yeah, that's a dramatic example. And I've got another meaning of 'what is thinkable and what is doable' here in Chapter 1. Mabbett says that across different policy areas there is a strong variation in the interest and action shown by the public. She gives the example of a high level of mobilization by residents and other citizens that might take place around a political issue like refugees.

Ewen   That's right. In a highly-charged policy area like that, people may perceive that they have a great deal to gain or lose from a decision like whether a refugee resettlement centre is going to be located in their area or not.

Jasmin   Yeah, and in contrast, in a policy area like pensions, where the outcomes may be much longer-term and less clear-cut, it's not so easy to get people worked up about it.

Vicki   (Pointing at a page in her book) I can see something interesting on the difference between the 'thinkable' and the 'doable' from Freeman's chapter too. It's about participation. What comes out is that patterns of participation by users of welfare differ – not only from country to country, and from one welfare sector to another, but from one local area to another and from region to region as well.

Ewen   (Drumming his fingers on the arm of the chair) What's the point you're making?

Vicki   Well, I guess he's saying that some people have the cultural resources, confidence and social values that enable them to participate much more effectively as users of welfare than others. And those in poverty, ill-health or who are homeless are maybe the least able to participate.

Ewen   (Slowly) This means that the gap between the 'thinkable' and the 'doable' doesn't only depend on the kind of welfare state you live in, or how complex it is, or whether it invites participation or not, or whether policy reform is being undertaken and whether it is popular or not.

Vicki   That's right, it also depends on whether you can – individually – be assertive and articulate. [short pause] If you don't have the power that comes from cultural resources, knowledge, confidence, in other words, what you '*can't* think' is also not 'doable'. What you 'can't think' also acts as a constraint.

Jasmin   (Nodding) Yeah, I can see how power affects the move from the 'thinkable' to the 'doable'. That's a good argument. There's also an international dimension to this, isn't there, like when Mabbett talks about the EU and globalization? What is 'doable' at the national level of policy making may also be constrained by international treaties and conventions. Mabbett notes that some policy problems can't be addressed effectively at national level at all.

Vicki   Like, in some areas of economic policy, international economic integration measures bolt down the capacity of individual governments to act. In this way, some national policy instruments have been 'rendered ineffective'.

Ewen   (Leaning forward) And Charlesworth and Humphreys noted this dimension too, didn't they? They talked about the influence of European Union legislation on health policy in the UK.

Vicki   Freeman also makes this point. According to him, the pressures on welfare states have 'been intensified by globalization'. He takes the example of the convergence criteria set for entry to the Economic and Monetary Union, the EMU. Freeman says that those criteria have proved, for almost all European countries, to be much more of a direct and immediate source of constraint than national or local factors are.

Jasmin   (Pleased) So that's three examples of the international dimension to round off our discussion of this discrepancy between what is 'thinkable' and what is 'doable' in policy making and policy delivery. Hey, not bad.

6   CONCLUSION

Vicki   (Starting to collect up her papers) And I'm starting to see why today's tutorial is called 'Talking about policy'. There are different ways of looking at the policy process, and we need to think about things like values and ideas and models, as well as the obvious things like institutions and political leaders. More evidence to take into account than I'd realized!

Jasmin   The example of the two models of health policy also showed us how evidence can lead to two very different and opposed policy conclusions. How you decide what policy to pursue then really is a *political* decision rather than just, say, a health expert's one. And a political decision is always one that needs to be debated and weighed up, very much involving argument.

Vicki   And I can now see that 'talking' about 'policy' also refers to different approaches to the *study* of the policy-making process. I'm feeling a lot more confident about it all now. So we've been dealing not just with actors directly involved in public policy, but also with political scientists trying to investigate and interpret what's going on. [Vicki looks at her watch]

Ewen   (Slowly) Yes, I'll have to remember that policy making isn't done by institutions somehow by themselves.

Jasmin   Or by robots or angels!

Ewen   And it isn't *studied* by robots or angels either.

Vicki   No, absolutely. What's involved in the making *and* the studying of policy is people with different perspectives and interests, passionate or dispassionate, under different constraints, and asking different questions about it.

Jasmin   (Turning to Ewen) And even if you can't write a question on the Chapter 4 case study in the exam, Ewen, perhaps you can bring in the general strengths and weaknesses of case studies to one of the questions you do answer.

Ewen   (Packing up) Yeah, I think I can see that now. We'd better get to the tutorial in a minute. My policy is always to get to things on time – life is less stressful that way.

Vicki   (Teasing) Got any evidence for that?

Jasmin   (Laughing) And what's your argument? Can you give me convincing reasons? On the face of it I don't find your statement persuasive!

Ewen   (Coolly) Well, we don't have time to discuss it now, do we?

Jasmin   (Smiling) Right, see you both at the tutorial in a minute.

Vicki   Sure, I'm just getting my notes together.

[Vicki quickened her step ...]

Acknowledgements

Grateful acknowledgement is made to the following sources for permission to reproduce material in this product.

Chapter 1

Figures

Figure 1.1: © Hulton Archive/Getty Images; Figure 1.2: © UPPA; Figure 1.3: © Luis D'orey/Reuters; Figure 1.4: courtesy of the Office for Official Publication of the European Communities, http://europa.eu.int/comm/internal_market/10years/postcard_en.htm

Chapter 2

Figures

Figure 2.1: courtesy of Medical Photography, Addenbrooke's Hospital; Figure 2.2 (left): © Ian Richards/Photofusion; Figure 2.2 (right): © Maggie Murray/Photofusion; Figure 2.3: courtesy of the European Public Health Alliance, Brussels; Figures 2.6 and 2.8: reprinted from *Health and Place*, vol.9, Mackian, S. *et al.*, 'Everywhere and nowhere: locating and understanding the "new" public health', p.224, copyright 2003, with permission from Elsevier; Figure 2.9 (left): © Vic Films Productions/RGA/Ronald Grant Film Archive.

Chapter 3

Figures

Figure 3.1: © picture-alliance/dpa, Frankfurt; Figure 3.2: © Vincent Kessler/Reuters; Figure 3.3: © Christina Ros/OU; Figure 3.4: The North East's Other Newspaper: *Muther Grumble*, no.6, June 1972, Parrot Publications, Durham.

Chapter 4

Figures

Figure 4.1: © Tom Olin; Figure 4.2: © Steven Bloch/Image of Disability; Figure 4.3: © Pierre Housseau/Rex Features; Figure 4.4: © popperfoto.com; Figure 4.5: courtesy of Jenny Morris.

Chapter 5

Text

p.161: Hooper, J. (2003) 'Southern poor force nuclear dump u-turn', *The Guardian*, 28 November 2003. Copyright © John Hooper; p.164: Younge, G. (2003) 'US state to allow gay marriage', *The Guardian*, 19 November 2003. Copyright © Guardian Newspapers Limited 2003; p.165: Watts, J. (2003) 'China takes steps to protect private ownership of land', *The Guardian*, 23 December 2003. Copyright © Guardian Newspapers Limited 2003; p.175: Wainwright, M. (2003) 'Reform at heart of Women's Aid mission', *The Guardian*, 27 December 2003. Copyright © Guardian Newspapers Limited 2003; p.179: Conaghan, J. (2003) 'Institutional sexism', letter in *The Guardian*, 24 December 2003. Copyright © Joanne Conaghan.

Cartoons

p.153: Centre for the Study of Cartoons and Caricature, University of Kent, © Stan McMurtry/Solo Syndication; p.162: Centre for the Study of Cartoons and Caricature, University of Kent, © Martin Rowson; p.178: © Steve Bell.

Photograph

p.164: copyright © Steven Senne/Associated Press.

Cover

Image copyright © PhotoDisc, Inc.

Index

abortion, and disability 140
accountability, and partnerships in
    health policy 73, 74, 167–8
Acheson Inquiry (1998) 53
action, and the policy process 1, 2, 38
actors
    and health policy 46–7, 64–6
        and centre–periphery relations
            66–8
    and policy making 9, 13, 16–22,
        39, 150, 151
ADAPT (American Disabled for
    Accessible Public Transportation)
    114, 134
administration, and policy 34
advocacy, and influence 20
ageing populations, and welfare
    policy 93, 95, 96
agenda-setting, and the policy
    process 13, 38
Alder Hey, Royal Liverpool
    Children's Hospital inquiry 50, 51
American Coalition of Disabled
    People 129–30
Anspach, R. 126
Aristotle 148
Armstrong, K. 26
asylum seekers see refugees
Austria
    corporatism in 83
    welfare policy 87

Bachrach, P. 13, 149
Baldock, J. 106, 110
Bank of England, Monetary Policy
    Committee 17
Banks, P. 121, 122
Baratz, M. 13, 149
Barker, C. 55
Barnes, C. 126–7, 139
Barnes, Colin 121
BBC (British Broadcasting
    Corporation), and the Hutton
    Report 159
BCODP (British Council of
    Organisations of Disabled People)
    128
Benelux countries, corporatism in 83
Bevan, Aneurin 69–70
black disabled people 132
Black Report on health inequalities
    53, 65

blind people
    organizations of 124–5
    in Spain 98–9, 156
Blüm, Norbert 84, 85, 86
BMA (British Medical Association) 69,
    70
bounded rationality 23
breast cancer, and inequalities in
    health care policy 54
Bristol Royal Infirmary Inquiry 50, 51
Bulmer, S. 26
buses, and disability politics 114–15
business associations, and social
    policies 83

campaigning groups see pressure
    groups
Campbell, J. 126, 128
capitalism, and disability 119
care insurance, in Germany 84–5, 156
caring, and inclusion and exclusion
    from participation in welfare 106–7
case studies in policy making 3–4, 5,
    146
    and political science 155–8
    welfare policy 84–5, 95, 98, 99,
        100, 101, 106–8, 156
    see also SEM (single European
        market)
Catholic church
    and the 'charity model' of welfare
        98
    and the principle of subsidiarity
        87–9
Cecchini report, The European
    Challenge 1992: The Benefits of a
    Single Market 25–6, 26–7, 36, 38
centre–periphery relations
    in health policy 3, 4, 44–5, 46, 47
        and health inequalities 52,
            53–4
        and health policy actors 65–6,
            66–8
        hierarchical policy design 71,
            73
        international influences 60,
            63–4
        and local communities 57–8,
            68
        and multi-level governance 71,
            73–4, 75–6
Chamberlayne, P. 106, 107, 108

Charlton, J. 123
    Nothing About Us Without Us 130
China, changing values in 165
churches, and social policies 83
citizenship
    and entitlement to welfare 80
    and health policy 49, 51–60
        and complaints procedures 59
        equality and equity 55
        and inequalities in health care
            4, 47, 51, 52–5
        rights and responsibilities 51,
            53, 54, 55–9, 71, 75, 176
    Marshall's model of 136
    rights for disabled people 136
civil citizenship 136
civil disobedience, and disability
    politics 115
civil rights movement, and disability
    politics 114–15, 128, 129, 130
civil servants
    and health policy 65, 66, 67
    and welfare policy 88
civil service
    and policy communities 18
    as a policy entrepreneur 20
    and policy implementation 34
    and the rational choice model 23
civil society, and the principle of
    subsidiarity 89
Claimants' Unions 101
class
    and disability 119, 132, 133, 157
    and health inequalities 44, 45, 52,
        53, 58–9
    and welfare policy
        attitudes to 92
        reforms 96
clientist approach to welfare 106
Coleridge, P. 126
collectivist expectations, of
    participation in welfare 105, 106
command economy, and health
    policy 68
commodification of welfare 93–4
Conservative governments
    and health policy 53, 56
    and policy communities 18
conservative model of welfare 87, 88,
    91, 92
    and cost containment 94–5, 96
    and values in policy making 160

Conservative Party, and European
    integration 30
constraints on policy making 174–6
consumerist approach to welfare 106
CORAD (Committee on Restrictions
    Against Disabled People) 121
Corker, Mairian 132
corporatism
    and cost containment of welfare
        94–5, 96
    and participation in welfare policy
        83–6, 103
cost containment of welfare 93, 94–6
Council of Ministers 11, 21
    and European integration 27
    and the SEM policy process 15
courts
    and anti-discrimination legislation
        on disability 22, 138
    as policy-making venues 22
Crow, Liz 131
Cutler, D. 98

Dahl, Robert, *Who Governs?* 11, 12–
    13, 149
DAN (Direct Action Network) 115,
    116, 134
deaf people, organizations of 124
decision making, and the policy
    process 12–13
Delors, Jacques 15, 19–20, 21, 27, 38
democracy, and policy making 28–30
democratic accountability 3
Denmark
    attitudes to welfare policy 92
    corporatism in 83
    and European integration 30
    organizations for disabled people
        125
devolution
    and health policy making 34, 65–6,
        71
    and welfare policy 83
difference, and disability politics 115–
    16, 134–5, 140
DIG (Disablement Income Group)
    126–7
Disability Alliance 127
Disability Discrimination Act 1995
    (DDA) 5, 136–9, 140
disability politics 5, 113–41
    and changing values 164–5, 166
    defining 114–16
    and difference 115–16, 134–5, 140

disability and disadvantage 121–3
    and disabled people as a minority
        grouping 123–31
    and discrimination 115, 121–3,
        127–8, 132
        anti-discrimination legislation
            22, 133, 135, 136–9
    and equality 115–16, 140, 154
        equal opportunities 121–3, 140
    and the European Commission 19
    and identity politics 134–5
    and recipients of policy 169, 170
    role of ideas in 167
    and the social model of disability
        5, 115, 116, 117–20, 128, 139
        critics 131–3
Disability Rights Commission 137
disabled people
    access to buildings 137
    and case studies 157
    and changing perspectives on
        evidence 154
    different identities of 123–4
    labelling 132–3
    organizations for 114, 115, 116,
        124–31
        classification of 126, 127, 130
        and identity politics 134–5
        paternalistic charities 125–6
        self-help groups 126, 127, 130
    rights of 132
    and values in policy making 159–
        60
Disabled People's International 117,
    124, 130
discrimination
    and disability politics 115, 121–3,
        127–8, 132
        anti-discrimination legislation
            22, 133, 135, 136–9
dissent, and welfare policy 80, 81,
    103–5, 109
doctors
    and disability 119, 120
    and EU directives on working
        hours 70
    and UK health policy 48, 49, 51,
        66, 67
        inequalities in 70
        and multi-level governance 71–
            3
        and the state 69–70
domestic violence, and constraints on
    policy making 174–5

Dreidger, D. 125

ECJ (European Court of Justice) 12, 38
    Cassis decision 22
    and health care policy 62
    and the SEM policy process 15,
        21–2
    and welfare policy 82
Economic and Monetary Union *see*
    EMU (Economic and Monetary
    Union)
economists, and the SEM policy
    process 25–6, 36
education, disabled people and
    discrimination in 121, 140
eighteenth-century Europe, activities
    of the state in 80
employment discrimination, and
    disability 121, 137, 140
employment patterns
    and welfare policy 93
        attitudes to 91–2
    and welfare states 87, 88
EMU (Economic and Monetary
    Union) 32
    convergence criteria for entry 92,
        181
Engel, D. 135
environmental policy, and changing
    perspectives on evidence 151
equality
    and disability 115–16, 140, 154
        equal opportunities 121–3, 140
    inequalities in health policy 4, 47,
        51, 52–5, 71, 75
        and changing perspectives on
            evidence 154
        doctors 70, 71–2
equity, and health care policy 55
Esping-Andersen, G. 87, 91, 147
ethnicity
    and disability 132, 133, 157
    and health inequalities
        doctors 70
        patients 44, 45, 52, 53, 54–5
EU (European Union) 4, 39, 180–1
    and European integration 26–7,
        29–30
    framework directives 34
    and health policy making 45, 60–4,
        70, 72
    and policy communities and issue
        networks 18–21
    policy-making venues 21–2

structure of the key institutions 11–12
welfare policy 88, 90
see also SEM (single European market)
Euro-sceptics 29
Eurobarometer survey, of attitudes to welfare policy 90
European Commission 11, 38, 39, 151
and the SEM policy process 10, 15, 19, 22
European Council 10, 11
and the SEM policy process 15, 16, 21
European countries
health care systems in 82–3
welfare policy in 87–9, 94–6
local participation 98–100
European Court of Justice *see* ECJ (European Court of Justice)
European monetary union, public debate on 29
European Parliament 12
European Public Health Alliance 63
European Union *see* EU (European Union)
evidence, changing perspectives on 150–5
exclusion
and disability politics 114, 115, 119, 121
and participation in welfare policy making 105–9, 110
exit, and participatory behaviour 103, 104, 107
expertise, in policy making 23, 25–6

families
and the principle of subsidiarity 89
and welfare states 87
feminism, and disability politics 116, 118, 131–3
Finland, health policy 62
France
and European integration 30
pensions reform 94, 95
welfare policy 87
French, Sally 131

gay marriage legislation, and values in policy making 163–4
gender
and attitudes to welfare policy 91, 92

and disability 132, 133, 157
and health inequalities 52, 53, 54, 59
and health policy making 44, 45
and values 158
see also women
Germany
care insurance in 84–5, 156
corporatism in 83–6
health policy 62, 92
pensions reform 94
welfare policy 87, 88, 156
attitudes to 91, 92
Gilligan, Andrew 159
globalization
and policy making 9, 180, 181
and welfare policy 93
goals, and the policy process 1–2
governance 3
see also multi-level governance
GPs (general practitioners), new contracts for 72
Greece, attitudes to welfare policy 92
Guibernau, M. 44

'having a policy' 1, 2
health care professionals
and disabled people 120
and health policy 48, 49
health education/promotion
and the European Union 62
government policies on 57
and the Internet 58–9
health policy 43–76
actors 46–7, 64–6
and attitudes to state welfare 92
and changing perspectives on evidence 152–4
and citizenship 49, 51–60
rights and responsibilities 51, 53, 54, 55–9, 70–1, 75
and disability 114
funding for health care 61
and health inquiries 50–1
international influences on 60–4, 82–3
and issue networks 69, 70, 71, 75
policy communities 69, 70–4, 75
and policy networks 68–70
restructuring 47–51
and the role of ideas 167–8
state intervention in 69–70, 75
what is 'thinkable' and what is 'doable' 178–9
Healthy Cities legislation 62

'high' politics 16–17
Hirschman, Albert, theory of participatory behaviour 81, 103–5, 110, 147–8
Hogg, C. 57, 58
hospital doctors, new contracts for 72
hospitals, Foundation Trusts 48, 49, 59
housing, and disabled people 121, 122, 137
human rights, and symbolic policy making 35
Hunt, Paul 127–8
Hutton Report 159

ideas, role of in policy making 166–9
identity politics, and the disabled people's movement 134–5
ideology, and values 162
ILM (Independent Living Movement) 128, 129–30
ILO (International Labour Organisation), *Time for Equality in Work* 121
impairment, and disability 117–18, 123–4
implementation of policy 8, 9, 33–5, 38, 39, 176–7
inclusion
and disability politics 134
and health policy 49, 51, 71
and participation in welfare policy making 105–9
incrementalism, and the rational choice model 24
individualism, and disability 119
individualist expectations, of participation in welfare 105, 106
industrialization, and disability 119
influence, and advocacy 20
institutional sexism 179
interest groups
influence on policy outcomes 31–2
and issue networks 18, 19
and policy communities 17
and the policy process 1, 2
power and policy making 13–14
see also policy communities
interest representation
and policy making 28–33
democracy and the media 28–30
International Alliance of Patients' Organizations 63

international influences, on health policy 60–4, 82–3
Internet, and health education 58–9
Iraq war, as a policy process 17
iron triangle, and US politics 18, 149
issue attention cycles, and the media 29
issue networks 17, 18–21, 39
    and health policy 69, 70, 71, 75
    and shifts in political science 149
Italy
    health care system 82–3
    welfare policy 87, 88, 95
        attitudes to 92
        'charity model' of 98

Kelly, Dr David 159
King, A. 106, 107
Kingdon, J. 39

Labour government (post-war)
    health policy 69–70
    see also New Labour government
Labour Party, and European integration 30
language
    and ideas in policy making 167
    and policy making 153
large interest groups, and policy outcomes 31, 33
Lasswell, Harold 80
Lawrence, Stephen 159
laws, and policy making 8
Le Pen, Jean-Marie 30
Leonard Cheshire (disability charity) 127
letter-writing campaigns, and participation in welfare policy 81
Lewis, Paul, Exploring Political Worlds 12
liberal welfare states 88, 91, 92
    and commodification of welfare 93–4
    and values in policy making 160
life transitions, and participation in welfare 107
Ligget, Helen 132
Lindblom, C. 26
Lister, R. 136
lobbying, and participation in welfare policy 81
local agencies, and health policy 44–5, 53–4
local communities, and health policy 57–8, 68

local participation, in welfare policy 97–102
London, and health policy making 34
'low' politics 16–17
loyalty, and participatory behaviour 103, 104
Lukes, Steven 13–14, 24, 32, 149
Luxemburg, welfare policy 92

Maastricht Treaty, and the SEM (single European market) 9, 19, 27, 29
managerial accountability 3
market liberalization
    and changing perspectives on evidence 151
    and the SEM policy process 9–11, 21, 25
    and values in policy making 162
markets, and welfare states 87
Marsh, D. 20
Marshall, T.H. 136
maternity care in Sweden 100
media
    and corporatism in Germany 85
    and health policy 50, 54, 57, 65, 66
    and policy making 28–9, 33
        'high' and 'low' politics 17
        values in 159
medical model of disability 115, 117, 119, 131, 140
medical model of health 55–6
medical profession see doctors
Mercer, G. 139
ministers, and UK health policy 65, 66, 67
models, use of in policy making 146, 171–3
modernization, of welfare policy 92, 96, 109
Moravczik, A. 20–1, 148
Morris, Alf 121, 137
Morris, Jenny 131
mortality rates, and health inequalities 52
multi-level governance 39
    in health policy 4, 44, 45, 46, 47, 51, 58, 66
        and centre–periphery relations 71, 73–4, 75–6
        devolved-power policy design 71
        and fluid policy design 72, 73–4
        and health policy actors 65–6

and the health policy community 70–4
    international influences 60, 63, 64
multinational companies, and the Single European Market 32
Munger, F. 135

National Centre for Independent Living 128
National League of the Blind 124
neo-liberal ideology 166
    and welfare policy 93
Netherlands, welfare policy 87, 92, 95
networks, and health policy 68–70
New Labour government
    and health policy 48, 53, 56–8, 74
    and the Hutton Report 159
    and policy communities 18
new public management 48
new social movements, and disability politics 114, 129, 134–5
Newman, J. 73
NGOs (non-governmental organizations), participation in welfare policy 98–9
NHS (National Health Service) see health policy
NHS Plan 56
NICE (National Institute for Clinical Excellence) 65, 66, 67
nineteenth-century Europe, welfare policy 80, 87
norms and values, in policy making 23, 26–7
Norway, corporatism in 83

Oliver, M. 117, 126–7, 128, 134
    The Politics of Disablement 119, 120
Olson, Mancur, The Logic of Collective Action 30–3
ONCE (National Organization of the Blind in Spain) 98–9
open systems, and policy implementation 34

parliament, and UK health policy 65
participation
    in welfare policy 80, 81–6, 110, 180
        and exit, voice and loyalty 103–5

and greater freedom of choice 100
inclusion and exclusion 105–9, 110
local participation 97–102
partnerships, and multi-level governance in health policy 72–4
path-dependent policies, and the SEM policy process 29–30
patients
    rights and responsibilities of 51, 53, 54, 55–9, 71, 75
    and UK health policy 66, 67
Patients' Charter 56
peace movement, and disability politics 115
pension reform 8, 9, 94, 95, 168, 180
Plato 148
pluralism, and the policy process 13
policy
    and administration 34
    features of public policy 1–3
    making and implementation 2
policy communities 16–18, 39
    bias in 30–3
    and health policy 69, 70–4, 75
    and interest representation 28
    and issue networks 17, 18–21
policy entrepreneurs 20
policy making
    case studies in 3–4, 5
    evaluation 36–7
    features of 1–3
    formulation 8
    and implementation 8, 9, 33–5, 38, 39, 176–7
    interests, democracy and the media 28–30
    and issue networks 17, 18–21, 39
    and laws 8, 33
    and mobilization around political issues 8–9
    and policy communities 16–18, 39
    bias in 30–3
    role of ideas in 23–7
        and expertise 23, 25–6
        norms and values 23, 26–7
        rational choice model 23–4
    and shifts in political science 148–50
    and the single European market 4
    use of models in 146, 171–3
    values in 158–77
        and ideas 166–9

venues 21–2, 38, 39
and the 'who governs?' question 12–16
see also SEM (single European market); talking about policy
political citizenship 136
political parties
    and care insurance in Germany 84–5
    and disability 121
    and European integration 30
    and the policy process 1
    and policy making 8
    and welfare policy 83
political rights, and disability legislation 138–9
political science 146, 147–58
    and case studies 155–8
    and changing perspectives on evidence 150–5
    shifts in 148–50
politicians, and welfare policy 83
Portugal, attitudes to welfare policy 92
poverty
    and the commodification of welfare 94
    and disability 119, 122, 127
    and health inequalities 52
power
    and disability politics 115
    and health policy making 47
        centre–periphery relations 44–5, 46
        and multi-level governance 73
    and the policy process 1, 2
    and policy making 4, 9, 12–16
        implementation 34–5, 39, 176
        and the SEM 14–16, 32
        and the 'third' dimension of power 13–14, 23, 32, 149–50
        venues 21
    and the rational choice model 24
pressure groups
    and corporatism in Germany 85
    and social policies 83
    and UK health policy 65
Private Finance Initiative 72
private insurance, funding for health care 61
private lives, and the policy process 2
privatist approach to welfare 106
professional associations, and social policies 83

public goods, and the policy process 2
public opinion
    effects on electoral outcomes 30
    policy making and the media 29
    and welfare states 81, 90–3, 96
public policy making see policy making
public transport, and disabled people 114–15, 121, 122
public/private partnerships 3
    and health policy making 48, 152–3
    and market liberalization 9–11

race
    racism and minority ethnic doctors 70
    and values in policy making 158, 159
    see also ethnicity
rape, and policy making 179
rational choice model, of the policy process 23–4, 34, 36
recipients of policy, and values 169–71
refugees, and policy making 8, 9, 179–80
regional differences, and centre–periphery relations in health policy 54
rehabilitation, and disabled people 126, 169
repetitive strain injury 137, 138
responsibilities, and health policy 51, 53, 54, 55–9
Rhodes, R. 20
Richardson, Jeremy 17
Riddell, S. 121, 122
rights
    and disability politics 132, 135
        civil rights and anti-discrimination legislation 136–9
    and responsibilities, in health policy 51, 53, 54, 55–9, 70–1, 75, 176
    and welfare policy 80, 81
Roberts, Ed 130
Rose, H. 101
Rothstein, B. 100
Russell, Bertrand 12

Salter, B. 51
Sandholtz, W. 20, 148

Saving Lives: Our Healthier Nation
53, 56
Scandinavian countries
organizations for disabled people
125
welfare policy 88
see also Sweden
Schröder, Gerhard 94
Scotland
devolution
and health policy 34
and welfare policy 83
overview of disability in 121, 122
SEA (Single European Act) 10, 14, 29
self-government, and policy
implementation 34
self-help groups
and disabled people 126, 127, 130
and participation in welfare policy
81, 82
SEM (single European market) 3, 4, 9–
11
and the Cecchini report 25–6, 26–
7, 36
decision-making phase of the
policy process 14–16
and democratic representation 29–
30
and the European Court of Justice
15, 21–2
evaluation studies 36–7
and the 'four freedoms' 10
framework of norms and values 27
and health care policy 62
media attacks on 29
and policy communities
bias in 32
and issue networks 18–19,
20–1
and policy implementation 34, 35,
36
and the rational choice model 24
and shifts in political science 148
stages of 15
and values in policy making 162
'winding back' perspective 15–16
'winding forward' perspective 15
sexuality, and disability 132, 133, 157
Shakespeare, T. 115, 123
Shipman, Harold 50
sickle cell anaemia 54
Simon, Herbert, *Administrative
Behaviour* 23
single European market *see* SEM
(single European market)

small interest groups, and policy
outcomes 31
Smith, M.J. 69
social citizenship 136
social democratic model of welfare
88, 91, 92
and cost containment 96
and values in policy making 160
social exclusion *see* exclusion
social insurance model, of funding for
health care 61
social justice, and welfare state
politics 4
social model of disability 5, 115, 116,
117–20, 122–3, 128, 139, 140
critics 131–3
and impairment and disability
117–18
materialist and structuralist
analysis of 118–19
social models of health 55–6
social rights 80
Spain
attitudes to welfare policy 92
health care system 62, 82–3
ONCE (National Organization of
the Blind in Spain) 98–9
Spicker, P. 89
Squires, J. 136
stakeholders, and multi-level
governance in health policy 74
state intervention
and health policy 69–70, 75
and policy making 2
states
and welfare policy 80, 83
see also welfare states
subsidiarity
and policy implementation 34
and welfare policy 87–9, 103
Sutherland report on the Single
European Market 35
Sweden
attitudes to state welfare 91, 92
corporatism 83
health policy 61–2, 82–3
maternity care 100
symbolic policies, implementation of
35

talking about policy 5, 145–82
political science 146, 147–58
and the use of models 146, 171–3
and values 146, 158–71
what is 'thinkable' and what is
'doable' 4, 146, 174–81

taxation
and corporatism in Germany 85
and welfare policy 80
taxation model, of funding for health
care 61
Taylor-Gooby, P. 91
thalassaemia 54
Thatcher, Margaret 27
Thomas, Carol 131
Thompson, G. 18, 20, 46, 68, 69, 71
Tocqueville, Alexis de 105
Democracy in America 97
trade liberalization, and bias in
political communities 31, 32
trade unions
and pension reform in France 95
and the Single European Market 32
and social policies 83
and voice 104
transport, and disabled people 114–
15, 121, 122
transport policy community 18

UK legislation
Chronically Sick and Disabled
Person's Act (1970) 136–7
Disability Discrimination Act 1995
(DDA) 5, 136–9, 140
Restrictive Trade Practices Act
(1956) 17
unemployment
and cost containment of welfare
96
and disabled people 121, 122, 124
Ungerson, C. 106, 110
United Nations, and equal
opportunities for disabled people
122
United States of America
Americans with Disabilities Act
(ADA) 135, 138
disability politics
and the civil rights movement
114–15, 128, 129, 130
organizations for disabled
people 114, 124, 128–30, 134
gay marriage legislation, and
values in policy making 163–4
local participation in welfare 97
youth service 98
US politics and the 'iron triangle'
18, 149
UPIAS (Union of the Physically
Impaired Against Segregation) 117,
118, 119, 128

values 146, 158–71
  and ideas 166–9
  and the recipients of policy 169–71
  role of 158–66
venues, and policy making 21–2, 38, 39
voice, and participatory behaviour 103, 104, 107
voter education, and policy making 28
voting, and participation in welfare policy 81, 82, 97
voting lobbies, and disabled people 123, 157
voting rights (universal franchise), and the unequal allocation of power resources 12–13

Watson, N. 115, 123
welfare policy 79–110
  case studies 84–5, 95, 98, 99, 100, 101, 106–8, 156
  and changing perspectives on evidence 152
  cross-national comparisons in 87–9, 94–5, 97–100, 110
  and disability 119–20
  and dissent 80, 81, 103–5, 109
  and participation 80, 81–6, 110, 180
    and exit, voice and loyalty 103–5
    greater freedom of choice 100
    inclusion and exclusion 105–9, 110
    local 97–102
    partnerships between providers and users 100–1
  pressure and change 93–7, 109
  recipients of 170
  and the state 80
  and values in policy making 160
  what is 'thinkable' and what is 'doable' 177–8, 180
welfare states 4–5
  and globalization 181
  models of 87–9 91, 92, 171–2
  and public opinion 81, 90–3, 96
  restructuring 4
welfarist approach to welfare 106

WHO (World Health Organization) 45, 62
Wilson, W. 34
'winding forward' and 'winding back' perspectives in policy making 176
  and the Single European Market 15–16
  and welfare policy 83
women
  and health inequalities
    doctors 70
    patients 52, 59
  and institutional sexism 179
  and organizations for disabled people 124
  and values in policy making 158, 159
  and welfare policy, conservative models of welfare 88
  see also gender

Yes Minister 39
Young, Iris Marion 134

Zola, I. 120
Zysman, J. 20, 21, 148